ROBBED OF HUMANITY

LIVES OF GUATEMALAN STREET CHILDREN

NANCY LEIGH TIERNEY

PANGAEA

Saint Paul

International Standard Book Number 0-9630180-5-1

Library of Congress Cataloguing-in-Publication Data

Tierney, Nancy Leigh.
     Robbed of humanity : lives of Guatemalan street children /
Nancy Leigh Tierney.
          p.   cm.
     Includes bibliographical references and index.
     ISBN 0-9630180-5-1 (paperback : alk. paper)
     1. Street children--Guatemala--Social conditions. 2. Human
rights--Guatemala.   I. Title
HV887.G9T54   1997
305.23'086942--dc21   97-34143
                                                                              CIP

Published in the United States of America
Printed in Canada
P A N G A E A
1997

I dedicate this work to the memory of my dear friend
María Imelda Hernández
12 January 1964 — 21 October 1993

and
to the children who never recovered.
May they find in God
the acceptance
that this world never gave them.

CONTENTS

Prologue

The sidewalk drama unfolded before the eyes of a Brazilian friend, a savvy newspaper editor who was taking a quick *cafezinho* at a cafe along Avenida Atlantica, Copacabana Beach. A little girl of nine or ten years, neatly if nattily dressed in pink fluorescent shorts and ribbed halter and balancing a fussy toddler on her skinny hip, stopped briefly at each table and whispered something with her eyes cast down. At each table the child was rebuffed, and one annoyed patron of the cafe sent her away with an audible scolding. Finally, the girl approached my friend's table. "Mister," she asked, "do you know any nice somebody who would want my little brother? *Mamae* can't take care of the whole bunch of us anymore."

How could this be? My friend asked later, "here in hyper-modern Brazil, one of the South's richest nations, not in Charles Dickens' squalid nineteenth-century London." Of course, his question was rhetorical. The journalist was well aware of the contradictory representations of childhood that increasingly separate real children in the Americas today into opposing camps of wanted/unwanted, acceptable/unacceptable, normal/criminalized, protected/hunted.

The "modern" idea of childhood as a special privileged and protected stage in the human life cycle is increasingly the exclusive province of more affluent households where the "house child"—*menino de casa* in Brazil—is pampered and protected to an extraordinary degree. In contrast, the child of the displaced urban poor is often depicted by the media and in the popular culture as a dangerous pseudo-adult—*feo, sucio, y malo*—ugly, dirty, and bad, as Laura Gingold recently put it. Childhood has become the preserve of the rich (relatively speaking), while it is almost non-existent for the urban poor.

In Brazil, for example, the "house child" is valued and coddled to an extraordinary degree. Well-dressed, articulate and bold, such children are graciously received in good restaurants, in shopping malls, and in the

streets and *praças* of towns and cities. They are treated with indulgence
by middle-class adults and with respect by low-status, poor adults.
These children count for a great deal and they are taught their rights and
worth at a tender age. Dona Goldstein captured the following interaction along a beachfront sidewalk in Recife. A well-dressed man and his
small son of about six or seven years old stopped to have their shoes
shined by a small, black boy, barefoot, and also about seven years old.
The father instructed his son on how to demand that a particular polish
be done in a certain way and for a certain price. The shoeshine boy was
keen to show off his skill. At the end of the shine, the father handed his
son the bills to pay the shoeshine boy. Both children seemed delighted
with the unequal exchange.

In Brazil, as elsewhere in the Americas, middle-class children learn to
"treat" the maid and her children as subordinates through a constant barrage of minute demands, even calling for help in changing a TV station.
While middle-class children are not allowed to enter the kitchen, which
is the province of the servants, and they grow up quite ignorant of any
domestic and especially kitchen skills, these proper children are taught
proper table manners and how to use silverware. The children of the
domestic learn how to slaughter and cook poultry and how to prepare
meals. They know only how to eat with a spoon, however, a definitive
class marker of the *favela* or *barrio* child.

But there is more to this story than representations of childhood and
stigma, as Nancy Leigh Tierney's careful account of the specific
Guatemalan situation illustrates. The deteriorating status of poor children in Latin America needs to be understood in the context of recent
shifts toward neo-liberal economics and World Bank policies of "structural adjustment" that have adversely affected the lives of poor.
Meanwhile, the greatly anticipated replacement of military police states
with newly emerging democracies has laid bare (rather than covered up
and controlled) the extreme social class cleavages that separate protected
and innocent "home children" from dangerous and vitiated "street children." Like the Kentucky coal miners' caged canaries whose song or
silence indicated the safety or danger of new mines, the healthy shouts
or the muted cries of sick and dying children are often the best indicators
of the consequences of major political and global economic transitions.

In fact, the situation for street children has degenerated over the past two decades following the economic and political transitions in much of Latin America. The optimistic decade of the 1970's witnessed high rates of economic growth and rapid "development" (such as, for example, the great Brazilian Economic Miracle) without, however, any appreciable improvement in the conditions and life chances of the region's poor, especially women and children. The worsening of their situations offered the first inklings that the new world economic opportunism of the 1970's was not all that the World Bank and International Monetary Fund had promised it would be. By the late 1980's, the world's economies were already mired in recession and decline, huge foreign debts were accumulating in the poorer nations holding them hostage to the U.S. and Brussels, and the World Bank was insisting, rather high handedly, on structural adjustment policies that often cut into public expenditures for education, health care and social welfare programs, resulting in adverse conditions for, especially, single women and children living in urban areas.

The 1990's will be remembered, in turn, as the decade of radical transitions to democracy and the global pursuit of individual and human rights. Military governments began to fall in Central and South America, while totalitarian regimes toppled in Eastern and Western Europe, and democratic revolutions were waged and won in Southern Africa. An international discourse on human rights—including children's rights—exemplifies the reformist spirit of the times. But while individual, women's and children's rights have been formally recognized in new constitutions or new civil codes (and those of Guatemala and Brazil are exemplary) guided by the principles outlined in the U.N. Convention on the Rights of the Child, these changes have not been claimed at the local level nor do they guide everyday practices toward street boys and girls who are more often seen as roving bandits than as rights-bearing children with special needs.

Democratization itself seems to have provoked the crisis of the new street child. The former police states had kept the social classes safely apart and "dangerous" poor children contained to the *favelas* or poor *barrios* "where they belonged" or else in "walled" prison-like reform schools. With the democratic transition, the detention centers, shantytowns and poor *barrios* ruptured, and suddenly poor children seemed to be every-where, flooding downtown boulevards and *praças*, flaunting their misery and their "criminalized" needs. Now there was both a more visible pop-ulation of desperately poor marginals on urban streets and new laws and liberal institutions that promised civil rights protections to children thought of as street bandits.

The brutal attacks and recent massacres of street kids in Brazil, Venezuela and Guatemala reflect the feelings of a great many ordinary people that their lives and property are threatened by these newly empowered children. Following the new liberal guidelines, children can-not technically be prosecuted or put into jails. Hence, street children (as vividly described here) are recruited and used by adult criminals as inter-mediaries in their crimes. Here Tierney's useful conception of "child-use" adds a new dimension to the annals of child abuse. Similarly, Tierney's description of "hybrid democratization" to describe the phenomenon of political reforms occurring in the absence of economic and social justice, helps explain the popular backlash against the increasingly visible popu-lation of urban street children.

Street kids in Latin America are often "working" children engaged in economic bargaining with their parents to delay a permanent ejection from the home. But to middle-class people, working kids on the streets are seen as too old to be children and too young to be citizens with rights. Instead they are often vilified as anti-social dwarfs, enemies of the fami-ly and of civilized society. And so, independent vigilantes collaborate with off-duty police in various citizen-supported projects of "urban hygiene" and "street cleaning" aimed at ridding the streets once and for all of urban "vermin," "flies" and "pests."

Unwanted and perceived as human waste, older street kids evoke strong and contradictory emotions of fear, aversion, pity and anger. In staking out the most elegant spaces of the city in which to live and to work, these "miniature adults" betray the illusion of Latin American hyper-modernity. Because they do not behave like "proper" children, they are not seen as children at all but as young criminals. The support given to various police actions against street children derives from the special vulnerability of the poor and uneducated to authoritarian control. Meanwhile, there is little trust in the new democratic process and its legal and judicial reforms from which most of the poor believe they are excluded. Consequently, a rough sort of popular justice through vigilante actions against juvenile "criminal elements" is often broadly supported.

The crisis of the street child is further complicated by a lack of precision regarding the actual numbers of street children, the varied nature of their existences (alternating between home and the street), and the number of crimes committed by and/or against them. Estimates of their population vary widely from the tens of thousands to millions, depending on whether to include those children who have homes but who spend most of the day and occasional nights on the street. Non-governmental organizations working on behalf of the needs and rights of street children are often accused of inflating statistics to achieve political or pro-active goals.

The choices offered street children today are extremely limited. They can return to their homes and to their "proper childhoods," which is not an option for most. Or, they can risk a semi-autonomous life on the increasingly dangerous streets of Rio, Caracas or Guatemala City. The true test of the new democracies will be their ability to conceptualize childhood in radically new ways. Will it be possible for children who cannot depend on nuclear families for support to find protection rather than abuse and bullets on the elegant urban streets of Central and South America?

Nancy Scheper-Hughes
Professor of Anthropology
University of California at Berkeley
Berkeley

Preface

It is so common a saying as to be trite, I suppose, but nevertheless it is true that a country may be judged by the way it treats its children. In the case of Guatemala, Nancy Leigh Tierney's *Robbed of Humanity: Lives of Guatemalan Street Children* is strong evidence upon which to base this harshest of verdicts.

As the title of this good book indicates, the focus is on street children. As such, it includes a fair bit of autobiographical testimony on what brought them to the streets, why they are still there and, importantly, what they hope for in the future. It should come as no surprise that the children are insightful and profoundly moving witnesses to their own lives. Some of the more painful entries occur when they weigh themselves in the balance and find that they are wanting. What can you say as a girl not only describes but evaluates the events surrounding her father's insistence that she submit to sexual intercourse with him? She does submit, but later says that she did so knowing he would give her a little money because of it. She makes it very clear that this is a sin and, in her mind, *she* is the sinner.

There is much more, of course, that is profoundly disturbing to contemplate: lives of thievery, glue and solvent sniffing, prostitution, ten- and twelve-year-olds, boys and girls, beatings and murder. But one of the most valuable elements of Tierney's work is that it is not restricted to the negative. These children are whole human beings. There is evidence of loyalty, laughter and love. It is reminiscent of a story that some years ago used to amaze listeners, only because they did not know the lives of street children but only their many horrors. Workers at a center for homeless children achieved a considerable success. After much effort, they convinced a thirteen-year-old boy to leave the streets. He gave up stealing and he gave up glue in favor of education and job training. It was, by all accounts, a remarkable success except . . . each night, after the lights were out he would slip out of bed, through the window and return to the streets for the darkest hours. The staff was left to wonder at the powerful hold these streets still had upon his life—until they learned what he did during those long hours. He was returning not to the streets but to a young friend he had protected for years and continued to protect each night even as his own life changed. It is important, in short, that we learn everything we can about these lives. We need not worry about downplaying the difficulties by portraying their strengths; there are horrors enough to make an impact on even the most uncaring reader.

One thing that impresses constantly in Tierney's accounts and in so many other instances of children telling of their lives is the literary beauty one often finds in the simple and direct manner of speaking. "My name is Ruth and my life has been very sad." It is difficult to imagine a clearer, cleaner, simpler, more accurate or more compelling way to start the story of this child. Many of these children may be uneducated, but they are acute observers, wise beyond their years and impressive analysts as well (at least until, for some of them, the glue or solvent works its effects on their brains). And this is true, of course, not only of Guatemalan children but children everywhere. One child in *Robbed . . .* speaks of dressing up as well as she could, doing the best with what she had and going into several stores. She knew immediately that she was not wanted there, that she was the object of scorn. One reads exactly the same sentiments from a child in New York City in Jonathan Kozol's excellent *Amazing Grace*.

There are powerful first-person accounts by children in this book but there is more, much much more. Tierney levels a damning indictment of the Guatemalan government simply by reciting its acts, its violation of its own laws and constitution and its wretchedly miserly allocation of funds for children's welfare. Tierney is right; ultimately the plight of Guatemala's children is directly attributable to a system, a system that is concerned about the military, the oligarchy and profits. It is a brutal system, brutal in what it does and what it refuses to do. The abundant data she provides rightly condemn that system.

Read well and learn something of Guatemala—and of the United States. Remember, our U.S. government has had no problem cooperating with Guatemala's; we have cooperated with the oligarchy; we have worked with the military and even hired some of them to do dirty work

for us. It is the children with whom we have found it impossible to cooperate. As you read of these children, their strengths, their hopes and the
nightmares that many of their lives are, remember that there are two
sides to this story. There is the children's and their government's. Never
forget whose side our own government—the U.S. government—
has chosen.

Read this book. But no matter how sad you find parts of it, do
not weep.

Do not weep at the stories of minds being destroyed by glue and solvent, nor of ten-year-olds selling their bodies for survival, nor of their
being beaten and murdered at the hands of agents of their own
government.

Do not weep.

The children of Guatemala do not want your tears.

Neither do those of us in the United States who have worked for justice and human decency for *both* our countries and with the non-governmental organizations of Guatemala.

Tears alone are not enough: your energy is needed; your commitment is needed; your labor is needed; your money is needed; your voices
of protest are needed.

A country is judged by how it treats children—its own and *all* other
children. So it is with Guatemala; so it is with the United States.

Nancy Leigh Tierney and the children of Guatemala have given you
all the evidence you need to make that judgment. For God's sake, and the
children's, make it. And then, please—*act* upon it.

Sister Alice Zachmann, SSND
Guatemala Human Rights Commission/USA
Washington

Acknowledgments

Upon completing this book, I express my deepest gratitude to the children and staff of Casa Alianza-Guatemala, particularly Eugenia de Monterroso and Hector Dionicio, who greatly facilitated my in-country research and shared with me much information and insight. The Hernández-Ramirez family also extended much support and love, as always, during my time in Guatemala.

I also thank Professors William Goldsmith and Billie Jean Isbell of Cornell University for providing critical feedback, editing, and invaluable insight, along with much encouragement and support.

I am grateful to the following Cornell University organizations which funded, in part, my research: the Hispanic-American Studies Program, the Latin American Studies Program, the International Studies in Planning Program, and the Mario Einaudi Center for International Studies.

Finally, I thank my friends and family for their understanding and enthusiasm during the writing of this book.

NLT
Boston

CHAPTER ONE

The Scene

There are over 100 million homeless children in the world.

And on a map called the Atlas of Shame, twenty countries are shown where children's rights are violated by the state or with its approval.

What most shakes my conscience is that in order to illustrate these violations, they use my country, Guatemala, as an example.

May no one, hoping to cover-up the sun with a single finger, dare to say that this work is 'part of the orchestrated campaign to discredit Guatemala. . . .'

We have already taken on that discredit ourselves, by permitting fear, cowardice, and shame to silence us.

Journalist Rony de León, reacting to a November 1991 *OMNI* article on street children, in "Prisioneros de la calle," *Siglo Veintiuno* special report, Guatemala. 9 March 1992, 3.

Striking physical and climactic contrasts mark Guatemala's landscape: majestic volcanoes give way to miles of flat plantation in the South; the penetrating cold of the highlands changes to oppressive heat along the coast; the North's tropical vegetation quickly becomes lost in the cactus-scarred East. These dramatic differences, all within a territory the size of Louisiana, make Guatemala stunningly beautiful. The equally severe disparities of the social landscape, between rich and poor, powerful and weak, and white and Indian, however, mar Guatemala's beauty. They provoke widespread suffering and have transformed the country's once tranquil fields into battlegrounds over the past thirty-five years.

Within this context of conflict, destitute children suffer perhaps the worst. Neglectful public policies spawn the high infant mortality, inadequate schooling, and low life expectations that plague Guatemala's children. More brutal and deliberate measures cause their death on the streets.

Over the past five to ten years, the government's violent mistreatment of street children in Guatemala, as throughout Latin America, has attracted international attention. Newspapers and magazines have depicted the daily harassment, frequent beatings and tortures, and occasional massacres of these children, shocking readers, even in those countries accustomed to teenage death on their city streets. Perhaps because police and paramilitary forces have organized and conducted most of the killings, or perhaps because so many Latin Americans have met this violence with silence, and sometimes approval, the murder of street children has seemed at least as pathological and perhaps less comprehensible than the equally tragic deaths of youths from gang and drug-related atrocities in the United States and elsewhere.

Tina Rosenberg, author of *Children of Cain*, a compelling study of the culture of violence in Latin America, has remarked that aggression in the region

> is significant in part because so much of it is political: planned, deliberate, carried out by organized groups of society against members of other groups. It is used to make a point. It is committed by the institution entrusted with the protection of its citizens. And it is justified by large numbers of people. It is

different from the purposeless, random, individual violence of the United States. It is more evil.[1]

To explore the "pathology" behind the abuse of street children in Guatemala, this text uses scholarly materials, interviews with child rights advocates and service providers, and the words of the children, themselves. It examines the treatment of street children in various settings: within their families, on the street, in private shelters and public detention centers; and considers their relationship to various social institutions, private individuals, and the larger, capitalist, order.

Children's rights advocates have identified the "gang of three"—Brazil, Colombia, and Guatemala—as the worst offenders in the Latin American region.[2] I have chosen to focus on Guatemala, though I make frequent reference to parallel situations in Brazil and Colombia, for several reasons. First, in Brazil, where three to four hundred street children die violently each year, the overwhelming scope of abuse already has attracted much analysis. Second, in Colombia, violence against young people has become inextricably linked to organized crime and the country's powerful narcotics industry. Rosenberg, for example, notes that "[t]he most common reason children under twelve are brought to the emergency room in Medellín is not the normal sprains and breaks of childhood, but gunshot wounds."[3] This context makes pure analysis of the abuse of street children more difficult than in other situations. Third, because I have lived and traveled extensively in Guatemala, I have a deeper understanding of the social, economic, political, and cultural forces in that country than in other parts of the region.

The presence of street children in Guatemala

The term "street child" in this work refers to youths with weak or broken ties to their families, who live and work on the streets and rarely, if ever, return to their homes. In Guatemala, boys constitute roughly two-thirds of the street child population, according to a recent Coordinadora Nacional de Acción por los Niños (CONANI) survey. The average age for these boys is twelve, only ten for their female counterparts.[4]   The same survey found few street children from Guatemala's Mayan indigenous communities, although indigenous peoples comprise approximately half of the country's total population and represent those hardest hit by the country's devastating thirty-five year civil war that left some 50,000 widows and 200,000 orphans.[5]   Perhaps because of Mayan solidarity and its particular conceptions of childhood, discussed further in chapter five, Guatemala's indigenous people have absorbed nearly all displaced and orphaned children back into their communities.

Following global trends, the number of children struggling for street survival in Guatemala has increased over the past fifteen years. Reports indicate a worldwide total of close to 100 million children on the streets, of which a disproportionately large share lives in Latin America.[6]   In Guatemala, a country of just ten million inhabitants, estimates of the street child population range from 600 to 5000, but most indicate a steady presence of roughly 1500.[7]   In addition, more than 335,000 children in Guatemala City work in street activities, such as shining shoes, begging, collecting garbage, and selling candy, but still maintain regular contact with their families. The daily lives and struggles of these children are revealed in their testimonies in chapter two.

Street children virtually vanished from the capital city, most likely returning to their abusive homes if not incarcerated or murdered, during the early 1980's, when General Efraín Ríos Montt imposed an iron-fisted "law and order campaign" against delinquents. By the mid-1980's, however, migration from the countryside and deteriorating economic conditions pushed large numbers of youths back onto the streets.[8] Guatemala also became a "refuge" for children fleeing violence and despair in neighboring El Salvador, Honduras and Nicaragua. By 1986, the presence of street children in the capital had grown so rapidly that the Magistrate of Minors solicited assistance from national and international non-governmental organizations (ngos) in finding solutions to the "problem."[9]

The social utility of street children

Guatemala's street children have emerged against a back drop of vast inequalities. Land ownership in the country is extremely concentrated, with less than three percent of deed holders possessing 65 percent of all cultivable land.[10]   In a nation such as Guatemala, firmly grounded in agricultural production, this concentration has translated into devastating poverty.   Destitution pervades much of Guatemala, but reaches its most acute levels among the indigenous.   The North (Alta and Baja Verapaz), and Northwest (Huehuetenango and El Quiché) regions of Guatemala, both predominantly indigenous, have the highest indices of poverty in the nation, 90 percent and 92 percent, respectively.   The largely ladino (non-indigenous) Department of Guatemala, which comprises most of the metropolitan area, has the lowest (although still excessive) rate of poverty, 64 percent.[11]   In 1988, annual per capita income was 7170 quetzales (Q.) for the Department (roughly US$ 2500 at that year's exchange rates), but dramatically lower outside of the capital.   Escuintla, another predominantly ladino department, captured the second highest per capita income, Q. 3640, while the indigenous departments of Sololá and El Quiché averaged incomes of Q. 459, and Q. 249 (less than $100 annually), respectively.[12]

Between 1950 and 1980, Guatemala's population grew 2.5 to 2.8 percent annually.   The intense concentration of land ownership has prevented the absorption of this increase by rural communities and has accelerated rural to urban migration as a result.[13]   The country's brutal civil war has added to this movement.   Ríos Montt's seventeen-month reign of terror, alone, internally displaced more than 1,000,000 Guatemalans.[14]   Census data show the outcome of such massive relocation. Population in the capital city grew between 1950 and 1981 at a rate one full percentage point higher than in the rest of the nation, and half of this growth resulted from migration, rather than births.[15]

Migrants fleeing destruction and poverty in the countryside, however, generally found little awaiting them in the capital: a shortage of housing, poor and scarce services, and high unemployment.   According to one reporter, Guatemala City

> has grown, surpassing its own economic and structural limits. Far away from the villas and mansions, where the comfortable families live in splendid isolation . . . the city has expanded like tentacles toward pestilent suburbs and landfills, where chil-

dren, chickens, rats, and dogs share a common precarious
existence.[16]

Roughly 700,000 Guatemalans, half of them children, live in the
squalor of the capital's poorest neighborhoods. In all, 176 precarious settlements, many of them born of illegal occupation, dot the urban
fringe.[17] Migrants to these communities, finding no housing readily
available, construct make-shift shacks at first, from corrugated tin and
waste materials, then over the course of a lifetime, if they are not first
evicted from their settlements by government forces, expand and
upgrade their structures. Often they survive with no electricity or running water until able to tap a neighbor's services. Such "self-help" strategies reflect the uncapitalized nature of urbanization in Guatemala as
throughout Latin America.[18] Largely due to depleted coffers and limited will, the government has spent miserly amounts on urban infrastruc-
ture. Official sources revealed a Guatemalan housing deficit of 763,000
units in 1987, and 816,000 in 1990. In the latter year, only 42 percent of
Guatemalan households had running water, and 50 percent electricity.[19]
Despite these shortages, in 1990 the government spent only 1.2 percent
of its total budget on housing, or 0.1 percent of its Gross National
Product (GNP).[20]

An astonishing rate of unemployment and underemployment—72
percent in 1990—plagues the quality of life in Guatemala City's poorest
neighborhoods.[21] Guatemala's long-standing reliance on agriculture for
exports to global markets and the eroding terms of trade for its products
on those markets have limited the availability of foreign exchange within the country. This limitation, combined with international competi-
tion, lagging technology, and confined domestic and regional markets,
has led to a "structural permanence" of unemployment and underemployment in Guatemala. Such restraints prevent industry from absorbing the influx of newly arrived immigrants from the countryside. Their
ability to improve productivity through technology and capital inputs
inhibited, capitalists exploit this labor pool viciously, holding wages to
abysmally low levels in order to maintain profits.[22]

Urban scholar and planner Thomas Angotti articulates the connection between this suffering on the local scene and exploitative practices

on the global level. He writes:

> Poverty and informality may not have been created by transna-
> tional corporations, but they serve their interests well. The
> majority of the population in Latin American cities survives at
> a level of subsistence far below North American standards.
> This allows for the suppression of wage levels in the North as
> well as the South. Latin American workers make up a ready
> labor reserve for transnationals. . . . Through the austerity poli-
> cies of the International Monetary Fund (IMF) and World
> Bank, Northern capital discourages national governments from
> making expenditures that would substantially improve the
> quality of life in Latin America, thereby sustaining the low
> level of subsistence that corresponds with low wages.[23]

Furthermore, when foreign capital all but ceased to flow to Latin America during the region's recent debt crisis, the position of labor became still weaker. This crisis, a "lost decade" of near economic paralysis, struck Latin America after years of unbridled, irresponsible, "petrodollar" lending by Western banks and the consequent collapse of finance. The results in Guatemala: Gross Domestic Product (GDP) shrunk by 3.5 percent in 1982, by 2.7 percent in 1983, and by an additional 0.6 percent in 1985; over the course of the decade, per capita GDP fell a total of 2 percent; disbursed foreign public debt balances soared from US$ 820 million in 1980 to nearly US$ 3 billion in 1986; and inflation rose to unprecedented levels for the country, 25 to 30 percent in 1985-86 and 60 percent in 1990.[24]

Trying to manage this economic chaos, Guatemala began implementing many of the International Monetary Fund's suggested "structural adjustment policies." As alluded to by Angotti, with these policies governments cut spending on social programs and public sector employment, and they end many subsidies, to food and energy costs, for example, which benefit the poor.[25] While they did eventually reduce inflation and re-stimulate production, though hardly solidifying the economy, the policies in Guatemala, as throughout Latin America, have had a crushing impact on all but the top layers of society. Poverty grew at an average 2.8 percent annually between 1980 and 1989 and now encompasses 80 percent of Guatemalans.[26] The country's Social Security Institute (IGSS) estimates that between 1981 and 1985, Guatemala *lost* 220,000 jobs, a debacle made even worse by an average *annual growth* in the Economically Active Population of some 62,000.[27] Real salaries deteriorated 15.1 percent during the 1980's, and by 1988, the minimum daily cost of food was Q. 9.93, with an average wage of only Q. 5.63 a day.[28] Agricultural workers in 1986 earned only 57 percent of the nominal salary they received in 1980, and this only covered one-third of the minimum dietary needs of their families.[29] Desperation pervaded the country.

That the population of street children grew precisely during these years of great economic strain is hardly surprising. Historically, since the early period of enormous European economic growth and inequality, concentrated in mill towns, like Manchester, street children have formed a sometimes prominent part of the urban landscape. Street children are central characters in nineteenth-century literature, familiar still today in Charles Dickens' *Oliver Twist* and Victor Hugo's *Les Miserables*.[30] Child advocates Judith Ennew and Brian Milne note that during historical periods of economic crisis, cyclical "downswings" or crashes, street children usually surface in greater numbers.[31]

The testimonies that appear below in chapter two reveal that children in Guatemala generally land on the streets following two sets of circumstances: either they begin working outside of the home to support the family and become increasingly accustomed to street life or they become increasingly endangered within the home and flee for protection. Both processes are accelerated by the increasing burdens placed on households during times of crises.

As seen, because of structural limitations within Guatemala's economy, wages are terribly low, providing incomes often below the level required for even a minimal existence. The poor, not accepting starvation, activate strategies centered around the family in order to survive.[32] In Guatemala, this has meant sending additional members of the family to work, usually women and older children, in order to bolster household income. Lacking education and opportunities, these new laborers have exploded the country's so-called informal sector. The capital's streets, packed with vendors of anything from toothpaste to tennis shoes, its buildings' lobbies lined with typists waiting to prepare your documents, and its market stalls filled with gadgets and trinkets, new and stolen, all attest to the ingenuity of the under-employed, exploited Guatemalan poor. So, too, do the huge numbers of their children shining shoes on busy corners or selling sweets on city buses.

The poor's survival strategies also have included "doubling up" in already overcrowded housing, a process which often builds tension even among close family members, and, as Lourdes Benería points out in her work with poor Mexican households, cutting back on social functions such as birthdays or outings traditionally meant to bring families closer together.[33] In addition, the absence from the home of the mother and older children, who have begun working to supplement household income, may also weaken domestic bonds. Single mothers generally must either

> resign themselves to underemployment or underpaid jobs more compatible with the care of their children, 'or they go out to work, improvising inadequate day care solutions,' which frequently consist of leaving the children locked up at home alone.[34]

The despair that young children feel in this environment will increase if one or both of the parents lose their ability to cope with the burdens of everyday survival and take to drinking or become more abusive within the home. Children sensing great mental and physical danger may then opt to leave the home, perhaps ending in the streets after being passed from grandparents to aunts and uncles to family friends all equally unable or unprepared to care for them.

As in the much earlier European settings of capitalist development, the presence of street children in Guatemala has become closely tied to the misery of the working class. This misery occurs within the context of a pervasive system of economic and social dominance which *structurally requires* the exploitation of the poor for its maintenance. The predominant upper class ideology in Guatemala obscures this connection, however, and protects elite interests, by vilifying street children and the families from which they originate, making their brutal treatment appear justified.

The State and other social actors

The government of Guatemala, the principal protector of upper-class privilege, has met the large number of children on the capital's streets with two primary responses: incarceration in juvenile centers and violent mistreatment on the streets. Government policies, as discussed below in chapter three, encourage the internment of street children in juvenile facilities, rather than emphasizing other, less punitive and restrictive, measures. National legislation on the treatment of minors also permits the government to breach its obligations, under other national and international law, to safeguard the rights of children.

Those who remain on the streets face an even more gruesome reality. Police officers harass and beat street children every day. At times brutality goes further, ending in the torture and murder of children. The cases described in chapter four will illustrate that this police violence is often premeditated, rather than situational. Officers attack street children as they gather outside a shelter, ride a city bus, or sleep in the park. Local newspapers and magazines report often on this abuse of juveniles. Newspapers have published four- to six-page special reports on the use of force against street children. Still, Guatemala City dwellers, like those in the United States responding to drug and gang violence, do little to protest. Coherent demands for change have come predominantly from internationally funded human rights groups in Guatemala, such as Casa Alianza and ChildHope, but have few roots in local communities, themselves.

This inattentiveness contrasts sharply with events during the same time frame, in which Guatemalans responded, some with extreme hostility, to the misperception that foreign visitors had come to kidnap their children to sell their body parts on the black market. Rumors of this nature have circulated throughout Latin America for at least a decade. While no proof of such sordid operations has surfaced, children do periodically disappear. In a very small number of cases, desperately poor women may have sold their children for adoption, hoping to give them a better life. In others, police have arrested Guatemalan nationals on child snatching charges, some ostensibly working in connection with lucrative illegal adoption agencies. According to *La República* columnist Mario

Rolando Cabrera, though, justice has seldom prevailed in these actual cases of child snatching, and it is precisely the uncertainty of justice that has fueled the new wave of frustration and panic in Guatemala.[35] Anthropologist Nancy Scheper-Hughes additionally attributes the practices of abduction and torture used by Latin American military regimes for so long to fostering such fears of loss and mutilation.[36]

Whatever the precipitating factors, these rumors recently sparked near hysteria in a number of Guatemalan towns, both ladino and indigenous. In early 1994, at Santa Lucia Cotzumalguapa, a municipality in the Southern department of Escuintla, angry residents stormed the town barracks after the police released a United States citizen they accused of stealing babies. It took law enforcement agents several days to pacify the protesters. A few weeks later, on 22 March, a group of fifty parents gathered in front of a local school in Zone 18's "Maya" settlement, demanding police protection for their children. Apparently, a few parents had spotted a pick-up with *gringos* on board near the school several times that week. The parents threatened to burn the barracks and drive the officers out if they did not begin patrolling the school gates.[37] Similarly, on 29 March of the same year, in the remote municipality of San Cristobal Verapaz, residents partially destroyed the court building, where police had harbored a U.S. woman thought to be a child snatcher. The mob left the woman badly beaten and comatose. Two weeks after, a violent crowd attacked three Guatemalan men attempting to kidnap a twelve-year-old girl in Villa Nueva, 18 kilometers from the capital. A similar response had occurred earlier in Bosques de San Nicolás, where residents nearly killed a soldier accused of raping a teenage girl.[38]

Coincident with these protests, street children throughout Guatemala City endured brutal attacks by police and "private" individuals. Yet when reports of *these* beatings, abductions, tortures, and murders appeared in the local media, no angry protesters gathered to demand protection for the children. In Bosques de San Nicolás, a discovery of four mutilated street children's bodies sparked no local action to punish the wrong-doers, but residents rallied to lynch the soldier they accused of raping a neighborhood girl. Has a fundamental distinction between street children and *barrio* children, and the consequent demands for their protection, occurred within Guatemala?

I believe that, for many, such a distinction has occurred. Chapters five and six of this book explore some of the mechanisms and motives behind the differentiation of street children from other Guatemalan children. The images of childhood conveyed through popular culture, religious doctrine, and mass media uphold the upper-class model of family life and discount the reality of poor households. Although this model bears no resemblance to the lives of the vast majority of Guatemalans, it prevails. Those families which deviate most from this model, those from which street children generally emerge, become viewed as condemnable and culpable for their own misfortunes, even by the poor, themselves. The propagation of upper-class ideals thus obscures the links between street children and the system of class privileges which operates in Guatemala and prevents others from identifying with street children's struggles.

Individuals also may have more personal reasons for condemning or disregarding street children. Some fear that these children will assault them, others feel appalled by their often filthy, ragged appearance. Still others, like drug peddlers and vendors of stolen goods, profit directly from the presence of children on the streets, and therefore contribute to their exploitation. Finally, as analyzed in chapter six, the repressive machinery of the establishment, besides brutalizing street children, also surely inhibits the effective protest of their abuse from within Guatemala.

Over the past forty years the government of Guatemala has systematically and brutally violated the human rights of its people. It is within this context that any analysis of street children's rights must be considered. Massive waves of repression, beginning with the crushing of popular unions during the mid-1950's, and culminating with the counterinsurgency sweeps of the early 1980's, dominate the country's recent collective memory. A short period of progressive reforms, in which the government for virtually the first time in history expressed concern for its citizens' well-being, came to an abrupt end in 1954 with the U.S.-manipulated overthrow of then acting president, Jacobo Arbenz. The subsequent change of power sparked a backlash against the urban and peasant unions that had flourished during the reform period and that had formed the backbone of Arbenz's support. According to historian Walter

Lafeber, the new military government, through its repressive tactics, successfully "wiped out" these popular organizations and prevented their resurgence for more than a decade.[39]

The army's inept governing and its reversal of many of Arbenz's social reforms sent living conditions spiraling back downward. Discontent grew not only among the populace, but also within the ranks of the military, as young officers protested the continued yielding of government officials to Washington's influence. Within five years, insurgent groups formed in response to the situation and "fought the U.S.-backed army to a draw in 1961 and 1962."[40] Although the rebel groups began splintering shortly afterwards, the perceived threat of revolution in Central America provoked massive U.S. support for and training of Guatemalan soldiers.[41] The "new" army became increasingly intent on annihilating its opposition and increasingly clever, too, as in 1966 it invented the practice of forced disappearance, the means of eliminating protest that later became wildly popular among military regimes in Latin America.[42] A statement on disappearance prepared by various international human rights groups describes its trauma:

> The government denies all knowledge and responsibility. *Habeus Corpus* procedures, where available, are ignored. Families are left with no financial means of support and the fear that any protest may lead to their own disappearance or the death of their loved one. The family does not know whether to mourn or hope, but is left in terrible uncertainty.[43]

The human rights organization America's Watch estimates that by 1986, the year of formal transition to civilian rule, some 35,000 Guatemalans had disappeared for political motives, the vast majority presumably murdered with impunity.[44] Other analysts, within Guatemala, emphasize that throughout more than thirty years of civil war, not one person has been charged with crimes against the state; although the military has abducted or "captured" thousands, it has recognized no political prisoners. Individuals simply disappear without a trace.[45]

In 1970, the military installed Colonel Arana Osorio as President of the Republic. Upon taking office, Arana vowed to "eliminate all guerrillas even 'if it is necessary to turn the country into a cemetery,'" and set to work by murdering 1000 people and arresting 1600 more during his first six weeks in power.[46] Fifty thousand Guatemalans died violently between 1966 and 1976, but the repression soon grew even more brutal, perhaps reaching its nadir during the 1982-83 dictatorship of General Ríos Montt, a fanatical evangelical Christian. Despite his religious affiliations, Ríos Montt's straying from morality soon became clear. During his seventeen-month rule, some 300 massacres left 16,000 dead and disappeared, 90,000 refugees and 1,000,000 displaced internally.[47] Massive migration of the population from the Western and Northern provinces at first made it difficult to assess Ríos Montt's thirst for blood. However, testimonies from survivors, later able to speak out through groups such as Grupo de Apoyo Mutuo (GAM) and the Coordinadora Nacional de Viudas Guatemaltecas (CONAVIGUA), lent support by the recent work of forensic anthropologists, have made clear that the murderous General desired no prisoners.

Most of the remains exhumed from the early 80's mass graves found in the Petén (Guatemala's northernmost department) have been those of women and children. This ghastly fact lends credence to the almost unthinkable, that under Ríos Montt whole villages were annihilated. Anthropologist Ricardo Falla, who spent years researching this period of violence, wrote from his own experience: "Before this . . . it was impossible for me to believe that human beings with hearts and flesh could be capable of reaching such mindless and merciless extremes of bestiality."[48]

Since the ousting of Ríos Montt in 1983, the scale of human rights violations has decreased. In the past decade, a shift has occurred in Guatemala, as throughout Central America, from massive to selective human rights abuses.[49] Yet violations are still prevalent enough to place Guatemala consistently at the top of the list for human rights abuses within Latin America.[50] State and paramilitary forces still regularly use torture, disappearance, extrajudicial execution, and intimidation, and this suggests that the smaller scale of violations (compared to the early 1980's) corresponds more to the diminished threat of insurgency (thanks to Ríos) than to any newfound respect for democratic principles among Guatemala's rulers.[51]

Ríos Montt's successor, General Oscar Humberto Mejía Víctores, did pave the way for positive change by establishing "free and fair" elections in 1985. Yet, for the army, the transition to democracy "did not signify a loss of control . . . the first civil government, that of Christian Democrat president Marco Vinicio Cerezo, had to develop within that control."[52]   Cerezo, himself, acknowledged this from the start.   In his inaugural speech he cautioned his supporters: "I remind you that I have received the government, but not the power."[53]   In seemingly bolder statements, during his October 1986 European tour, Cerezo claimed to have pacified political violence, leaving untackled only an increasing wave of common delinquency. GAM argued, nonetheless, that in just 1986, up to the point of the president's statements, 400 incidents of political assassinations or disappearances had occurred.[54]

Analyst Carlos Figueroa Ibarra notes that a type of hybrid state now seemingly has emerged within the country, one which exhibits "scraps of democracy (clean elections, separation of powers, progressive constitutions, civil governments)" alongside the remnants of dictatorship (an active terror apparatus, decisive power for non-elected officials, in this case the army directorate).[55]   The indecision with which Cerezo and his successors have acted on key human rights issues and, indeed, the military's two coup attempts against Cerezo illuminate the limits of Guatemalan democracy. Figueroa Ibarra asserts that while the hybrid state remains in tact, while fundamental social and economic reforms continue on the shelf, "[t]error will remain, only sleeping, not at all dead."[56]

For the Guatemalan street child, terror has not been sleeping.

CHAPTER TWO

A Street Child's Reality

'I believe that I will never again return to my house, I will never enter a school, I will never have a profession. I know that I will never again leave the street.'

Interview with Caolho, a Brazilian street child, one year before his death in a Rio de Janeiro massacre by military police, as appeared in "Morte Consumada," *Istoé* (4 August 1993), 63.

These girls are like the circus clowns, they fake a good time, when in reality they carry around a profound sadness.

From Manolo García, "Pequeñas esclavas nocturnas," *Prensa Libre Revista Domingo*, Guatemala (17 July 1994), 8-9.

They have to take everything, however ghastly, in their stride.

From Susanna Agnelli, *Street Children, A Growing Urban Tragedy* (London: Weidenfeld and Nicolson, 1986), 37.

A few years ago during my service as a Peace Corps volunteer, I formed my first impressions of Guatemala's street children. Stationed outside of the capital, I traveled into the city weekly or every two weeks to attend meetings or run errands. On these trips, I would see dozens of children congregated on street corners, or in alleyways, or in parks. Generally they wore shabby clothing and appeared physically ragged. I often saw them, eyes glazed, inhaling thick substances from small bottles or plastic bags. Young children would approach me as I ate at McDonald's, Pizza Hut, or a local favorite, Pop's Ice Cream, reaching out their hands to request spare change or left over food. Others boarded city buses to sing or tell stories of their difficult lives on the streets, hoping to elicit a few cents from the passengers. Many others tried to sell me watches, cassettes, candy, juices, or a million and one other trinkets.

In the capital I also would see adults scorning these same children, pushing them out of stores, ignoring their presence and sometimes, more damaging, insulting or hitting them. As I rode the 50 kilometers back to my town on the bus, I would think of what I had witnessed that day on the streets and my thoughts almost always turned to the kids. I would remember older boys teaching newcomers, seven and eight years old, to inhale drugs, police beating small, defenseless children, and whole groups of tiny bodies sprawled across alleyways, sleeping. I felt bitter, confused, but most of all, profoundly sad.

These dark impressions of street children that I first held paralyzed my ability to respond. Thanks to a fellow Peace Corps volunteer and friend who worked with a small group of them, though, my views of the kids as mere victims gradually faded. I began to understand the vitality and the strength of street children in their ability to respond even to life's toughest blows. I returned to Guatemala a few years later in order to learn more about their perspectives and everyday experiences, and I began to assess, on a deeper level, Guatemalan society's responses to them. Asociación Casa Alianza (ACA or Casa Alianza), the Latin American branch of New York's Covenant House and Guatemala's most prominent ngo attending to street children, supported my efforts by allowing me to work in several of their group homes and shelters. Through this direct contact during 1994, I lived among and came to know thirty boys and girls, seven to twenty years old, who had spent between two days and several years on the streets and who had entered ACA's programs anywhere from two weeks to seven months prior. Because of the diversity of their street experiences, ages, and sexes, I believe that this small sample represents well the overall population of children living on Guatemala's streets, with the obvious exception of a bias toward actually leaving the street and seeking services.

Of the thirty children with whom I worked, all responded enthusiastically to my brief presence in their lives. Contrary to my misconceptions and fears, I found them friendly, funny, extremely sharp, caring, and, in most cases, polite and respectful (more than I can say about many of the middle-class children with whom I have worked in other settings). They appreciated my attention and seemed to like having an "outsider" involved with, if only for a short while, their everyday lives. While all of the street children I met generally distrusted people who arrived solely to ask questions, during my two months in ACA homes about half of the thirty shared their life experiences with me. The other half was either too young or too guarded about "information." From the fifteen who willingly spoke to me, I conducted lengthy interviews with nine and taped the life stories of four. All four of these tapings involved young women in ACA's newly-opened child-mother home. Their stories appear, transcribed and translated, at the end of this chapter. My hope is that through making available their testimonies and my own observations from less formal conversations with children, I will deepen the reader's understanding of a street child's reality.

Leaving Home

Within Guatemala, similar sets of circumstances generally trigger the loosening or rupture of bonds between street children and their families. At times a particularly dramatic incident will provoke a child to leave home, as with Bernardo,[1] a fourteen-year-old boy who fled his family and his highlands village after an uncle caught him raping a younger cousin, then threatened to burn him alive if he returned. More often, however, the break occurs after a process in which a child who works outside of the home, or leaves sporadically because of trouble within it, becomes increasingly accustomed to street life. The child generally spends a night or two on the streets, returns home, then leaves for another three or four, until finally he or she remains outside, rarely, if ever, visiting the family.

Although the absence of one or both parents from the home in no way ensures that children will land on the streets (many single parents, grandparents, and aunts and uncles provide stable and supportive environments for children), all but one of the fifteen ACA kids with whom I spoke in depth reported a loss of at least one parent to death or abandonment. Fifteen-year-old Angelina's father died when she was one, leaving her mother to support alone the household's seven children. Her five older brothers and sisters, she informed me, all went to school, "showed good behavior, and good manners," but she and another brother developed "problems with vagrancy and the vice of drinking." Corina's father also died, when she was three years old, Jorge Mario's when he was one, and Marco Antonio's when he was nine. Vicente's father and mother both passed away when he was young, forcing him to survive alone on the streets. Graciela's mother reportedly died when she was young, as did Elida's, Carolina's and Ines'. Claudia's, Ruth's, Otoniel's, Edgar's and Marianna's parents all had separated. Later, Ruth's father also died, when she was thirteen.

The strain of separation or death on the remaining parent frequently led to abusive environments within the children's homes. At times the parent began drinking heavily or found a new spouse who resented children from the first marriage. Almost all of the kids within ACA homes exhibited scars as evidence of this abuse. Leopoldo was the size of a ten- or twelve-year-old but was actually seventeen. Massive burns on the back of his legs had prevented his normal growth since childhood. I noticed the burns for the first time when the boy played a soccer match in his shorts. Because of the grotesque appearance of the scars, which seemed open and infected, I questioned him about what had happened. He became embarrassed and did not want to discuss his legs, but his counselor later told me that Leopoldo had been burned when very young and that, as a result, the skin on his legs would no longer stretch; this had complicated his growth. Casa Alianza had paid for plastic surgery for

Leopoldo prior to my work there, but he had fled the hospital after the operation and prevented proper healing.

After fifteen-year-old Ines' mother died, her father took a second wife. The girl's father and stepmother both severely beat her. During one beating, Ines reports, her stepmother gashed her mouth with a kitchen knife, producing a large scar still visible today. After that incident, when she was roughly six years old, she left home to live with a grandmother on the southern coast for a while, but when a wealthy woman lured her to the capital, only to treat her as a servant, the girl's abuse continued. Ines landed in a government shelter after a few years and, finally, on the streets. Magdalena María, a nineteen-year-old mother of three who survives by prostituting herself, also suffered abuse in her home. She left for the streets when she was eight and explained to me, in her own simple terms, why: no one in her house loved her. She usually laughed about such things, but once revealed how serious her abuse had been. In a group meeting at her ACA home, she recounted how her father used to hang her by the ankles *"por ser tan malcriada"* (for being such a brat).

Graciela's father and older brother abused her for years until a group of nuns took charge of her. Later when she met her "partner" on the streets, he also beat her severely and threatened their one-year-old son. Corina's stepfather behaved so dictatorially in the house that she fled when eleven and "disappeared for two years" before attempting to return home. When her stepfather still behaved abusively toward her, she told herself to "be brave" and began "walking Eighteenth Street" (prostituting).

Carolina's father neglected her after her mother died, as did Claudia's when her mother left home. Both men began drinking heavily in response to their circumstances, forcing Carolina to live with abusive relatives and Claudia to become interned in a government shelter. Young Vicente experienced similar turmoil. When his mother's first husband died she relied on prostitution to support herself and her eight children. Through this activity she met a second husband, Vicente's father, who apparently treated her well. Nonetheless, she left him for a third man after roughly eight years of marriage, and Vicente's father began drinking out of despair, becoming a chronic alcoholic and eventually dying on the streets. His mother later suffered a stroke and while she recuperated at home, a younger sister arrived drunk one day and murdered her, an act which Vicente witnessed. Evangelicals brought him and his young siblings to their grandparents' home, but his grandfather was blind and his grandmother earned so little from washing that they could not maintain the large family. Vicente left, at the age of ten, to support himself.

Edgar, a boy of twelve, fled his home because his stepfather, too, drank excessively and would beat him, his mother and his sister. According to Edgar, his mother never intervened to protect him and one day, when the stepfather drove Edgar out of the home with a pitchfork, she wouldn't allow the boy back. He went to a relative's house and later to some neighbors', but never felt welcomed anywhere. As a result, he "found" the street at age nine or ten.

Marco Antonio and Otoniel both spent years moving between the street and their homes before finally separating from their families. For Marco Antonio, household economic hardships led him to work, cleaning city buses, from the age of eight or nine. The long hours he worked often required him to stay the night in a bus or a near by gas station. His stepfather's abusive behavior also discouraged him from sleeping at home. According to Marco, the man drank, smoked marijuana, and would terrorize the family when intoxicated. The boy finally fled the home more permanently when his stepfather gouged him with a machete (a wound that left a large scar on Marco's hand).

Like Marco Antonio, Otoniel cleaned buses to supplement his household's income. His family had lived relatively comfortably and he had studied until the age of twelve (fifth grade), but when his mother had an affair and became pregnant, her husband (Otoniel's stepfather, he never knew his real father) left the family and the boy's grandmother evicted all of them from her house. Otoniel's new stepfather drank and demanded that he work, ordering his mother not to feed him until he gave her money. He would sleep in the buses he cleaned for a few days, then return home, but finally left for good when his mother threw him out of the house for fighting with his stepfather.

The circumstances described by these youths represent the norm for Guatemala's street children. According to a 1993 study by the Centro de Desarrollo Integral Comunitario (CEDIC), a local ngo supporting street and working kids, 80 percent of the 275 street children they contacted reported physical abuse in their homes, 90 percent verbal abuse, and 10 percent sexual abuse.[2]   A second study conducted by a different ngo showed that 23 percent of street children have been sexually abused by their parents and many more by other relatives.[3] Further, CEDIC reports that 40 percent of the surveyed street children left home because they felt unloved, 41 percent because they were thrown out, and 9 percent because they were abandoned.[4] Fifty-seven percent of the children came from homes with alcoholic parents and 33 percent from homes with a drug-addicted father or mother.[5] These figures, along with the above descriptions of familial abuse given by the street children, strongly evidence that Guatemala's kids leave their homes for the street not because they desire more freedom or lack discipline, a popular misconception, but rather because they fear for their lives.

Hitting the streets

Once they leave home, many children become quickly assimilated into the street environment. According to ACA street educator Marvin Castillo, kids often have acquaintances on the street even before they break with their families, either through working relationships, or through older brothers and sisters or neighborhood kids. These acquaintances introduce the new arrivals to the small groups with which they coexist on the streets, sharing resources, sleeping together, and protecting each other.[6] Even those who have no prior contacts on the streets soon find *compañeros* (mates) with which to form their own groups and bolster security. Street children almost always congregate with two or three others, rarely walking alone or forming part of larger gangs (although this latter does occur sometimes, as Claudia's testimony will evidence).

Despite the fights which periodically arise on the street, within these small groups and among street children, in general, a fierce sense of loyalty exists. When I asked some younger boys to share with me one memory from their street lives, eight-year-old Ricardo said "by asking for money I bought all kinds of fruits. I shared them with my friends, we all ate. . . ." Twelve-year-old Wilder recalled that he had hitchhiked all the way from Honduras with a *compañero* and then spent time with him on Guatemala's streets before entering Casa Alianza. The girls also often spoke of friends who had helped them in their struggles. Claudia and Carolina's testimonies will highlight this mutual support, although Corina seemed to possess the strongest sense of solidarity of all of the kids that I met. She deeply moved me when she recounted the death of Toby, a street boy murdered in 1990 in a fatal argument with another youth. Corina cried when she spoke of Toby. It seems that he had been a great friend to her. She remembered that before he died they had spent much time together. When she felt cold, she said, Toby would give her his jacket, when she needed money, Toby would obtain it for her. When he saw her inhaling glue he would take the bag from her. So, when she heard of his death, she said, she could not accept it. She would sit for hours in the same places they had frequented, waiting for his return. "It's sad," she said, "to see a friend die like that."

Within the city, street children generally concentrate in specific sectors, major streets, parks, or markets, drawn by the relative safety they perceive in numbers. In these locations, focal points or *focos*, children find the necessary means for their survival. They gradually weave relationships within their *focos* and, thus, transform their locations from mere physical to social spaces.[7] Because street children eat and sleep in the same spots day after day, people working around the *focos*, in cheap hotels, cafeterias, and markets, know them. Owners of small food stands may sympathize with them and allow them to eat for free at the end of the day. Other market vendors, however, bitterly complain about the presence of street children, as they believe the kids drive away customers afraid of being assaulted or robbed.

According to Edgar Alay, the coordinator of CEDIC's street programs, younger children, seven and eight years old, generally survive on the streets by begging or singing on buses for money. Many city residents sympathetically give a few coins to these kids because of their tender age. Once these youngsters begin to mix with older children, who generally steal to survive, however, they often lose their satisfaction with pocket change and begin stealing, themselves. Moreover, once kids turn twelve or thirteen, begging becomes a less feasible means of survival, for then adults view them as old enough to work.[8] Still, some street children resist stealing either because they fear being caught or because they believe it morally wrong. Seventeen-year-old Otoniel claims that he never stole, preferring to "ask ten times before taking something" that didn't belong to him. Despite his rocky familial relationships, he attributes this virtue to the positive influence of his mother.

Those children who do steal generally engage in petty theft, robbing passers-by of their sunglasses or wallets, or breaking into cars. They sometimes use the articles that they steal, but more frequently sell them to vendors at one of the city's several markets that feature stolen merchandise. In spite of the small scope of their thefts, the risk for street children involved with stealing proves high. Victims of their robberies have beaten them mercilessly. Police also often foil the kids' attempts and haul them into Guatemala's dreary juvenile jails, where they may spend indefinite periods suffering harassment and performing mundane chores. Alternatively, police may brutalize children they suspect of stealing directly on the streets. A recent incident, in which a security guard caught a seventeen-year-old who had stolen a tourist's sunglasses, then shot the boy through the head, graphically illustrates this danger.

Even when not breaking the law, street children constantly face an abusive police presence. Guatemala's beat cops stop kids to ask them for identification but, according to many children, merely rip or confiscate their documents. Cops also extort money or goods from children who have no identification in exchange for allowing them to remain on the street. Tellingly, 100 percent of the street children in CEDIC's survey reported that the police had abused them.[9] This relationship between street children and security forces will be discussed in chapter four.

In addition to stealing and begging, many street children survive through prostitution. While only 21 percent of the children surveyed by CEDIC admitted engaging in prostitution (as opposed to 83 percent who said they stole and 34 percent who reportedly begged or sang),[10] the actual percent may be higher. The children's rights group ChildHope estimates that 80 percent of girls on the street turn to prostitution.[11] These girls, like Magdalena María, often sing or sell candy on buses during the day in order to pay for a night's hotel room. Their hotel rooms, in turn, generate profits of a more sordid nature. Although the practice is more common among girls than boys, the latter represented 25 to 30 percent of those who admitted prostitution in the CEDIC study.[12]   ACA's Castillo notes that boys commonly extend sexual favors to gay men in return for food, money or other gifts.

The degrading nature of prostitution and the dangers involved with stealing frequently provoke street children to consume drugs to, as they say, "get up the courage" to engage in both means of survival. Of the 275 children in CEDIC's survey, 96 percent reported regular drug use. They most commonly use shoe glue (85 percent use the drug according to the survey), solvent (67 percent), marijuana (36 percent), paint thinner (34 percent), "tip top" (28 percent), and cocaine (only 6 percent).[13] Because several of these narcotic and hallucinogenic substances temporarily alleviate cold and hunger, many children inhale them throughout the day instead of simply before stealing or walking the strip. While I spoke with a group of children in the city's Central Park one morning, two teenage girls began inhaling solvent in front of me. It was nine o'clock and already they were escaping into their own private world created each day through reality distorting drugs. A street educator accompanying me explained that many children, especially girls, prefer solvent to glue because they can inhale it from discrete containers that fit easily inside a child's palm. Solvent is also less expensive than glue and neater, as glue frequently sticks to children's faces and mouths.

In walking around other focos that same day, by noon I already had seen dozens of children inhaling glue or solvents from plastic bags and jars. Even standing a few feet away from the children I began to feel light headed from the strong odor. The effect, and eventual cause, of this near-constant drug use is intense addiction. Dependence on such substances inhibits many from leaving the street because shelters rarely admit children under the effects of drugs. Of the street kids in CEDIC's study, 82 percent had entered shelters in the past, but 54 percent of them had left because of "the need to drug themselves."[14]

Inhalant abuse proves further self-destructive because of the serious physiological damage it causes. Inhalants can wreak havoc on nearly all body parts: the brain and central nervous system; the heart and lungs; the liver, kidneys, ovaries, and digestive organs. Bone marrow loss, blood disorders, muscular atrophy, hearing loss and blindness also may result from extensive misuse of these toxins. As I spoke with two street girls one afternoon, Arturo, a sixteen- or seventeen-year-old boy, approached and claimed to have stopped consuming drugs. Not likely—he looked at me through glassy eyes and spoke in halting rhythmic speech. Still, he said he had quit because of a recent hospitalization for liver problems; the result of eight steady years of inhaling glue. Friends apparently had brought him to the hospital when his eyes turned a deep yellow. In 1993 another street child, sixteen-year-old Joel Linares, died of kidney failure after ten years of glue use.[16]

Children also suffer a host of more common health problems while on the streets. Lice: 92 percent of children in CEDIC's study suffered from them.[17] Upper respiratory infections: 88 percent had contracted them on the streets from exposure to dampness, cold, and torrential rains during Guatemala's wet season, as well as exhaust from cars and buses (thick clouds of black smoke frequently pollute Guatemala City air at street level) and continuous exposure to dirt and dust.[18] Skin infections stemming from the inability to bathe, dysentery from the inability to secure safe food and drinking water, and festering wounds also pose common problems for street kids. I was with a young prostitute, Alba, when a street educator cleaned a deep gash on her foot. She had been run over by a motorcycle a week before and the foot had become badly infected. Merely being outside all day, then, exposes children to countless physical dangers. In addition, 53 percent of the children in CEDIC's study had contracted sexually transmitted diseases through unprotected intercourse with clients and other street children.[19]

Leaving the street, however, does not ensure children greater protection. Within the government's juvenile detention centers, children held for loitering or failing to carry identification cohabit with those having committed more serious offenses. Equally, first time detainees bunk beside those incarcerated for perhaps the fourth or fifth time. Thus, younger or "less experienced" children may quickly acquire the behaviors of their older, perhaps more "hardened" counterparts. Several children that I interviewed also reported widespread homosexual activity within the government centers, making time there unbearable for those not inclined to such behavior. Even within private institutions homosexual advances sometimes occur. Vicente has a particular interest in young boys. At age twelve or thirteen, he lured two younger boys into a bath-room in an ACA home and sodomized them. ACA expelled him from the home as a result, but allowed him to return in exchange for his promise to attend counseling. He still has difficulty controlling his urges. Educators in his current home have surprised him several times during intercourse with a nine-year-old boy in the same program. Apparently the nine-year-old consented to relations after Vicente promised to give him money or sweets. Staff members also have found other boys togeth-er in the same bunk on numerous occasions.

Within ACA boys' homes many residents get shame or blame when expressing confusion over their sexual identities or asserting their bi- or homosexual preferences. Most receive, willingly or not, professional counseling around this issue, with the implication that they may be "cured" with appropriate treatment. Girls, too, often enter homosexual relationships, especially while in juvenile jails. On the street one day I encountered two teenage women, Alba and Brenda, who, while prosti-tuting themselves with men, also had a sexual relationship with each other. Alba, the mother of a two-year-old boy, had tattooed a heart on her hand with Brenda's name inside.

At the government's shelters for younger children (the courts cannot send those under twelve to detention centers), boys and girls often cohabit, an often detrimental arrangement. Ines, the fifteen-year-old who landed in a government shelter after escaping abuse in her home and slave-like conditions in her "employer's" house, explained that she had fled her shelter for the streets after a boy there repeatedly tried to rape her. Although social workers intervened to counsel the boy, Ines still felt unsafe. She and other children also report abusive attitudes among staff members and degrading treatment within government shelters and detention centers. Tragically, all of these negative attributes combine to induce youngsters to flee the facilities designed to protect and "rehabili-tate" them. (A more detailed analysis of the government's treatment of street children appears in chapter three).

Children's experiences on the streets and in institutions may have devastating impacts on their self-images. Writing about parallel circum-stances that exist in Brazil, sociologist Rinaldo Vieira Arruda notes that street children "on one hand develop creative behaviors which make possible their survival," but on the other they internalize negative images of these behaviors "because while it permits their daily survival, in the long run it only leads to prison and death." The street child, thus, "perceives that his daily life is an impossibility, it is death in life."[20] Vieira Arruda asserts that the biggest step in prolonging street children's delinquency comes with their introduction to the official "rehabilitation" process because from then on, he states, "they become recognized, catalogued, stigmatized, and watched over. From then on model behavior is demanded from them, but anti-social behavior always is expected."[21] The commentary of Jaime, a Peruvian street child, reflects this expectation, as he says that "once they have written you down you are marked . . . and now, you know, I am working honorably and something happens tomorrow, they rob a stall, and the police, who do they look for? Huh? They look for Jaime."[22] Vera da Silva and Helena Abramo, who, like Vieira Arruda, study Brazilian street kids, refer to this process as a "criminalization of their [street children's] condition, of their strategies, of their spaces."[23]

Street children's self-images generally deteriorate the longer they spend on the streets or in detention centers, for in their effort to survive they become accustomed to and always expect exploitation and abuse. Among the boys I observed, a generally abysmal level of self-confidence existed. As I tried to teach ten-year-old Ignacio a basic grammar lesson one day, for example, the boy paid attention but would not try completing any exercises on his own. When I asked him why, he didn't reply. "Do you think you can do them?" I asked. "No." "Should I explain it again?" Silence. "Do you think that if I explain it again you will understand?" "No," he replied. After I finally convinced him to listen again, Ignacio answered all of the examples correctly. He felt proud that day, but such positive lessons rarely occur on the streets.

Another boy, Otoniel, constantly seemed sad or worried and often told me that he felt no love from anyone. Vicente always sought physical reassurance, a hug or a pat, of his acceptance by adults. At age fifteen he still wet his bed every night. Moreover, his sexual counseling seemed only to reinforce his negative self-image. When his home started attending, as a group, lectures on reproductive health, Vicente searched for pretexts not to go. The first week he provoked a fight with another boy and refused to go on the basis that he was still angry. The second week he fled the home, conveniently, the day of the talk and did not return until the following afternoon. And, what of the self-image of the nine-year-old boy who allowed himself to be sodomized by Vicente in exchange for candy or an article of clothing?

The deepest schisms in self-respect, however, existed among the young women that I observed and interviewed, perhaps because of their double exploitation, as children and as women, and their economic and physical dependence on either "clients" or street boys. In an innovative study of homeless mothers with substance abuse issues, U.S. researchers uncovered the extent of violence suffered by women on the streets and the impact such trauma has on sobriety. Nearly 50 percent of the 84 women in a St. Louis, Missouri, rehabilitation program, similar to ACA's child-mother home, had been raped, and about 75 percent had survived some form of violent attack as adults. Half again, had suffered physical abuse in their relationships, 20 percent had attempted suicide, and most had extensive histories with loss of family, friends, and lovers to violence. Even while in treatment, the injury, abuse, or death of loved ones continually loomed over the women and complicated their efforts to remain in the program.[24]

To assess the damages heaped upon Guatemala's street girls and adolescents, one must add to these personal attacks on women and their loved ones the trauma of being targets in police and government crusades against street children, and also examine the overall insecurity and chaos of living in a deeply troubled, war-torn society. During my first three weeks in the child-mother home, I spoke the most with Magdalena María and I believe that she best exemplifies how street girls internalize violence and negative self-images. When thinking of her life, her conduct, and her outlook, I felt, and still feel, a sense of despair. Magdalena, aged nineteen, had two children and was expecting her third when I began working in the home. She had just returned there two weeks before, after spending months back on the streets. Her eleven-month-old son, Oscar, lived with her in the home, but the police long ago had placed her other child in state custody. During this past episode on the street, she had Oscar with her. She told me that she sold gum and sang on buses in order to buy food for herself and her baby. But, she also prostituted herself.

Even within the home, little Oscar suffered. Magdalena neglected him, leaving him in his crib most of the day and rarely changing his diaper. He developed a severe skin infection as a result. Magdalena could not nurse him since she was expecting again. Instead, she often gave him dirty bottles that she retrieved from the floor, and sometimes "forgot" to give him lunch. Once, he tipped over in his walker and fell into a puddle. A friend Ruth grabbed the poor child, crying and covered with mud, but when Magdalena María saw him, she only laughed. How could she laugh at this? I remembered, then, that she also had laughed at her own abuse. She had left her home at age eight and spent eleven years moving between the street and juvenile detention centers. She said that she knew what is was like to be tracked, hunted by the police. She recalled how the cops had taken her son away, and said that she felt terrible every time she thought of him. You couldn't tell through her treatment of Oscar, but really, how must she have felt? A failure.

After only five weeks back in the home she left again. The immediate factors precipitating her departure seem almost irrelevant. She had to leave. Another woman in the home said that she needed sex, that Magdalena's body had become too accustomed to it over the years. I sensed more that she needed to continue destroying herself. As she walked out the door of the home, a housemate asked her where she would go. "Eighteenth Street," Magdalena replied. Oscar was in the hospital that day. She probably has lost custody of him by now. She did try to get him once, but she went to the hospital drunk.

After Magdalena, two other women left the home within a week. The home's supervisor suggested that being outside was part of the women's lives, that they had spent more time outdoors than in, and that that was where they felt more comfortable. Many street youths both male and female do change their lives dramatically. The testimonials, below, attest to some of these great transformations. CEDIC's Edgar Alay estimates, however, that 50 percent of Guatemala's street children never "make it out." They continue stealing and drugging themselves until they die on the streets or society locks them away in prison.[25] Unless educators convince children to enter shelters quickly, Alay warns, the street becomes too powerful of a force for educators to intervene later. Even when children experience near-death, humiliation, and extreme exploitation within this environment, the street powerfully lures them. "It's as if the street has absorbed them, practically killed them."[26]

In their own words

In August 1994, I interviewed and taped four young women from ACA's child-mother home narrating their life stories. I have formatted their testimonials in the manner they appear, below, in order to convey speech patterns, indicate pauses, and make the material more readable.

Ruth

The first time I met Ruth, she was squatting on the kitchen floor of Casa Alianza's child-mother home, lowering herself to the height of her one-year-old son in order to feed him a late lunch. She spoke with the home's cook and one of its educators about her experiences in other ACA homes, and although she complained about the child-mother program's rigorous 4:30 am wake-up call, she seemed animated that day, much more than in most subsequent days. The cook told me that Ruth had returned to the home two weeks earlier, after five months "on the street."

A few days after that first meeting, I tried to find out more from Ruth about her past and the events that led her to Casa Alianza. Helping her with her daily chores, I began asking her about her family. She told me that she came to Guatemala from El Salvador when still a child, with her father and two brothers. Her older brother, she said, had returned to El Salvador, and the other, along with her father, had died. Her answer, although polite, stopped there. She offered no explanation, no further details.

Ruth's guarded nature almost never eased. During meetings, at meals, on excursions, Ruth remained withdrawn, seeming incapable of trusting even those women in the home who had the experiences most similar to her own. Periodically, she would tell me things about her past, but only scraps, very selective scraps. To my surprise, when I asked the women in the house who would willingly talk about their lives on the streets, their lives at home, and their lives in institutions on tape, Ruth volunteered, but sought assurance that her information would be treated responsibly and without humiliating or embarrassing her in any way.

On the day of the taping Ruth, normally quiet and reserved, revealed the most intimate and formative events in her life, in great detail, from start to present. As we finished, she told me, almost trying to defend the break with her normal silence, "[I]n order to be able to say all of this, I have prepared myself. Because I want to get out a little of, of what it is I have inside."

This is Ruth's story, as she told it:

My name is Ruth
and my life has been very sad.
When I was small,
my mother and brothers lived together
and they never got along well with my father.
My mother began to distrust my father,
and my father
also.
And my father began to say
that my mother had other men,
that she had other husbands, like,
and he no longer permitted us
to spend so much time with her.
The time came when
the war began.
When the war began
we came here,
to Guatemala.
And my father brought us here
without knowing that my mother already knew. . . .
In that time my father was
a shoemaker

and he'd go out to
fix shoes
and one time . . .
he took the three of us
to work with him . . . we went to Ciudad Real,
by the railroad tracks . . .
to a woman's house . . .
and I noticed that my father began to ask her
if they rented there
or if it was their own.
And he began to tell his life
of how he didn't have anywhere to live,
that there were only three of us,
that my mother had drowned in Puerto San José
[*a Guatemalan tourist spot*] . . . and from then on
my father told us
to say that to whomever asked us,
and we believed my father.
And we grew up believing in that.

You believed that she had died?

Aha—that she had died.

*Ruth says that she and her father and two brothers were given a small parcel
of land in that settlement, by whom it is not clear, and between them they constructed a shack, a small house made of corrugated tin and other inexpensive
materials. Once they settled, she says:*

My father began to
fix shoes
he'd go out and take along all of us.
When my older brother was seven,
my father made him his little shoeshine box.
And he told him that he was going to shine shoes.
Then, after that,

my little brother also began,
and I came and said to my father that I also wanted
to help him because it wasn't right that my brothers also worked
and not me.
So they decided to dress me as a man.
They dressed me like a man
and they made a little box for me, also.
And I went out to shine shoes. . . .
I went to shine in Bellos
to the Justo
to Guajitos
[all poor settlements in the capital]
I would go out to shine, like that
sometimes in our same colonia.
Or I'd go to Zone 1
with my little brother I'd go to the center,
to Zone 10.
And sometimes my brother shined
or sometimes no
or sometimes he would begin to clean car windows
and I would begin
to ask for money when the cars stopped
at the traffic lights.
And when we had gathered up a quantity
we would arrive at the house already really late,
like eleven or twelve at night.
And always when we went in my father would hit us.

*Not understanding why, if they earned money for their household, Ruth's father
would hit them when they returned, I ask her and she explains:*

Because we arrived really late
and he thought that perhaps
we were, like . . .
that we had stayed out doing something bad, and no.
And we would hand over the money to him, because to him we gave it.

We gave him some 25
some 20 quetzales
every day . . .
There were nights when my little brother told me that we should ask
for lodging
and we would stay out, sleeping in some other place.
And this, having our own house.
But . . . my little brother perhaps didn't feel comfortable
or who knows.
And my older brother began . . . well.
We went to Castañas to shine,
and my father to fix shoes.
Who knows what was wrong with my brother
and he said to me,
'You go there, I'm going there,'
and from there my father told us 'at six we'll meet here' . . .
When it was six, only we met up with my father.
And my older brother didn't show up.
And my father was really panicked . . .
really frightened.

He began to look for him,
file police reports, and everything.
After a few days we went to look for him in the hospitals,
in the cemeteries,
in the morgue,
we went to look for him in the
police precincts,
and nothing.
He didn't show up.
And a few days later
they came to tell my father that my brother was sleeping in the Bar
Triunfo
[*a bar is a prostitution house in Guatemala*]. . . .
And my brother began to have vices.
He began to become lost and to distance himself from us.

How old was he?

He was eight years old.
No, seven-and-a-half. . . .
And days and days would go by when
we would know nothing of him.
Then, with my little brother,
I began to go out to shine.
We would stay out of the house.
When I was perhaps six years old
my older brother was with us one night
and my father began to play with us,
to spin my brothers
and not me.
So I came and I said to him:
'Dad do to me what you did with my little brother,'
I said to him.
And he mounted me on top of his shoulders
and began to spin around.
When he spun me,
when I felt it
he kissed my parts.
And I felt really bad,
and from there he carried me outside and began to have relations with
me.
And I began,
I felt really bad,
and then I began to cry,
and I asked God forgiveness for what had happened.
But before that my father would tell us a lot
that my mother had said perhaps he had brought us
because perhaps he was going to take me as his woman. . . .
And my father said no,
that he was always going to take care of me. . . .
My father said that he was going to take care of me and my mother
answered

'you're going to take care of her, but for you, wretched old man.'
My mother treated him like that.

And when, after that happened,
and I found that out,
I didn't feel like going home anymore.
And my father paid me to wash his clothes,
or at times when he didn't give me money
I stole from him,
or he had to do it with with me for there
to be money.
Then at times I became very sad,
I would begin to cry
and I would leave the house,
and I would go to sleep, like that,
in the neighborhoods
or to places, like, to ask for lodging.
And they gave to me.
They gave to me and my little brother.
And . . .

I interrupt because I want to know more about her interactions with these people. I ask her if she would stay with people she didn't know,

yes . . . with people I didn't know.
They gave to me
and gave me clothes, like.

And what did you tell those people when you asked to stay the night?

I told them that if they wouldn't give me lodging
for the night
because I lived very far away
and at night I couldn't find my house
only during the day,
and . . . I told them to help me in that I hadn't eaten.

And with my little brother I went around like that.
We told the person that we were lost
that we lived in Escuintla, something like that.
And . . . that's how it went,
they gave to us,
they told us that it was alright.
Now when they gave us a place to stay
they said to us that where, that why were we like that,
and we told them that my father had thrown us out of the house
and that's why we were in the streets.

Well, days later my little brother got lost
he got lost in . . . in the center it seems that he got lost.
[*She says in a distressed voice*]
And he didn't come back to the house anymore either!
And we hardly knew anything of him anymore.

How long ago . . . how many years after . . .

After the disappearance of my brother?
A year,
my little brother became lost.

Aha. And how old was he?

He was . . .
he, yes, he was like maybe seven years old.
Six years old, my little brother.
And my father started looking for him,
also, to go around for him,
and nothing.
We didn't find him.
And my father continued with me, having relations.
And I always felt bad,
right?
And I at times even

did it with him also
because of money.
And he always gave to me,
or sometimes when he didn't give me money,
I stole from him.
And I met friends, like,
who told me 'lets go to sell,' they told me,
'and we'll give you your cents.'
'OK,' I told her,
and I would go with her to sell.
And I would go to the houses
to ask for clothes,
shoes,
food.
As I couldn't work, they gave me huge bags of clothes,
of stale bread,
old tortillas,
cold food,
or shoes, like.
And money. . . .

And my father began to distrust me . . .
he began to treat me badly
and whenever I would arrive really late he would hit me.
And the people around the house would say to him 'don Israel,'
'don't hit your daughter,'
'no, she's your only kid that helps you.'
And my father would say to them 'this son of a bitch
doesn't help me for shit,'
'What happens is that she's a vagabond,
drug addict,
she likes to be out until ten o'clock at night. . . .'

Ruth tells how at one point she ran away for a few days and lived with a woman she helped to sell food on the streets. She went back home, though, when the woman and her daughter said they were leaving and Ruth feared

they would take her out of the capital with them. When she returned, her
father acted happy to see her, but within days, she says:

Those relations that I had with him
began again.
And nobody knew it.
[*Her sense of shame really comes through here.*
Her voice becomes quieter, more despairing]
And at times people would say to me 'And your father
doesn't touch you like that,'
and I would tell them no.
At times I came to think that my father wasn't my real father,
because he was a big Jehovah's Witness,
he was a great believer in the *Bible,* and everything.
I began to think,
and in my mind I said 'If he's
as religious as he says, he wouldn't have hurt me so much.'
And how he hit me, too.
I was around nine years old
when I got lost in the center.
And some policemen . . . brought me to the first precinct and. . .
they began to file reports,
and nobody came to see,
to look for me
or anything.
From there they brought me to the house. . . .

Confused by this I ask how the cops knew where she lived. Ruth replies that
she told them. This is a seeming inconsistency. Why did the cops wait to bring
her home, why did she wait to tell them where she lived? Perhaps she didn't
want to go to her house, or perhaps she wanted her father to worry. It is
unclear, but she says no more about this and goes on to narrate what happened
when the police did bring her home:

They told my father not to leave me lost
because I was a good girl.

And my father told him that
I hadn't gotten lost, that I had gone away from him.
And after that, my father hit me.
After [the policeman] left me
he told him, 'Don't hit your daughter, sir,'
he said.
And after the police left, he got me up really early
and he beat me,
he began to hit me . . .
with a belt he hit me.
So I came and I said to him 'You know what
old asshole, that's why I had left,
because what happens is that for me you don't worry,'
I told him.
'For my brothers, yes,'
I told him.
'Shut up son of a bitch!'
and he would beat me.
Or would bow me down, like,
in the path,
and people would stop and look at me, and everything. . . .
From there
I heard that my little brother
that the older and the younger,
were in the Ayau
[*a state-run shelter for children in the city center*]
So I went and asked admittance and they gave it to me.
And I stayed in the Ayau, for some months. . . .

[Later] I escaped from the home,
from there, from that home,
I went to the house.

Having heard of many kids who "escape" the Ayau, and always wondering
how they manage it, I take advantage of this opportunity to ask her how she
did. She says that she escaped through the church doors and began running to

Eighteenth Street to catch a ride on a bus to her house. During her time back
at the house, Ruth tells that she "found" a lost girl, and brought her to stay
with her and her father. Ruth felt happy to have a playmate, but the situation
turned into another nightmare for her when police arrested her father and a
neighbor for kidnapping the girl. Before the arrest, though, when the girl went
to live with the neighbor, Ruth decided to leave home again.

I left again for the street

I did.

But I didn't go to the street, rather I went around with my brother.

Well that night . . .

my brother told me, 'lets go stay over there.' . . .

Then I met some of his friends

that had been in the Ayau . . .

and we went that day to Ninth Avenue,

where the train parks,

and from there we slept in front of the Concordia Park

on the ground.

We got up and started begging,

we had taken to the streets.

But I didn't consume vices

or anything.

And by the blessed grace

I never consumed vices in the whole time that I was outside, in the

street.

I slept in the street,

or with my brother we slept

beneath, like,

the buildings.

After we shined shoes.

During this particular period in the street, the police brought Ruth back to the
Ayau, but she escaped during an excursion one day. Thinking about what
she'd just told me about her life, I wondered what could happen at the Ayau to
make so many kids want to leave there for the streets. Although I had
forgotten at this time, in an earlier conversation she had told me that the Ayau

is horrible. In what sense? I asked her.

In everything.
They hit you there, boys and girls are together,
they sell and use drugs there.

Here, I ask her: But why did you want to escape?

Because I didn't like being locked up.
And one time we tried to escape, me and my brother,
through the big door,
and they caught us, and made us go in.
And, after they moved us inside
another time when we left on an excursion
I fled.
And I went to the house,
and when I arrived, my father had been in prison
and had gotten out.
And I began to cry,
and I told him to forgive me,
but it was not my intention to have done it.
But I was guilty, it was my fault that he was in jail.

But why? I ask, completely not making the connection.

Because I had brought the girl, right?
And she said that my father was a kidnapper
and because of that they sent him to jail with a woman.
After a few days, the woman got out.
After the woman got out
she died shortly afterwards.
She died of sadness.
Because she was locked up in jail
for something that is very unjust,
because even she
went to the can because of me.

And I lived with that great guilt,
and it is something that,
that I'm not able to survive.
After that, my father always had relations with me.

*Ruth's sadness over her father's suffering seems almost too poignant when
juxtaposed with his abuse of her. Her deep love for her father despite this
aspect of their relationship becomes clearer later when her father suffers a series
of strokes and she cares for him single-handedly. For now, she responds to his
grotesque treatment, as always, by leaving the house as often as possible.
Only this time she encounters far more serious problems than before on the
streets. While selling* chuchitos, *little tamales, she and a friend went into a
few bars to sell them for snacks. In one bar, she recounts:*

They told me to come in the afternoon
but to come alone to sell *chuchitos*
and that they would give me presents.
And I arrived,
I reported in the evening
and they told me to wait.
It was perhaps eight or nine o'clock at night. . . .
And she [the matron] had dolls in her room.
I told her to lend them to me,
and I began to play dolls, and all. . . .
And once in the room
she began to ask me if I had ever had relations.
I told her no,
that I did not know.
And we went to sleep.
When we went to sleep,
during the night
I felt that they were touching me and it frightened me
and I kept looking,
and what, it was a man that was sleeping beside me.
So then, after, I began to cry and to scream
and he told me that if I did it with him,

that he would pay me.
In other words, the woman had sold me to the man.
And she told me 'Look, this is how you have relations,'
and she had relations in front of me.
And the man grabbed her breasts and I said no,
and no.
And then they told me that they were going to give me money.
And they were going to buy me a dress,
and clothes,
shoes.
And then when I left that day,
in the early morning,
I had to do it,
the man grabbed me by force.
And when I was with him, afterwards . . .
when I went to bathe
I was bleeding.
And I began to cry and I was really frightened. . . .
I thought that my father was going to notice that they had made me
bleed,
that they had done something to me.
And I began crying, and it was a trauma
something that I have had within me,
that I haven't been able to get out of my mind.

I later ask her if the same bleeding had happened with her father.
She explains:

It's that when I had relations with my father
[*here, when she says my father, she lowers her voice*]
he didn't hurt me,
or anything. On the other hand, when
the man grabbed me like that,
forcefully,
and when I got up,
I was full of blood.

I went to bathe
and I was bleeding. . . .
It's that he practically broke me.

And that [abuse] . . . with your father, how often would it occur?

Sometimes every day,
but it lasted a long time.
Perhaps we spent . . .
around three years . . .
or two years
like that . . .
having relations. . . .

Sometime after her rape in the bar, it is unclear how long after, Ruth's father suffered a stroke during an argument with her little brother. When he returned from the hospital, Ruth dedicated herself to looking after him. She began working in a cafeteria and would bring jars full of leftover food for his dinner. One evening when she arrived, she discovered that her father had suffered a second attack:

It was six in the afternoon.
I was very happy . . .
And I entered the room, very happy.
From the door I said, 'Dad, Dad, I'm here,
And . . . look what I brought you,'
I said to him.
'Today I brought you fresh tortillas,'
I told him.
'Look I brought you food,'
I said to him 'come, let's eat,' I told him.
When I entered the room
my father was passed out underneath the table.
I began to cry,
and I started to shout,
and I said

'Help me! Help my father!'
And foam was coming out of his mouth.
Who knows even how long he had been passed out.

Then, a woman said to me,
'We always come to see him
but today we haven't come.'
And he had his machine . . .
he said that it was for one . . . of my brothers.
But because my brothers left,
he had to sell it.
It was around nine at night,
and I said to him, 'Dad, tell me where you have the money
hidden.'
And he only said to me 'Aahh, aahh'
[because he couldn't talk]. . . .
When I found the money
they took him to the hospital
and I paid for the taxi with the money,
they took him away to the hospital.
When I went to see him, my father was already,
he already looked healthy to me, and all.
The second time I went to see him,
my father had his eyes really pasted over . . .
The next day I didn't feel like going to visit him.
And a woman said to me 'Let's go,' and I changed.
And after I changed,
I saw that some men in black entered and
someone said 'The funeral home entered [the house of] doña Fina' . . .
and I went in there
and I heard that,
that they said
'Who is don Israel's wife?'
he said.
'No, he doesn't have a wife,'
she told him,

'but I am the one with the children,'
she told him.
'Is your name Delfina López?'
'Yes,' the woman told him.
'Well you have to come with us,' he said. . . .
And I began to scream,
and I began to scream
all along the railway line,
passing from one side to the other.
And I told the people that my father had died,
that he had died.
And I didn't know what to do. . . .

When we arrived,
I saw my older brother again,
after so many years that I hadn't seen him,
and I saw him. . . .
When it was seven, at night,
they took him out of the hospital room
and my brother wanted to see him.
They opened the coffin.
He had cotton even here,
in his mouth.
He was going like that, as if . . . he was alive.
And I didn't believe it.
And in the funeral home,
we took him in the car to the funeral,
some women paid the funeral parlor,
others the burial.
In the end,
he was buried.

And I got in the back with the coffin with my father
and the women were up front,
and I was embracing the coffin,
I couldn't stop crying for my father.

Then, in the night, my little brother arrived.
And I . . . said to him
'Look, my father's come back now,
but he's dead,' I told him.
'No!' he said to me,
'my father doesn't have to be dead,
he's alive.'
And he began to run in back,
around the coffin.
'How good that you have come, Daddy,' he said.
'When are you going to get out from there?'
'I want to see you,'
he told him.
My little brother,
how he cried.
And he was going crazy.
When we went to bury him,
it was really sad because
my little brother wanted to see him,
and they didn't let him.
They didn't permit it.
And my little brother opened the coffin,
and he was getting into the coffin,
and he was embracing my father tightly.
And I saw that my father cried.
He cried.
And my little brother said,
'Don't cry Daddy,' he told him,
'but don't go in there,'
he told him.
'Stay here with us,
we're still small.'
And he began crying, my little brother.
I told him, 'don't cry, come here,' I told him.
'No, let me go,
I want my father.'

And when I was going to approach the coffin,
they closed the coffin,
and they closed him.
And they were laying the bricks when my brother threw himself down
and said 'Daddy, Daddy, don't go.'

And then after they finished closing him in,
my brother was already in Casa Alianza, the older one.
And there, through him, they took the little one.
And my little brother went
to the *refugio*.
I . . . I did not want to go.
And in the *refugio* he began to have vices.

After a few days, I went to the house.
I was going crazy for my father. . . .
I went to stay with some girls.
For one 31st [*New Year's eve*], I remember,
no for a 24th [*Christmas eve*],
the dawn of the 25th [*Christmas day*],
they had gone to a party and I felt like going to a dance.
And I had on a miniskirt,
and a short blouse,
and pink shoes. . . .
When she came back,
at around two in the morning,
she sent me and I went.
I met a friend there . . .
and she told me that there was a disco below,
and we went.
When we came up,
the man, I saw a man that was coming
and what, he grabbed me.
He wanted to try to rape me,
and I began to scream.
And I told him 'Let me go! Let me go!' I said.

'But I want you,
son of a bitch,' he said to me, like that.
And he had a pistol.
'If you move I'll kill you.'
'Let her go,' [my friend] said,
'because we weren't doing anything bad.'
'You shut up!' he told the other girl,
and with the butt of the pistol he opened all this here, see.

*[She gestures to her own forehead to show where
the man beat her friend].*

And he wanted to grab me
and I prayed to God.
My father had died, perhaps a month,
a month before, my father had died.
So then, I came and said that I would let,
that I would let him.
And I began to cry,
and pray, and really ask God to help me . . .
And I began to run and run,
my whole skirt ripped.
And I started running fast,
and I asked everyone to help me
and nobody helped me.
And from there I arrived at the house
where I lived.
I was very shaken
and she said 'What happened to you?'
'Look at what they did to me,' I told her.
He had given me a huge lump.
They left me black and blue in all this part here,
here and here, see *[she points to parts of her face]* . . .
He hit me with the pistol . . . .

Ruth periodically saw her younger brother in the year after her father died. He left the ACA refugio, and two separate families were helping them. They studied in the same school, however. Although then fourteen years old, she had only studied through the second grade previously. She counted on her brother for support. "When I told him 'look, Nahamán, I haven't eaten,'" she says, "he quickly went to find food and gave it to me. Or I would say, 'Nahamán, look I've got problems,' and he would help me." Ruth remembers vividly her last encounter with Nahamán, the last time she saw him alive.

January arrived
and my little brother was already into vices.
He was into vices,
and I didn't know, right?
One time I saw him . . . and I said to him 'Nahamán, where are you
going?' . . .
and we started talking and everything.
And I told him 'Look, boy, I'm going to leave,'
I told him.
'I'm going to leave for . . . for Coatepeque.' . . .
'What are you going for?'
'With a couple,
they're going to take me,'
I told him.
'I'm going to go there,'
I told him.
'I'm going to work,
then I'll come to get you,'
I told him,
'and we'll go.'
'Don't leave,' he said to me.
'I know,
I know why I'm telling you not to go,'
he told me.
'No, Nahamán,
I don't want to be here anymore,'
I told him.
'They treat me so badly.'

'Don't leave,' he told me.
And he had the odor of glue . . .
And I 'Nahamán come here,'
I said to him.
'What?' he said,
and he didn't get close anymore.
'Breathe on me,' I told him.
And he had the odor of glue.
And I cracked his face.
I told him, 'You idiot, boy!
Why are you into those vices?'
I said to him.
'Look at my older brother,
he became lost because of that.
My father told me to take care of you.
Don't lose yourself, Nahamán,'
I told him.
'You, don't say anything to me!'
and he began to kick me.
And he took off running . . .
Then he returned again and said,
'Don't leave girl,' he told me.
'Get away from here!' I said 'boy,
boy drug addict,' I said to him.
'My father didn't teach you that,'
I told him,
'My father taught you to work,'
I told him,
'Why don't you work?' . . .
And he began to hit me that time, too, right?
Then I came and hugged him.
I told him, 'Forgive me boy,' I said.
'But don't get into that,'
I told him.
'Leave those vices of yours.'
'Look,' I told him, 'I'm going to go,'

I said, 'and I'm going to come back,'
I told him.
'When I come back,'
I said, 'I'm going to take you with me.'
'Take me with you girl.'
'No, no because the couple won't give me your fare,'
I told him.
'Take me . . .' he said,
'don't leave me here alone,
take me with you.'
And I didn't take him,
and I left. . . .

Months later
I had already been there awhile,
I left in January, around June or July I heard about my brother's death.
I didn't believe it.
They told me that a car had hit him
and that the owner of the car had paid the expenses.

Who told you that? I ask, wondering how anyone found her in Coatepeque.

The girl,
the daughter of the woman where I was.
And I didn't believe it
and I decided to come.
That was like Tuesday
or Wednesday that they told me.
Sunday I came here, to Guatemala.
When I heard about my brother's death
I didn't return anymore,
I stayed here
and I started to cry.
They told me that he died in March,
that four policemen had killed him.
They had beaten him with pure kicks.

Where did you go when you returned to the capital?

> To the line, the same place,
> where I had my shack.

Uh huh, but how did you find out how he died?

> Because he came out in an extra,
> and they read me the extra.
> In other words, the people that I knew
> had put away an extra where that came out,
> about my brother.
> And they read it to me.
> And I didn't believe,
> and they told me 'Take it, read it,'
> they told me.
> When I read it I believed,
> and I said 'It can't be my brother,
> no,' I said.
> A few days later two bruises appeared on my leg,
> a little one and a big one.
> And I showed the woman, and she told me that,
> that my brother and father had come to visit me,
> and not to cry because I was going to trouble his soul.
> And I began to resign myself.
> Because there was no other [way], right?
> But always something remained with me
> of why I didn't take him with me. . . .

On another occasion, Ruth told me that she became desperate with Nahamán's death, wanting to die herself. She would remember the days that they went around the city together working or begging. She felt as if her own son had died. In fact she later named her son Rolando Nahamán and felt a sense of relief, a kind of peace, when she noticed how much he resembles Nahamán. When we went out together one day to see her brother's tomb, at Casa Alianza's mausoleum in Ciudad Vieja, a quiet town about an hour's drive from the capital, Ruth cried a bit, but seemed to find the place in some way soothing. She commented on the peaceful surroundings and the beautiful stone and marble works that Casa Alianza had donated to the cemetery. In the mausoleum, itself, lie the remains of ten or twelve other street children, some seven, eleven, seventeen years old when they died. Each one has a tombstone with an inscription from the Bible or that pertains to the suffering of children. Nahamán's says his last words: "I only wanted to be a child, they didn't let me."

On the tape, Ruth continues by telling how her older brother went to look for her at the shack shortly after her return:

> He came . . . to ask me if I had heard about [Nahamán's] death.
> And I told him that yes,
> and he embraced me,
> and started crying.
> And he said to me 'courage,'
> he told me,
> 'now we're only two,
> and both of us have to support each other,'
> he told me. . . .
> He told me where he was.
> And one day I had trouble.
> I had my first husband at fourteen
> [*here she refers to a common law husband*] . . .
> and I lived with him.
> For six months he treated me well,
> afterwards he began to beat me,
> and my in-laws also hit me. . . .
> And he was really jealous.
> If I put on make-up, he hit me.
> If I made myself look nice, he hit me.
> If I went out, he hit me. . . .
> I lived a year with him.
> After that, I left him
> and I didn't have anywhere to go.

And I went to look for my brother, the older one,
that was in El Cortijo . . . of Casa Alianza. . . .
He was the cook there.
I told him I needed help
and he said he would speak
on my behalf,
so that they would take me in at the *refugio* for girls. . . .
I was . . . there months.
After, they transferred me to Flor Bella
[*an ACA transition house for girls*].
In Flor Bella, I stayed about fifteen days.
Then they transferred me to Antigua
because I wanted to be close to my brother. . . .
And he came to visit me, and I did too.
Afterwards I knew nothing of him,
he almost never came to visit
or anything.

Ruth had told me on a different occasion that her brother returned to drugs and became suicidal. When this period of instability began again for him, is unclear, though, perhaps shortly after he lost touch with Ruth.

From there, I misbehaved in the home.
They transferred me to Flor Bella.
In Flor Bella I had problems with a girl . . .
and I had to leave the home . . .
They sent me to the *refugio*.
From the *refugio*, I left, too.
And I decided, better, to make my living independently. . . .
I began to work,
to look for a room,
a girl helped me to pay for the rent.
She helped me to buy a bed,
she gave me dishes,
sheets,
and I had a job.

Ruth goes through a series of boyfriends who all treat her badly. She becomes pregnant by one and loses the baby in her third month of pregnancy. Within a month, she becomes pregnant again, by a different boyfriend. This man does not recognize his responsibility (Ruth says "his error"), however, and never supports her, although she does live with his parents for a few months. She also learns, through Casa Alianza, that her mother is still alive and living in El Salvador. It seems that Casa Alianza located her regarding its lawsuit against the four cops who killed Nahamán. With Ruth five months pregnant, the organization takes her and her brother there and they see their mother for the first time in more than ten years. Ruth continues:

> I didn't recognize her anymore. . . .
> I started living with her,
> but our relationship never went well.
> She pointed to my errors,
> and I also pointed to hers.
> And to this day I am here in Guatemala,
> and she is there,
> and neither one of us knows anything . . .
> Afterward, I left.
> I came back here again.

Ruth stayed with Delfina López, her old neighbor. The woman saw her through her ninth month of pregnancy and accompanied her during labor. After a few months of movement between her 'in-laws' house, back at her mother's in El Salvador, and another old neighbor's, she heard about the newly-opened child-mother program at Casa Alianza and went to ask for a place in the home. She says:

> When I went there,
> I brought the baby in very sick.
> And they told me that . . . if I hadn't brought the baby in
> at that time,
> that I would have brought him in dead.

She left the home only a short time afterwards, however, because of problems with the other women in the house. She went to live with in-laws. She would wash and iron and sell eggs, moving from colonia to colonia. She could not maintain herself and her son, though, and often had to forego eating in order to feed the baby. After five months she could no longer survive and asked for a second chance in the home. She now has begun to study in a beauty school and expects to graduate soon and to find employment. I ask her to reflect on her life as she has just narrated it to me. Her father's abuse has profoundly affected her, making her feel stained. She only feels better, she says, when she asks God's forgiveness for the sin. Wondering how she could interpret this abuse as her own sin, I say to her:

'But that, what happened with your father, for you is not a sin because. . . .'
She interrupts to correct me:

It is a sin because
I, in spite of everything,
I did it with him so that he would give me money.
And because I had no one else to give it to me,
that's why I did it.

So I take it as a sin for me. . . .
I feel bad because sometimes things come into my head
that's when I begin to . . .
I become really down.
I begin to think about the past.
And it is something that has been difficult for me
to move beyond,
because whenever I . . . it's like
everything that I have lived through
doesn't let me live so peacefully.
Because maybe I have a bad character,
because of that I have problems in the home. . . .
And because I don't find anyone to tell
everything I've lived through,
that's what happens also.

During one meeting in the home about the young women's relationship with their babies, Ruth indicated that she thought of herself as a bad mother. The social worker pointed to the good ways in which Ruth helps her son and then asked her to rate herself on a scale of zero to ten, with ten representing a good mother. Ruth gave herself a zero. Her relationship with the other young mothers in the group and with the home's staff also has suffered because of her inability to trust. She constantly feared that one of her compañeras *would attack her outside the home, and she had difficulty talking even with her counselor because she believed the counselor would tell her problems to the other women.*

When I left Guatemala that summer, Ruth was struggling to change, to become more integrated into the home. When I asked her what she hopes to do in the future, she replies:

Graduate,
look for a job,
support my son,
and have, buy a parcel,
a house for me
in order to have a place to live with my son
so that nobody says to me
'Look, move out of there,
because its mine.'
Rather its something that is going to be mine
and my son's.

Elida

Elida, a twenty-year-old woman, is small, rather timid, but sweet, and extremely polite. When I first met her, she had lived in the ACA home with her one-year-old son for less than a month. We talked frequently. She asked me many questions, more so than the other women in the house. She was trying to fit in as much as possible within the home, but often felt alienated. Knowing that she had never lived on the streets, *per se*, the others sometimes would not associate with her as freely as with their *compañeras*. In spite of that discomfort, Elida seemed deeply appreciative of Casa Alianza for the help they had given her: shelter, food, clothing, a trade, and most importantly, medical treatment for her son, Amilcar. Amilcar was a small baby with soft skin and hair, but obviously quite sick. He cried desperately and inconsolably at times. He could not sit up by himself, despite his age, and his gaze was empty, as if he had trouble focusing.

Elida told me on one occasion that the baby was born at seven months (something she and the other women attribute to a gynecological exam she had two weeks prior to her premature labor), and that he has suffered many illnesses. In my short time at the home, Amilcar recovered from a bout of amoebas (probably contracted prior to Elida's entrance in the home), a bronchial infection, and one day his temperature shot to 105 degrees and he began vomiting blood. I sensed her deep fear that she would lose Amilcar that day and I had trouble separating myself from that sadness and despair.

Elida blamed herself for Amilcar's inability to walk or sit. She said that she never listened to the doctor's advice about moving the baby's arms and legs to "exercise" them, as she was always too afraid that she would break him because of his tiny size. When Amilcar was still a newborn, Elida would often have others change him because of this fear.

When she told me her "story" late one night in a back room of the home, Elida spoke quietly and timidly throughout our taping, as if she were almost fading away herself. Her ability to weather the many difficult circumstances she has encountered, however, attests to her strength. She begins, very haltingly, on tape:

Well I am,
I am Elida Esperanza Pérez,
and my story, well
is that when I was a girl,
well I . . . was happy when we were all together:
my family,
my mother,
and everyone.
The day my mother died, well,
I felt that my family ended there and all
all of us separated . . .
When my mother died,
well, then I and my sister had to leave together,
because my mother wanted it like that.
And . . . that was when
they separated us because they didn't want us
to be together.

Who didn't want that?

Eh, the woman where I had gone to live . . .
she is Salvadoran
and her husband's a colonel.
And then, the day that they told me
that my sister couldn't be with me,
I started to cry and I told her [the woman] no,
that I was sorry but . . . she was going to be
far away form me,
and my mother had entrusted her to me and everything.

*Elida mentioned during an earlier talk that the colonel's wife did not like her
sister, although she never explained why. Elida's initial objection to her
separation from her sister became undermined, though, when the woman made
her sister's life unbearable and she "began to cry and cry that she wanted to
leave." Elida says that when this happened:*

I told the woman that
on the condition that I would always see her again
and she told me yes.
And so . . . she left.
Monday,
I remember that it was Monday.
And I never saw her again.
Never.
She was eight years old.

And you?
I was around thirteen.
And well, yes, I suffered a lot
because I couldn't see her.
Nothing.
And a day came when the woman, well,
came to distrust me a lot,
when she thought that I had stolen some money from her.
And she hit me,
she gave me a beating like . . .
like my mother had never given me . . .
She humiliated me and everything.
I was even on my knees that day
And . . . I felt bad.

Later in the interview we return to this incident and her relationship with the colonel's wife:

When that woman, when I met her,
she took me away.
She told me, she offered me schooling
and everything.
And when the moment came, well,
I went.
And at the last minute, she didn't give it to me.
And I lived two years there with her.

She treated me like,
I could say, like . . .
a servant girl.
And the day that I left, well,
she insulted me
and she didn't even pay me one cent. . . .
The day that they came for me they
they told me that I wasn't going to be a servant in their house,
that I was going to be a daughter,
like their daughter.
But at the last minute it wasn't like that . . . .
She scolded me a lot,
she made me do housework.
And I did everything.
And even though I did it,
well, I felt tired because I wasn't accustomed,
very accustomed
to doing it.
And because
I have suffered from a sickness on my hands . . .
a son of the colonel sent me
to the doctor, right?
He sent me, and [the doctor] prescribed medicines,
but the woman didn't even believe me.
And she told me that she wouldn't,
that she wasn't going to buy me the medicine
because it wasn't true.
But, I put up with all that.
And at times she humiliated me in the sense that . . .
I couldn't touch something
because she said I would leave a disease on it.
And so all that was what bothered me.
I lived all that, two years I lived, bothered with them.

Elida says that the day this woman accused her of stealing and hit her, she decided she had to leave, that it did her no good to continue living there. From there, Elida lived with a series of families. All, she says, treated her well, but for various reasons she had to leave them. In one house, she recalls "a woman, well, had problems with her husband, in that there were a lot of people, the family was very big and the house very small. So she told me, 'with pain in my heart, daughter, find some place to go.'" After that particular incident, Elida began working in a house where she met "her partner" Amilcar's father, and eventually they lived together. She continues narrating:

I met him and . . .
with him I also suffered a lot.
I suffered a lot in the sense that
he would hit me, he,
who knows what he thought of me.
We had already lived together two years
when the baby was born.
And then, he told me that the baby wasn't his . . .
You know there came a day when I couldn't take any more
everything he did to me,
that he hit me, and . . .
many problems.
And so, I got to the point where I lost hope.
And my son was born
he was born very sick.
Then I got to the point where I lost hope also.
And the baby was born with a disease
and I thought that God wasn't going to leave me him.
But thank God,
here he is.
And . . . and . . . [*a very long pause*]
and then I, well, looked for the family that had taken my sister.
And that was how I found out about
Casa Alianza.

Confused by this jump, I ask her to explain: "How did you find out about it?" She doesn't answer right away, though, instead she first reveals other things obviously on her mind.

Well, it was difficult for me [*she responds to my question*]
because it was difficult for me.
I had to suffer and . . .

Suffer in what sense?

Suffer in the sense that I had . . .
troubles,
in that I had nothing to eat,
I had to work.
At times,
as I don't know how to read or write,
at times it was very difficult for me because . . .
When one doesn't read or write its not,
not so likely that they lend you a hand to give you a job.
So I couldn't support myself.
And . . . I suffered in that sense
that I went hungry . . .
I suffered, I didn't have anyone to talk to,
nobody to tell my story to,
everything that I felt inside me.
And . . . and in my life
I also have suffered
disasters.
Well in that
[*these words come out very slowly*]
my first, ummm
my first disaster was that I was . . .
was raped like two times.
And that was when I . . .
began to, to . . . feel bad.
I couldn't . . .
it's like when I met the baby's father, that affected me a lot.
Because I saw that he
also was the same,
that he also only hurt me.

He hurt me
and I felt that it was the same.
But he did it differently
because he hit me, and all . . .
and to this day I feel that it affects me a lot.

I ask Elida more about the rape later, although, naturally, she has difficulty discussing it. When I ask her if she knew who raped her she responds:

No, I don't know them.
No, I didn't know them.
Because um . . . my mother's work was
selling,
selling you know *elotes* [*cooked ears of corn*]
things like that.
And I was the one that sold them.
So one day a man arrived,
right?
and said that he needed some *elotes*
in his house.
He said the quantity
and my mother said that it was alright.
That time my mother sent me
but she didn't know
that the man really wanted . . . to abuse me.
And . . . the day that he did it,
well,
I didn't say anything to my mother.
I didn't say anything to her because,
out of fear that she was going to hit me,
or something like that.

She becomes shaken when remembering the scene and starts to cry a bit.
I don't press her, but when she regains her composure I ask:
More or less how old were you when that happened?

Twelve years old.

And you never told you mother what happened?

No.
To nobody.
I had told it to no one.
[*A pause*].

*After telling me of the rape originally, Elida answered, in part, my question
about how she learned of Casa Alianza. During a long period, eight years, she
says, although the math doesn't add up, she searched for her sister and finally
found her again, in a Casa Alianza home in Antigua. She says:*

She was already grown,
she was about fourteen years old.
And . . . then I felt really happy
and I told her of my problems, and everything.
And she told me
about here, about this program 'child-mother,'
of Casa Alianza.
And I wasn't really interested because I thought
'who even knows where it is,
who knows even what it's like.'
But, the colonel also told me
that it was nice, that they were going to help me.
[*Why she still communicated with the colonel remains unclear*]
And I thought quickly of the baby.
I said 'he needs a lot.'
And he [*the colonel*] sent me here.
So when I came, well,
they lent me a hand,
and . . . thank God,
my life now has been different
than it was before.

*Elida had mentioned to me on several occasions that she came from a large
family, of ten brothers and sisters but she never had talked about their fate,*

beside that of her one sister, Flor. I wanted to find out if the others, too, had
experienced the same troubles as she and Flor, moving from place to place,
barely surviving, after their mother died. She informs me, here.

Well, eh,
they have . . .
they separated
because no,
we haven't been able to be together.
When my mother was alive, well
she also suffered a lot because my father,
my father hit her.
My stepfather you could say.
And . . . she suffered and she worked for all of us.
Then, there came the day when
she couldn't support all of us.
Or perhaps, yes, she could have,
if she would have exerted herself.
But she couldn't take it anymore because
she had her sickness
that was already advancing.
And . . . well my brothers and sisters
some were, are, with my aunts and uncles.
And, and as she had a
baby of eleven months,
she then began to think about what
could she do, if she couldn't leave him with me because I was young.
Well she had to . . .
give him away to a person that she felt very close to.
She gave him to her,
she gave him away to her
because he was small.
She handed her his papers, and everything.
Well, up to now I've noticed,
I myself have gone to visit them, they are very well . . .
They are much better than we are.

Because they send them to study.
They know more than we do,
even though they are younger.

Aha. And so when she died, who was still in the house?

Well, I was there,
my sister Flor,
and my brothers and sisters that my father has . . .
he has three.

*And you didn't want to go with your father? She explains that she did live
with him for awhile when the baby was born, but there was no health center in
the town where he lived. With the baby so sick, she couldn't stay there and had
to return to the capital. I ask: But before having the baby you didn't live with
your father?*

No . . . I left about fifteen days [after my mother died]. . . .
I left because, well because the people said to me,
they thought badly . . .
they told me 'Ahh, you better leave,
find your own path.
Because your father, well
he can hurt you,'
they told me.
'He isn't even your father, but your stepfather.' . . .
Even my mother when she died told me that . . .
well that I was already big.
She said 'I, yes,' she said,
'I'm going to die,
find your own path.'
So then when that woman, when I met her,
she took me away.

*Just as Elida has had experiences of abuse similar to those of Ruth, she also
shares her goals of moving beyond her past. When I ask her what she hopes to*

do in the next five to ten years, she replies:

> If I set myself, like, to study,
> to get ahead,
> well, God willing,
> to get a good job in order to give my son a better life.
> Because . . . when I was pregnant, I suffered,
> because I didn't eat,
> and that even affected the baby a lot,
> in that an ulcer formed in him.
> And, then, I defended myself in washing and ironing
> in houses.
> And that was my work.
> Well now, well
> I would like . . . to be a, a bit more
> in the sense of . . . knowing how to earn money.
> Like dedicating myself to study,
> like what I am studying,
> dedicate myself to getting ahead.
> In order to receive that diploma.

Elida currently studies sewing and design and takes her literacy classes within the home very seriously. She maintains contact with Amilcar's father, who spends every Sunday with them. She has seen changes in him since she entered the home, but his long years of abusive behavior toward her have made her unable to fully trust in him.

Claudia

After leaving Guatemala, whenever I thought of the women in the child-mother home, I thought first of Claudia. Despite her past life on the street (Claudia is the one that everyone in the house agrees was the wildest), she almost always projected an air of determination and maturity within the home. Although at her tender age of eighteen she has already seen and experienced devastating events, her self-confidence seems to have weathered these rather than been folded by them, as occurs with many street children, especially girls. During my time in the home, she always took very good care of her ten-month-old daughter and performed her household chores without reminders. Of all of the women in the home, I thought of Claudia as the most stable, and the least likely to fall into trouble in the future. Even she, though, abandoned the home one day, apparently depressed about her baby's father. She returned after a few hours, and explained that while back on the streets she realized that she needed the program in order to give her daughter a better life.

Because I had rarely spoken to Claudia in depth prior to our taping, I knew little of what she revealed about her life that evening. Perhaps also because we had such little knowledge of each other beforehand, she asked me to conduct a formal interview, rather than beginning by openly discussing her life, as Ruth and Elida had. Claudia appeared uncomfortable, a little tense, at the start of the interview, but during the course of the taping she became more relaxed and willing to expand on her earlier concise responses. She was also the first one to want to hear herself on tape. Immediately after the interview, she borrowed my recorder and replayed almost the entire tape. This is what she heard:

[*After a few nervous laughs she begins*]

Well. I left,
let's say that my parents never lived together.
They separated when I was very small.
Afterwards,
I began, because my father drank too much,

he would leave
and I would stay alone with my little brother.
I took care of my little brother,
and he would go.

And your mother?

They separated,
they separated when I was very small.
With that I began to play with my friends,
I began to know the street more.
At age six
I got lost with my little brother.
I knew the Elisa Martinez home
in Antigua, Guatemala.
I was there.
At age eight they transferred me to
Rafael Ayau.
I was there a year.
At nine I found out about Casa Alianza.
I was there,
in Casa Alianza a good while.
I had some friends there,
they call themselves friends . . .
.one time I left for the street,
they showed me how to
inhale glue, drugs . . .

How old were you?

I was already around ten.
I began to use drugs . . .
I was in several homes,
in many homes
in Zacapa.
I was in Santa Mónica,

I was in Santa Ana,
in Santa Isabel . . .
mmm . . . in the *refugio*,
in Solo Para Mujeres.
I spent a good while in Solo Para Mujeres.
I would leave,
I would return,
same as in these homes of Casa Alianza.

*Tell me how . . . in that first home, why did you leave . . . were you still with
your little brother or did they separate you?*

They separated us
because
the girls were apart and the boys apart.
We didn't see each other.
It was like a jail
And . . . they would hit you.
My father would arrive,
but he would come to see us,
but drunk.
He would take us out,
they would return us again to the . . . home,
because he drank too much.

And how long were you in that home?

Umm. . . a year and a half,
or two years.
[Then] they transferred me to Rafael Ayau.

And what's it like there?

It's a jail there also.
They hit you there,
abused you.

I escaped from there.

How long were you in Solo Para Mujeres?

Exactly a year.

Why did you leave?

Because they just had you locked-up there.
The director is very coarse when she speaks to you.
I didn't like the home.
They didn't let you leave with,
with your child,
to travel or anything.
They always wanted you isolated.
And I didn't like that.
That's why I left.

The first time you decided to enter Solo Para Mujeres, what was your life like?

Mmm . . . the first time I entered Solo Para Mujeres
I wasn't pregnant.
I liked to be there,
but just to pester.
I would go out and in.
Then when I got pregnant,
I stayed stable.
My daughter was born there.

In Solo Para Mujeres?

Yes.

Why did you decide to take part in the program?

Because I feel that

> my daughter is growing,
> she notices what you do.
> Good or bad, they always notice.
> And I don't want,
> I wouldn't want her to be in the street like I was,
> getting to know drugs and all the bad things.

But you always went to Solo Para Mujeres before you got
pregnant, why did you go?

> I felt like pestering,
> I always went.

I laugh and say: Oh, okay, then . . . there wasn't any other reason why you
joined?

> No . . . because in the street
> you always had problems.
> Even though you can be in the street for a long time,
> know everyone,
> but there are always police,
> people that want to hurt you.
> Because in the street like that,
> they've beaten our own friends,
> they've taken them to prison,
> some have shown up dead.
> The majority now are dead. . . .

Although we talk about different aspects of her life in institutions and on the
street from here, we later come back to this theme of abuse on the streets when I
ask her to tell me about the problems she and other children have had with the
police. I ask her:

Did you see police more in some zones or streets than in others?

> Mmm . . . yes there are some where there are a lot.

In Zone 5,

Peronia,

eh, Mezquital

[*these last two are poor settlements on the urban fringe*]

which are the ones where the gangs are the strongest . . .

on Ninth at night

there . . . is a large number.

Um hum, and when you saw a police officer, what would you feel?

Almost nothing, but

supposing that when my *compañeros* saw a police officer and they had

money,

they would give us the money right away, because

they stop you,

they search you, and everything.

But at times they hit you,

but, supposing if you have money they let you free,

and if not they take you to jail,

or they hit you.

If you didn't have money?

They almost always searched you for money.

Do they take money away from the person?

From the majority.

They only search you for money

or some object of value,

something you are wearing,

jackets, like that.

And if you have something they let you free? [Here she interprets my 'you' to
mean specifically her, instead of in general, as I had meant]

Ummm . . . they hardly search the women.
Practically only the men.
But yes, they looked over women.
Before, there were a lot of police women,
they would search you,
and if you didn't have anything,
they would take you to prison.

Aha. And how often would the police approach you?

Ay, they stopped you almost every day on Ninth.
For papers,
why were you drugged,
anything.

Um hum. How have the police treated you, in general?

In general? They only hit me once.
And one time that
they were going to grab us there, by the Trebol
[*a hectic intersection with a popular movie theater*]
with Alba,
the one that was here.
Once we were standing around
and three police cars surrounded us
and I was in the middle
with Alba. . . .
They were talking with the boys
[*here her voice becomes more animated, excited*]
and I grabbed Alba by the hair and we started running.
With that, they threw a bottle,
you know, of glue, at us,
at our head.
A little more and
they would have hit us in the head with that jar,
because it was a jar,

and I don't know how, I turned around towards the back and
I just managed to duck.
And we started running,
we went in through the whole market,
and they were in back of us, with the patrol car
chasing us. But they didn't catch us,
but they did catch several of our *compañeros*.
Several went to prison, several of them.

Um hum, and the other time, that they hit you?

Ummm . . . we were there . . .
by the Presidenta
[*a market for stolen goods on the edge of the city center*]
and, there were several of us.
They only kicked me in the stomach.
And with the rest, they really gave it to them.

And what did you do?

Stay like that,
stay quiet.
Because if not,
at times they took you in.
It depends,
they kill you sometimes,
they do different things.

You didn't feel, then, that you could complain or denounce?

No, because,
for nothing,
because the denunciations here, in Guatemala,
are worthless.
Because one time . . .
they already have killed several *compañeros* and

they have complained.
Once, they realized who had beaten
a boy,
they went to denounce it.
What the judge did or I don't know who,
he sent them to Mexico
[*it is not clear who she means, I think the cops*].
And everyone in Casa Alianza knows that.
They transferred them to another home so that
nothing would happen to them
[*here I understand the kids who complained*].
And the police they transferred to there.
And it depends, if they hit you
they didn't say anything anyway
because in a short time they let them free.
They didn't comply with what they should
[*their sentences, perhaps?*]

Now, you mentioned before that you have known several that have died in the street . . .

Yes.

or that have been abused . . .

That they have killed.

Can you talk a little bit about those cases?

Ummm . . . once a car with polarized windows . . .
was on Eighteenth
and they forced them [a group of kids] into the car,
and there were six of them.
One's name was 'el Catracho,'
he wasn't from here,
another 'el Soruyo,'

the brother of Jorge Luis,
my daughter's father,
his brother was there.
Luis was there.
There were about six
and they turned up tortured.
They killed them.
A woman was there, too,
that it seems they sprayed her eyes
but she saw that they were torturing them.
It seems that they removed their nails,
they gouged out their eyes,
their,
their,
their eyes.
They branded names on them with hot irons.
And it seems that, last,
they shot them three times in the forehead.
And she saw, and with that she says that they were in
in. . . the public cemetery.

When she saw from a distance that the men
got out to urinate,
and in that one of them [the boys] was still alive.
And he told 'Cheni'
[*here I do not understand clearly the name she says*]
to run because she was the only one that was with them,
to run.
And Cheni ran.
It seems that they were going to rape her and they were going to tor-
ture her.
She ran.
She went to Casa Alianza and told everything.
But they had already killed them.
And they were going to kill Cheni also.
And Bruce left with her.

[*Bruce Harris, ACA's regional director*]

They left the country, or what?

They got her out
of the country in time.
They later brought her back
and they were going around looking for where she was.
The men were looking for her.

The case of the tortures and the female survivor that Claudia recounts here is discussed further in chapter four. Some of her details obviously come from hearsay and, while not fully accurate, reflect the truth. Wanting to know more about the source of her information, I ask how she found out about all that had happened.

Because I was in the street
[*she replied as if self-explanatory*].

And it was known, what had happened?

Yes.

Um hum . . .

They were our *compañeros*.

And how did all of you in the street feel when you found out what had happened?

Bad.
That time almost the majority went to their houses.
After six
or almost a year passed,
they returned again.
Because whenever they kill, like that

a group,
kill several,
everyone leaves

They don't stay in the street anymore?

They don't stay in the street,
fear that they'll kill them, too.
And after a good while they return,
when everything has passed.

And did you know others?

Mmm . . . several that they have killed.
Among themselves.
And at times they kill each other like that,
in gangs.

Have you ever been in prison?

I was in prison, like . . . no more than three,
four times.

For what?

Sometimes I was drugged,
or because I was in the street
at a very advanced hour of the night,
or because of problems,
or without papers,
without anything.

How long did you have to stay?

It depended on how long they gave you.
Sometimes they gave you three months, four.

And you, how long did you stay?

One time I stayed three months.
Sometimes you escaped.
If you were sly, you'd escape before,
you wouldn't stay the three months.

Uh huh. And in the jail, how did they treat you?

Bad.
Because in the jails
there's almost always lesbianism.
Almost everyone is a lesbian.
Lesbianism,
they treated you like an animal.
Supposing someone had problems . . .
there was a pig there
and they'd send you to clean there.
Or sweep,
or do sit-ups . . .
or they put you in a dark room.
Horrible
[*she says this with a tone of disgust*].

And when they sent you to jail did you always go before a judge?

No.

You never went before a judge?

Mmm . . . they took you, but to,
to the police,
from there they told you where they would take you.
Almost never.

On the tape, before we started talking about the police, she told me about other aspects of her everyday life on the streets. I had asked her: You said that you

were in several homes, and you left, but how long would you spend in the street
between each program?

Mmm . . .
around two years, you know
stable,
stable, like that in the street.
I drugged myself,
I went to discos,
at night we'd arrive, you know,
at Sixth [*Avenue*]
or at Eighteenth [*Street*],
there were always problems,
like, with gangs.
We had to go see what happened.
At times they'd take someone to jail,
we had to go see how we arranged to get him out.
At times they took us to prison,
the cops hit us.
And, thank God,
I was in the street,
I never prostituted myself.
My friends helped me.
Several that, yes, they helped me *a lot, a lot.*
Thank God I didn't fall into that.
And . . . yes I suffered because . . .
imagine at times one didn't have anything to eat
or anything.
You had to see *how* you made do.
Go back to your house or whatever because if you don't
know how to rob,
don't know anything,
you die of hunger.
The humiliations that they gave you,
You had to see where you could stay and sleep,
you had to see *how*, you know, you took care or yourself in the street.

And those humiliations, for example?

That they looked at you funny,
they insulted you,
they hit you.

That was whomever?

Yes, whomever.
At times you were like dirty,
you didn't have anyone on your side.
Instead of helping you, they pushed you aside.

Did you feel like going back to your family, your father?

I went back.
I was with my mother almost two years,
when all of this happened to me.
And I became desperate,
I returned to the street.
And I was *never* in my house.

How old were you when you spent a while with your mother?

My mother . . .
I met her at fourteen years old
for the first time.
It seems that she fled, very young.
She went to Belize.
And I didn't know her,
and one time . . . I said to my uncle that I wanted to meet my mother.
And . . . one time she came from Belize,
she took me to Belize.
I was with her a good while.
Who knows,
I had a deep grudge against her.

I treated her badly,
I treated her the lowest.
And I would tell her she wasn't my mother,
because if she had been my mother, she wouldn't have abandoned me
nor would I have gone through all that.
But she would tell me that it wasn't her fault.
And that's how I got to know her, how I treated her.
And now I am in contact with her.
She calls me, or I call her.
I just went to Belize to see her. . . .

When you were in the streets, what did you do to get money?

Mmm . . . I almost always went out to steal
with my *compañeros*.

Um hum, just that?

Yes, almost always,
I always accompanied them.
Their work was breaking into cars
and stealing the radios.

Oh, and you would sell them?

They would.
And if you helped them,
or something like that,
they had to give you money.

Would you say that there was a typical day?

Mmm . . . What do you mean?

*For example, would you get up at a particular time, what would you do when
you woke up?*

When I got up we went to bathe.

Where?

In number one,
Betty's home,
[Betty de Rueda, the director of the Solo Para Mujeres drop-in shelter]
where you only go to eat,
you enter at nine in the morning and leave at five at night.
We would go there to eat,
to bathe,
then we would go back.
At night we went to discos,
to the movies,
or to pizza,
depending,
depending if we had money . . .

So you most often went around with other people?

Um hum.

Did you ever stay alone?

No, I almost always was with . . .
my friends or with boys.

Um hum, and what kinds of problems did you have among yourselves?

Problems?
At times because someone . . .
perhaps is robbing, and
as there is a person who has to . . . to watch that no one comes,
sometimes the person doesn't watch well
and at times they grab that person and they beat him.
There are problems because of that.

And supposing that I have a good friend
that I really get along with well,
and I see that another person wants to hit him,
one gets involved, another gets involved to defend him,
and to the point that there are problems between gangs. . . .

And supposing that there are gangs,
there is a gang on Eighteenth,
and a gang on Ninth.
Those hardly get along.
Supposing that . . .
someone from Eighteenth wanted to hit someone from the Ninth,
all of Ninth would get involved.
And there were always problems, like that,
between gangs.

And how many people were with the gangs?

Oooh—a lot!
[*she says almost amazed*]
Like 60, 70.

In each gang?

[*still with wonder*]
There were gangs that had more. . . .
I was in the Milagro gang,
the Charcos,
the Zone 19,
the Killer,
the Peronia,
the Zone 7,
the Bethania,
the . . . in the . . . Ninth,
the Barajuste,
various things.

How did you start in the gangs?

They call the Barajuste the gang of the little kids. . . .
There were only little kids,
they were like nine years old and they drugged themselves.
I began in that gang.
I was one of the, in the Barajuste gang, one of the first.

*Um hum, and those kids, were most of them kids that, like you, slept in the
streets or did they have homes?*

They had their homes, but they had problems.
And they would lose hope and leave.
And because there is no one to take refuge in, and all,
we had to take refuge in one another.

Where did you sleep?

I almost never slept in the street,
almost never.
We would always stay in hotels you know,
in groups.

Oh yes, and they always let you in?

Yes, they knew us already. . . .

Um hum. The people that worked in those places, how would they treat you?

They were good people.
They knew us already.
But there were people in the hotel that . . .
that didn't care about you, perhaps,
because if they would have wanted to help you or something like that,
they would have said to you 'don't do that,'
or whatever. But,

at times, they saw us drugging ourselves,
and they wouldn't say anything.
It was like nothing to them,
they never supported us like that, directly.
Rather the street educators always came,
Bruce came,
Seño Eugenia, [*former ACA-Guatemala director*]
to visit us.

And you felt support in them?

Yes, a lot.

Um hum. What kind of drugs did you use?

Marijuana,
glue,
solvent,
pills,
mmm . . . tip top,
mmm . . . that's it.

And was it something you did every day?

Most, *most*, I used solvent.

In this program here, in Lourdes [child-mother], how is it going for you?

Well,
here I feel that my life has changed totally.
I don't think about the street anymore,
or about drugs,
or *any* of that.
I don't feel despair.
In November I graduate.
Mmm . . . I'm trying to see what . . .

what to do for tomorrow.
Let's say specialize in something in the morning
And . . . work at night.
And supposing, save
and set out to live, with my daughter.
And in the home, it's going well for me.

Why do you think that you have changed?

I've changed?
In my character,
because before I was really aggressive,
I fought with everyone.
I went out of and into a place,
I insulted half the world,
and, like *truly*.

But why have you changed? For what motives?

Because of my daughter.

And you think only for her?

Yes, because
I at times have started thinking
that if my daughter weren't here, I wouldn't be here.
I wouldn't be.

What was it that attracted you so much to the street?

Mmm . . . perhaps,
perhaps like clowning around,
the drugs,
going to the dances,
being in gangs,
all of that.

The streets attracted me very much.

Lately you haven't wanted to leave?

No. Not until after I graduate.

And afterwards?

Let's say that
the baby's father was also in the street.
And I met him there.
He didn't want to pay attention and enter a place,
he wanted to continue drugging himself.
And I spoke seriously with him, that if,
he didn't enter a place . . .
a home, his house, or something,
he couldn't come to the home to see the baby.
And I talked to the director, *Seño* Eugenia,
and she gave him another chance to enter the *Comunidad*
[*an ACA home for eighteen- to twenty-one-year-old youths*].
They talked with him,
they found him a job,
and he's working, he's in the *Comunidad*.
And [with his earnings], each month they're going to buy him something,
like a stove, things that he needs.
And if when I,
next year, begin to work,
I begin to save also,
you know, so that when the two of us leave
we can be together . . .
but leave, you know, ahead,
not with our hands empty.

Um hum, and do you think you'd like to stay with him?

Umm, yes.
He is a good person.
He has helped me a lot.
We're going on four years [together]. . . .

Oh, a long time.

Yes, a long time. . . .

Carolina

When I first mentioned to the staff of the child-mother home my desire to interview some of the women about their life experiences, they all agreed that I should approach Carolina. Carolina, it seemed, had spent a long, difficult, time in the streets. She has spent years battling a drug addiction and the lure of the street, moving between periods of relative stability in ACA homes, or dreary juvenile detention centers (simply referred to by her and other street children as "jail"), and the chaos of the streets. Moreover, Carolina willingly testified about her experiences on a prior occasion, at a national conference on children's rights.

Her son, Danny, was five months old when I first met Carolina, and was the youngest baby in the home. I had difficulty remembering his tiny age, however, because of his gigantic size. He already seemed at least double his age. Carol takes good care of Danny and demonstrates her affection for him regularly. She buys bracelets with his name on them and often doodles his name inside of big hearts. In spite of this tenderness, though, and her good nature towards me, most often I would think of Carol as a "tough" young woman. Like several other women in the home she had small tattoos of boys' names on parts of her hands and arms. These souvenirs of prior loves accompany a host of scars, not only on her arms, but also her face and legs. She was often fiercely protective of herself and her son.

Even after eight months of relative stability in the home, Carol sometimes appeared "trapped" in street problems. One morning in mid-July, she entered the office while I was there to speak to her educator about an incident the night before. Apparently, when she went to run an errand, a girl still in the street threatened her. According to Carol, the girl is a lesbian and became offended, provoking a fight, when Carol refused her advances. Carol had no scars or bruises, but she claimed to have cut the girl's face and hand with a piece of glass. Two weeks later, while on the street myself, I met the girl that Carol had spoken of, and, indeed, saw fresh scars on her face. Later, at a "narcotics anonymous" meeting at the home, Carol publicly admitted that she had reacted rashly and expressed remorse.

At that meeting, Carol also discussed her deep despair for her sister, who was still on the street. She said that she felt so desperate she had considered leaving the home, herself, to return to the street. The night that we began to tape, her worries for her sister became vividly real. We sat in the back room of the home. Since it was still early evening she had not put her son to bed yet. His gurgling sounds are heard on the early part of the tape while we speak. The tape picks up Carolina's voice when she is in the middle of a sentence:

It's that my uncle,
the problems that I had in my house, well
my mother died
my father began to drink,
and he didn't take care of us anymore,
he only spent time in the street,
drinking.
And, it's like an aunt took care of us, but my aunt's husband
tried to abuse me.
[*Here, as elsewhere Carol uses 'tried' to mean 'did'*]
And, like, I told her,
and she never believed me.
And I told my grandmother, my father's mother,
and she told me that I could go with her
[*the doorbell rings twice, loudly, in the background*].
I went for a while, but I felt desperate and returned again.
And then, afterwards, eh,
when I returned to my aunt's house, eh,
the same thing happened,
that he always was abusive.
And my aunt never believed me.
That was how I lost hope
and I left for the street.
I began to use drugs.

How old were you?

Eh, I was thirteen years old.

When you left for the streets?

Yes.

And when your mother died?

When my mother died I was ten years old.

And the abuse there . . . with your uncle, did that happen all the time or only part of the time?

He, it's that it was a short time,
but I would tell my aunt
and she never believed me.

Did you tell anyone else?

Yes, I told my brother.
My brother had problems, because of that,
with my uncle.
My uncle wounded him very badly,
that as a consequence, my brother has an operation in his stomach.
[*Perhaps the uncle stabbed him, although it's not clear*]

How many brothers and sisters do you have?

She is distracted so I repeat the question, but just then a voice is heard on the tape frantically calling "Carol." She holds up her hand for me to wait and she goes to see what's the matter. When she doesn't come back right away, I take her baby and see what's happening. Her sister, who had come by the home earlier with some sort of problem, is at the front door with two young men. When I get out that way Carol and the staff members are on the sidewalk in front of the home and I can hear a lot of speaking in raised, excited voices. I do not go out, but later one of the educators tells me hat Carol's sister was bleeding profusely from a cut on her face, and that the two youths broke into a fist fight right on the sidewalk. Apparently, one had broken up recently with Carol's sister, and the other had just become her new partner. The youths were inflicting serious damage on each other. It is not clear to me exactly what happens, but the three leave after a period of perhaps ten minutes. Carol comes inside and she is visibly shaken, crying, and one of the educators supports her and brings her to her room for a *reflexión*. The incident set a kind of depressed air over the home, at least I sense that. The baby is in my arms beginning to cry and wondering where his mother is. The interview, obviously, cannot continue.

After a few days I call Carol to see how she is doing. She doesn't want to talk about her sister, but says that she would still make a tape with me. On 11 August, I stay overnight at the home and we plan to tape after dinner. However, we wait until about 10 pm because I had brought a video about human rights abuses and Guatemalan street children with me. I had shown the program at a boys' home earlier, and I asked Ruth if she wanted to watch it while I worked with Carol because it contains a large segment on the death of Nahamán Carmona, Ruth's brother. Hearing this, all the women want to watch the video, including Carol, and the educator on duty also expresses interest. So, before taping I sit down with the group to watch the video.

It is my third time watching it that day. Consequently, instead of paying full attention to what is shown on the screen I can observe the reactions of the women. All of them are drawn to the video. It portrays well the grizzly treatment of street children at the hands of Guatemalan police, and it is depressing. Depressing. The women more or less interact with the video, they know almost everyone shown. They say "there's so and so, there's so and so." I am also playing with two of the babies so that the mothers can watch. That distracts my observations for part of the video. At the end, the father of Mirna's daughter is shown. They laugh because someone says that he actually looks half-respectable there. The segment on Nahamán makes Ruth cry, but she is dignified, discretely wipes her eyes, and tries to keep ahold of her son. After the video as I am getting ready to tape Carol, the women comment on the cases shown, especially the Bosques de San Nicolás case mentioned by Claudia,

involving the torture of four teenage street children. It is in this context
that Carol sits down to finish her story, but she is now much more determined to talk. On the 5th she seemed uneasy and asked me to conduct
a formal interview. Now she speaks freely, of her own will. This, finally, is what she chooses to say about her life:

My name is Carolina Elisabeth.
Eh, I'm going to talk about my problem,
my life in the street,
why it was that I left my house.
The problem, because of which I left my house, was that
my father drank,
and . . . it's that my mother died when I was ten years old.
We were left with only my father.
My father began to drink.
About a week after my mother had died,
the house burned down on us.
We were left with nothing . . .
we received help from my aunt,
she gave us a roof, a place to live . . .
my father worked a while to provide food for us,
to dress us, put shoes on our feet.
And afterwards, my father began to drink.
And he wouldn't come home anymore.
He would stay passed out in the streets.
I, with my sister, would go out to pick him up.
Then, afterwards, he wouldn't come home anymore.
We would go out to look for him,
we wouldn't find him. . . .
And my aunt brought us to live with her.
There, her husband tried to abuse me.
And I told my aunt, but she didn't believe me. . .
Then . . . when that happened, I headed for another aunt's
[*previously she had said a grandmother's*]
I was around eight months
or a year, perhaps, there.

And I despaired,
and I returned again, to my other aunt's house and . . .

Why?

It's that she, she did treat me well from time to time, but
at the same time she treated me badly . . .
She insulted my father and everything.
And she told me
that my father had killed my mother.
And, like, since I was young . . . they made me testify against my
father.
And I testified
against him.
When they were going to send him to prison,
eh . . . I rescinded, and . . . they brought me there again.
And then I said the opposite,
that it hadn't been him.
And . . . I was face to face with my father.
And . . . afterwards,
that woman,
my aunt, that is,
because of everything she did to me, I couldn't love her . . .
I wanted to go with my father,
and she didn't let us.
And one time my grandfather, my mother's father,
came to get us.
And because he was the father of my,
of that aunt of mine . . .
he could take us.
He brought us back to my father.
And, like, I began to stay with my father again.

*Carolina doesn't mention it here, but in group meetings within the home she
has revealed that her father was abusive, even smashing a bottle over her head
one time.*

After a while, I began to use drugs. . . .
I would go to the store,
I didn't go to the,
directly to the store,
but to consume drugs. . . .

How old were you when you began with drugs?

Eleven, around twelve.

And what did you use?

I used glue,
I used pills,
And . . . eh . . . thinner,
I began to sniff thinner. . . .

Then later, I left for the street.
I began to live in the street.
When I began to live in the street, I began,
in order to survive, they told me,
I had two options,
either sell my body
or steal.
And I decided . . .

I interrupt her to ask: Who told you that?

to steal.
[she finishes her sentence in the middle of my question]

But who told you that?

A girl,
the one they call 'Mota' in the street.
Its like, she told me,

'Look, Carolina,' she told me,
'you have two options to survive on the street,'
she told me,
'because you're not going to live off the air,'
she told me.
'You have . . . either you steal,
or you sell your body.'
And that was how I began to steal.
But . . . I never sold my body
because I said for me to lie down with a man that
I don't love,
or, or it's going to be an old man, something like that . . .
So, I began thinking of all that,
I preferred to steal.

And when I stole,
they detained me one . . .
let's see . . . the first time they took me in . . .
because we were going to break into a car.
And . . . they grabbed me by the hair
And . . . I told him that he shouldn't grab me like that
because he, some day,
someday he was going to have kids,
and he didn't know what punishment God could give them.

Um hum.

Because one should never say never.
Because that never comes around.
And when I said that to the police officer,
he continued beating me.
With the handcuffs he gave it to me here
[*pointing out a scar on her face*].
He drew blood,
he broke my head.
And . . . I cursed him.

And the more I cursed him,
the more he beat me.
And I told him that they were a bunch of 'good for nothings,'
because they only, if one gave them their share
of what one stole,
they grabbed it.
But if one didn't give them anything,
that's when they got angry.
[*Here she corroborates Claudia's testimony about police behavior.*]
So then that officer said to me
'if you give yourself to us, we'll let you go, and if not, we'll take you in.'
So, I preferred that they take me in,
and that was how I landed in jail for the very first time.
Because I'd rather be in jail than give myself to them.

How long were you there?

I was there six months,
six months I was detained.
One time when they brought us to an
exposition, here, in the Palace
[*the National Palace, a few blocks from the home*]
I escaped from there.
And I went to Casa Alianza's main offices
and they helped me there.
They gave me clothing because
I only had a uniform from there.
They gave me clothing, and brought me to the *refugio*,
so that I would be there.

And . . . I was there for a while,
and I returned to the streets.
And . . . I landed again [in jail].
When I arrived again,
they isolated me.
They put me in

[*she says a word I cannot make out,*
but from the context I take it to mean 'solitary confinement'].
And they hit me.
And they put me in a *pila*
[*a large water storage sink*].
And just like that, wet, they isolated me.
And I was really afraid to be there,
but there was a friend who told me
that just, whenever I was in there,
to just think about God,
and that He was going to help me.
And . . . after five days they took me out of there.
Then about a week later, I escaped again.
From there . . . that's how I landed there six times.

And . . . I met a boy named Billy,
and I was with him, that is,
we went around together in the streets.
He helped me,
I helped him.
He didn't like me consuming drugs,
he didn't like me stealing.
He, himself, brought me to the *refugio*,
and told me that I had to get into someplace,
so as not to be on, not to return to the street. . . .
During that time Flor Bella opened
and I was one of the ones to go to that home.
We inaugurated it.
And I was there three months.
After three months they opened the group home Ixmucané.
We moved to that home.
I was there about a year and a half
and in time . . . I drank again.
I went with a friend to the beer festival
and I drank.
And when I arrived [at the home], they noticed.

They returned me to transition
for one month.

Carol goes on to narrate a series of destabilizing moves between transition and
the group home. After a final serious incident in the group home, in which
Carol comes close to throwing one of the educators off a staircase, they send her
to transition again, but she becomes frustrated and leaves for the street. She
makes it a point to mention, though, the deep hate she felt for the educator,
whom she blamed for the incident.

She then relates an incident which I cannot confirm, but it is horrifyingly simi-
lar to the known experiences of several other street children in Guatemala.
When back on the streets, she says:

That's when, that is,
when they tried to burn us with a cigarette.
[I was] with . . . the father of Ines' baby,
his name is Julio. . . .
That time we were in front of the *refugio* for boys.
And a car came . . . and
they began to insult us, and everything.
And they forced him into that car.
They forced him into that car,
and they forced me in, too.
And they were beating him.
They told me that what they were going to do was
rape me.
I said to that one: 'Why?
If we haven't done anything to you.
You shouldn't harm us because
that harm that you do us
will also fall on you,
and you will suffer more than us.'
And he told me to shut up,
And . . . he put out a cigarette on my leg,
it left a scar.
And . . . you can't see it much anymore,

but I have several scars on my legs.
I have one here [*she signals to a part covered by her shorts*],
that is, they burned me with a cigarette.
And with him, they left this part here [*his arm*] almost destroyed.
Just from cigarette burns.
And they forced us out there by. . .
the Zone 3 ditch [*at the municipal landfill*].
They let us go
and told us that they were going to throw us
from the ditch. . . .
And he asked that they at least let me go.
That at least,
if they wanted, that they harm him,
but that they not harm me.
And I . . . I had him by the hand
and I said to that man that if they were going to throw us off,
that they throw both of us.
And with that, a truck came,
one of those for the garbage.
It stopped short. And when they saw,
they started up the car and left.
In that moment, he looked me in the face
and said to me
'I believe it was God who saved us.'
And we kneeled down,
and he cried,
and I cried. . . .
And he embraced me
and we went back again.
But both of us crying.
And whenever I see him, I remember all of that.
And it makes me sad to see him. . . .
But if it hadn't been for that truck,
we would have been dead, me and him.

And where did they burn you? Right there in the car?

Yes, in the car.
That man laughed
and he said that at last he had us,
and that there were many more left still,
and that, little by little, they were going to die.

Had you seen them before, those men?

No.
I had never seen them,
but after that happened,
yes, I saw them again.
Eh, with that boy named Billy
that had brought me to the home. . . .
We were talking
when a car with polarized windows passed by. . . .
It stopped in front of the *refugio*, and they began insulting us.
And . . . it took a turn
and in a while it came back and
they just lowered the window,
they began firing at us.
And there were some educators upstairs, and they shot at them, too.
They knocked down the sign that was there.
And when they took the turn,
he said 'Let's go . . . because if we stay here,
they're going to kill us here,'
he said.
And we left, but we were really scared. . . .
We went to a hotel.
I don't even know what was wrong with me,
but I saw that, that they wanted to open the door,
and I spoke to him, and he told me to calm down. . . .
He told me, 'if they kill us here,
they're going to kill both of us here,'
he told me.
'We just have to entrust ourselves to God.'

Then that's when I told him,
'but they already tried to kill me,' I said.
And he said to me that if I was going to die,
he was going to die with me.
Then, after . . . he told me that we should leave there. . . .
And I went back to my house.
And when I went to my house,
Eh . . . I went for three months.
After three months, I returned to the street, again.

That house . . . that was still your aunt's?

Yes, and that was where I landed in prison again.
But I didn't land in the juvenile one this time,
rather in with adults, in Zone 18.

How old were you?

I was. . . seventeen.
Excuse me . . . I was sixteen years old. . . .
And I said my age, but they didn't believe me.
And they brought me to Zone 18. . . .
There was a fine there,
they paid the fine,
and I went back to the street. . . .

Who? Excuse me, who paid the fine?

Eh, a friend.
A friend,
he paid the fine, and I left.

She had already mentioned to me that Casa Alianza knew of her detention, so I wondered if they hadn't tried to help her. But, they didn't do anything to help you get out of that jail for adults?

Eh, Casa Alianza?

Or whoever, nobody helped you in that situation?

No, because when you land in jail
and you're out of the program,
the program doesn't get involved in anything,
in anything.

*This is not quite true, although ACA has a more limited legal role in cases
pertaining to kids outside of their guardianship. Carolina tells me at this
point that shortly after leaving jail she returned home and met Danny's father.
She found out that he was married only after she became pregnant, but
immediately broke contact with him. She says that she plans never to go back
with him again.*

And now I am here [*she continues*]
and I want to move ahead. I want to graduate
in order to give the best to my son.
Because if I was in the street,
I don't want my son to experience
what I experienced.
Because life in the street is really sad,
it's really hard.
The one that learns to survive lives,
and the one that doesn't, doesn't live.
And it's that I want to give more to my son. . . .
That's why I am studying.
I had opportunities to study before, when I was in other homes,
but I didn't take advantage of them.
And now, yes, I am determined
To . . . to graduate,
to work,
give the best to my son.
Because I wouldn't like to see him with a bag of glue
or a marijuana cigarette,
like I was . . .
I am determined not to go back to the same

in the street . . .
my life now
is another.
My son has changed me a lot.

*I ask her to explain a bit more about her day to day life in the street here, after
she finishes her narration. I ask her where in the city she'd be on any given
day. She responds:*

I would be in the Hipódramo [in Zone 2],
in Central Park. . . .
Eh, I didn't walk along Eighteenth because it made me scared.
I was all over the place.

Scared of what?

You know, because of what happened before,
with the boys that they've killed there.
I thought about all that.
And . . . it made me scared.

And when you heard about that case, about the four boys, how did you feel?

I felt bad because I said . . .
instead of helping them,
they destroyed them.
And I don't think it should be like that because
being in the street,
you have rights,
because you're still a human.
And if others deserve respect,
we also deserve respect.
Because we are not
garbage,
animals,
or anything.

We are people
and, just like the rest of the people in society deserve respect,
we also deserve respect.

Did you know them, or some of them?

No, I didn't know them.

Did you know other kids that have suffered in the street?

Nahamán,
Toby,
one that they called Nenón,
the deceased Chico,
Com . . . the deceased Compotas,
one that they called,
the one named Joel Linares
And . . . I knew many that are now dead.
Alvaro Contreras.

When those incidents happened, how did you know about what had happened?

She explains that she found out in the street about most of them, or in ACA homes. Then she says:

In the death of Alvaro Contreras
I was there.
I saw how he died. . . .

What happened in that case?

In that case,
we were consuming glue
by the ditch of the Hipódramo.
Eh, there were five of us,

two of us were on a little incline,
and the others were drugging themselves,
on the edge of the ditch.
The deceased . . . he was hallucinating giant rats.
And when we saw that,
we took the glue away from him.
And he said
that you don't deny a vice
and that we should give it back to him please.
Because we knew what a vice was,
we gave it to him.
But, without knowing that that was going to cause his death.
Because he again began to hallucinate rats
and he took off, running.
He was with me, and I had him held by the hand.
With that, he told me 'let me go,'
he told me,
and he ran away. . .
but when he took off running,
we only heard a scream,
and he went to the . . .
very bottom of the ditch. . . .

I told him to answer me.
And my mind was blocked because I,
I very much loved that boy.
And each . . . when I remember that
it makes me really sad because
he was
he was a kid, like
he was very sweet, affectionate.
He was fourteen years old and . . .
We went to call the firemen
and some others arrived.
But nobody could reach where he was.
The firemen came,

it took them an hour to get him out.
I had the hope that they were going to bring him out alive,
even if broken, but alive.
And when they brought him out,
they covered him with some leaves.
And I threw myself on him, it didn't matter to me that he was dead. . .

He was dead, but I didn't believe.

They brought him to the morgue
And . . . to the Alcazar funeral home . . .
They waked him there.
The next day, at 10 in the morning,
we went to the burial, that was in the Antigua cemetery,
the cemetery of Casa Alianza.

*Carolina's telling of this boy's tragedy affects me deeply. On the tape a long
pause is heard. Not knowing how to respond to such a story, I finally opt for
leaving it and continue with my questions: When you were in the street, how
frequently did the police approach you?*

You know, when I was
consuming glue,
stealing,
or we were having a fight,
or they simply grabbed us for being there.

*But was it an everyday thing? Did they approach you every day or some days
did you have no problems?*

Yes, there were days when I had no problem,
but there were days
when the problems came piled up.

And the times that they took you to jail . . . did they bring you before a judge?

Eh, no.
They only took our
prints,
and they frisked our whole body,
and they brought us from there to the jail.

Can you tell me a little bit about the treatment in the jails?

Ah,
[*she begins as if she could tell me a book*]
. . . the treatment in the jails is very hard
because, before, what they would do was
that one would bathe, like, naked in front of the police.
[*It's not clear that she means this practice has now changed*]
Eh, for a rude answer.
they made you do,
they gave you a really hard punishment.
For a fight,
they isolated you,
or they forced you into the *pileta*
and they isolated you in any event
and they had saturated you.
They hit *me* several times,
they isolated me,
and, like that, they stripped us in front of the men.
And if we didn't do it,
they ripped our clothes,
they beat us.
The food there is . . . something that not even a dog would eat. . . .
Some beans, really hard,
they seem like bullets,
really white rice, without salt,
without anything.
And it is, life in the jail is really hard.

When you were in the adult jail was it different?

It's even harder still.
Because . . . in the juvenile one there are still beds.
On the other hand, in the one for adults,
they are slabs of cement. . . .
To do the cleaning,
you have to stick your hands in the dirty toilets
and if you don't do it,
they hit you.
You have to obey the police officers,
and if you don't, they hit you. . . .
To receive food,
if you don't have a plate, you have to receive it in a bag . . .
if you don't have a sheet, you put up with the cold
because you just stay on the slabs,
without, without anything.
They treat you very hard.

When you were in the street, did you have problems with other people, that weren't cops?

Yes,
with the people in the street
because the people in the street are disgusted by you,
they are afraid of you . . .
it's something like they can't see you because they
are talking, they're whispering,
they're moving away from you.
And you feel bad.
And if you, if you approach a person,
that person moves away,
they cover their nose.
And . . . never . . .
the person doesn't know
what their future will be like later.

Did you have problems with other boys or girls?

Yes, there are always problems among oneself.
That, perhaps because of a boy,
because you took that one from me,
because you took the other,
there are always problems.
They stab each other . . . among oneself,
and, they fight. . . .
There have been many boys killed there, among
among . . . the same gang.

*I find her earlier expression "among oneself" interesting because it connotes
unity or solidarity, despite the obvious divisions.*

You have several scars . . .

Yes.

*from other girls, right? [I know this because she has mentioned her fights
several times in the past.] Can you talk a bit more about the problems?*

Yes.
Eh, I had problems
with a street girl,
over a jar of glue.
She was going to stab me in the stomach with a *verdugillo*.
[*a type of small knife*]
And they had told me that if you get stabbed
by a *verdugillo*,
it kills you
because blood cannot escape.
And I, where she wanted to give it to me,
I raised my leg,
and she hit my knee.
And up until today, I have that,
because that stab went right to the bone. . . .
I feel a lot of pain.

I have a scar on my hand,
problems, also, over a boy
that . . . liked me
and the other girl liked him.
I honestly was not to blame,
but rather it was him for not knowing how to choose.
And the girl told me that I was taking him from her . . .
And . . . in that moment . . . she took out a knife,
and I said 'this one's going to kill me here,'
because I didn't have anything.
We began to go at it with our hands . . .
when she saw that she couldn't hit me just like that,
she took out a knife.
And I took off my blouse
and I was just in my bra. . . .
And I defended my face because
she was looking for my face.
When she struck a blow toward my face,
I covered myself with my hand,
and she gave me a blow to the hand. . . .
They had to put eleven stitches in that hand.
And it hit a tendon,
a vein . . . I was being drained of blood.
And when I saw my hand, I couldn't fight with one hand,
but, yes, I could fight with the other,
and I really hurt her, too.
Because I managed to get the knife from her
And . . . I stabbed her twice in the face.
And once in the stomach.
And, you know, you always have problems in the street.
And without realizing that those problems
can even bring you death.

When you had those wounds, those blows, where would you go or how did you cure yourself?

The street educators cured me.
They were always there,
curing me.
And . . . they yelled at me, yes, but
they cured me.
They brought me to the hospital . . .
to cure my hand.
And . . . they went to get me,
they brought me back to the *refugio* for my recovery
because I was very weak, because of so much blood.

If you could say just one thing . . .

Um hum

to the people that don't know you, that perhaps know nothing of life in the
street, that know nothing of Guatemala, what would you say?

What I would say is this:
That they take good care of their children,
that they never take to the street, because the street,
life in the street is very difficult.
And when a person asks them for help,
that they give it to him,
because that person . . . is asking for help
because he needs it.
And when they see a street child,
that they not scorn him,
but that they give him affection and love,
because that is what he needs . . .
support to be able to get off drugs
and the street.
That's all.

CHAPTER THREE

At the Mercy of the State: Street Children and the Government of Guatemala

The government, instead of protecting children and safeguarding their rights, ignores them, considering them a nuisance and a social stain. The gorgeous universal letter on the rights of the child which Guatemala has signed is a myth of fantasy in this country.

Instituto Austriaco Guatemalteco. *Seminario Los niños de la calle: Una realidad alarmante*, (Guatemala: IAG, 1992), 139-40.

[The Guatemalan] government has no strategy towards urban youth, in general, despite the fact that it is a time bomb. . . . The state does not reach into the population. . . . [It] has developed no programs that might begin to alter the state's traditional lack of relationship with the young and their troubles. . . .

Deborah Levenson. "On Their Own." No. 4 of AVANCSO series, *Cuadernos de Investigación*. (Guatemala: Inforpress Centroamericana, 1988), 39-40.

As in most countries, in Guatemala a specific set of rules governs the treatment of citizens, in general, and children, in particular. While formulating the current national constitution in 1985, Guatemalan lawmakers, as part of the transition to "democratic" rule in the country, paid close attention to this relationship between people and state. The very first articles of the Guatemalan Constitution define the government as protector of individuals and families and obligate it to guarantee rights to life, liberty, justice, security, peace, and "integral development" to all Guatemalans.[1] The violent excesses of government and guerrilla forces during the previous ravenous decades of civil strife clearly left their mark on the framers of the Constitution, as seen in the philosophy of respect for human rights which underlies the document. As Blaustein et al., observe in their interpretation, "The 1985 Constitution is much more specific in 'affirming the primacy of the human person' [and] the family . . ." than previous national charters.[2] Four chapters of Title II define in detail the freedoms (not only individual, but also political, civil, economic, cultural, and social) that the Guatemalan government must promote and respect, and later chapters create a congressional commission on human rights and a national attorney's post to monitor the government's compliance with its duties, to investigate and denounce abuses.[3] Perhaps most importantly, Article 46 of the Constitution elevates the status of human rights by setting international agreements on the subject above domestic law. Few national constitutions pre-empt the decision-making authority of their governments in such dramatic fashion.

Beyond the rights extended to all Guatemalans, the Constitution grants special protections to children and adolescents. It obligates the government to safeguard the physical, mental, and moral health of children and to guarantee their rights to food, health care, education, security, and social insurance.[4] It declares the protection of orphans and abandoned children as a matter "of national interest" and requires the government to combat familial disintegration through alcohol and drug treatment and prevention programs.[5] Furthermore, it establishes minors who violate the law as "unindictable" because of their purported limited ability to reason and it mandates their rehabilitation in special juvenile centers, rather than incarceration in adult jails.[6]

Five years after adopting these liberal tenets, Guatemala also signed and ratified the United Nations' Convention on the Rights of the Child (hereafter, the Convention), a nearly utopian instrument of international law which binds states parties to protect and promote a wide range of children's rights. In some instances it requires governments to introduce programs or legislation to meet with specific goals. Several of the accord's articles, in particular, relate to the treatment of street children and the problems they encounter, as revealed in chapter two. Recall that Article 46 of the Constitution grants preeminence to international human rights agreements and doubly binds (nationally and internationally) the government's compliance with the following principles:

Article 19: States Parties shall take all appropriate legislative, administrative, social and educational measures to protect the child from all forms of physical or mental violence, injury or abuse, neglect or negligent treatment, maltreatment or exploitation, including sexual abuse, while in the care of parent(s), legal guardian(s), or any other person who has the care of the child. . . .

Article 33: States Parties shall take all appropriate measures, including legislative, administrative, social, and educational measures, to protect children from the illicit use of narcotic drugs and psycho-tropic drugs . . . and to prevent the use of children in the illicit production and trafficking of such substances.

Article 34: States Parties undertake to protect the child from all forms of sexual exploitation and sexual abuse. For these purposes, States Parties shall in particular take all appropriate national, bilateral, and multilateral measures to prevent: . . . the exploitative use of children in prostitution or other unlawful sexual practices. . . .

Article 37: States Parties shall ensure that . . . no child shall be subjected to torture or other cruel, inhuman, or degrading treatment or punishment. . . . No child shall be deprived of his or her liberty unlawfully or arbitrarily. . . . Every child deprived of liberty shall be treated with humanity and respect for the inherent dignity of the human person. . . .

Every child deprived of his or her liberty shall have the right to prompt access to legal and other appropriate assistance. . .

Article 40: States Parties shall, in particular, ensure that . . . every child alleged or accused of having infringed the penal law has at least the following guarantees: i) To be presumed innocent until proven guilty, ii) To be informed promptly and directly of the charges against him or her.[7]

These legal principles, however, have little influenced the Guatemalan government's actual treatment of children—particularly street children. The testimonies in chapter two illustrate the indifference of policymakers to children's needs and their blatant disregard for even the most basic rights of street children and abandoned children. Badly biased government spending patterns also reveal a break with *principles of decency*.

The high cost of government neglect

Despite constitutional guarantees to education and health care for all Guatemalans, public expenditures for those services amounted to only 2.6 percent of total GNP in 1990 (in contrast to the average 4.1 percent spent on education, alone, in the rest of Latin America).[8] Spending in health and education dropped even further after Structural Adjustment policies took effect, from roughly 2.8 percent of GDP between 1985 and 1989, to about 2.2 percent of GDP between 1990 and 1995.[9] In 1990, according to UNICEF, only 63 percent of adult males and 47 percent of adult females in Guatemala were literate. Data from 1986-87 reveal that only 36 percent of students who enroll in primary school reach the final grade—as opposed to an average 66 percent in the remaining countries of the Central American/Caribbean (CA/C) region—and a mere 20 percent of those eligible students continue to secondary school.[10] The health standards of Guatemalan children fall even further below (already low) regional levels. The average number of deaths per 1000 children under five years old is 80 for Guatemala, while 48 across the region. Guatemala has double the regional average of moderately and severely malnourished children (34 percent as opposed to 17 percent) and a lower rate of measles vaccinations among children than any other CA/C country except Haiti.[11]

A *Siglo Veintiuno* report on the status of Guatemalan children indicates that 42,000 die each year from preventable illnesses, such as dehydration, dysentery, and upper respiratory infections, in part because there are only minimal health facilities available to them. Although children under sixteen years of age comprise roughly half of the nation's population, Guatemala has no pediatric hospital. In fact, only 36 hospitals, most of them in the capital, serve the more than ten million Guatemalans, with 1.6 beds per 1000 inhabitants and just one doctor for every 2300.[12] Equally devastating, treatment provided by doctors often proves inadequate. Only a fifth of child burn victims assisted by doctors survive, for example, and of these 70 percent remain permanently deformed or incapacitated, like Leopoldo, after their treatment.[13] Not surprisingly, then, UNICEF ranks Guatemala as the *worst* performer on children's programs in the CA/C region, even after allowances that take into account differences in GNP among countries.[14]

Guatemala also has failed terribly in making protection of orphaned and abandoned children a national priority. The Department of Social Welfare oversees three child- and family-related programs: Dirección y Asistencia Educativa Especial (DAEE), which assists the mentally retarded and learning disabled; Tratamiento y Orientación de Menores (TOM), which services juvenile delinquents; and Bienestar Infantil y Familial (BIF), which manages government orphanages and child care centers. The coverage of these programs, however, is abysmal. According to Deborah Levenson, the author of a study on youth gangs in Guatemala:

> By BIF's account, it services 1.69 percent of its potential clientele . . . The state's failure to organize social welfare has led to shortages of skilled and well-trained professionals . . . A TOM official described the agency's situation as 'no leadership, no motivation, no communication, no training . . . a lack of human resources, lack of trained personnel, programs that do not represent the needs of the majority, inappropriate solutions, lack of rational and scientific planning, lack of evaluation and supervision.'[15]

A recent CONANI briefing supports Levenson's findings. According to

the report, of the 3685 children interned in juvenile centers and orphanages in 1992, the ten institutions operated by the government harbored
only 974, while 82 private institutions cared for the remaining 2711.[16]

Furthermore, the state provided no special services for street and
working youth until January 1993, when it opened its "Tio Tom" shelter.
Analyzing child-oriented programs in the country, Universidad de San
Carlos (USAC) student Emma Samayoa de Medina reported that public
agencies serve orphans from birth to twelve years old and private estab-
lishments serve those from birth to seventeen years old. Abandoned or
imperiled children up to twelve years old are also served by public institutions and those up to seventeen years old by private ones. Only the
state treats juvenile delinquents (twelve to seventeen years old), and only
the private sector assists street children (birth to seventeen years old).
Samayoa concludes from this coverage that for the state "no orphans
older than twelve exist, or if they do exist, they are destined to become
juvenile delinquents. . . . [Similarly] for the public sector, the minor in the
street can only be a juvenile delinquent, as it provides no other programs
for him."[17]

Articles 33 and 34 of the Convention require Guatemala to safeguard
children from illegal drug use and "all forms of sexual exploitation,"
including prostitution, yet the government has failed to take even the
most basic steps toward this protection. No public programs exist to
treat child addicts in Guatemala, and no legislation effectively restricts
the sale of glue or solvents despite the high rates of addiction among
street children. Child rights advocate Bonnie Hayskar notes "it is striking that . . . armed guards with automatic weapons protect fast-food
restaurants, but 55-gallon barrels of narcotic shoe glue sit in the open for
public sale in local stores."[18] Child prostitutes also sit for public sale
every day and night in the open of Guatemala's streets. National police
officers readily observe their "negotiations" with clients but rarely intervene, and when they do, they arrest the child, not the client. As Carolina
attests, officers sometimes further the child's exploitation by demanding
sexual favors in return for release. Hotel managers rent rooms from
which child prostitutes conduct business. Yet government officials rarely
take action against this practice and, thus, enable it to continue.

Moreover, the government has provided little protection to children with abusive parents or relatives (as required by Article 19 of the Convention) or to families plagued by alcohol and drug abuse (as mandated in Article 56 of the Constitution). Ruth testified that her father sexually and physically abused her for years. Neighbors suspected, they asked her "And your father doesn't touch you like that?" They pleaded with him "no, don Israel, don't hit your daughter." Don Israel displayed Ruth in public, where everyone saw her, bent over and humiliated. The police even witnessed him strike her and admonished him not to do so in the future. They later arrested him for kidnapping. In short, countless signs of danger existed, yet no government intervention occurred on Ruth's or her brothers' behalf. When Claudia and Carolina's fathers began drinking excessively and neglecting the girls, no social workers "rescued" the families. When they and other children escaped from or left the Ayau and juvenile detention centers, the system failed once again, as counselors provided no follow-up to re-evaluate the children's safety.

Although some of these incidents occurred prior to Guatemala's adoption of its present Constitution or the Convention, little evidence suggests that the plight of endangered children has improved since then. To the contrary, the steady flow of children leaving home and hitting the streets suggests the continuity of familial abuse and governmental neglect. Of course, staff in some public agencies do make valiant efforts to assist children in need, and many, undoubtedly, feel a sense of impotence or despair at their limited impact. These sentiments came out clearly when I interviewed TOM administrator Franklin Azuldia. Azuldia explained some of the government's new, seemingly beneficial programs (discussed below) and indicated that he and several other acting administrators, who had "grown up" in the organization, had pressed for the reforms for years. Only now, however, they had found the necessary political climate for change.[19]

Unfortunately, it is the elite agenda that dominates government policy and programs in Guatemala, and thus, as Paz and Ramirez conclude in their study of the country's juvenile justice system:

> The State . . . does not act with [constructive] social policies but rather waits until the moment in which these children constitute a 'threat to society,' either because they become delinquents or because their irregular situation becomes deeply

socially troubling [as in the case of prostitution or addiction]. The child passes unnoticed on poverty's stage, nobody worries for him, and when the state finally intervenes it does so to impose a sanction on him. . . . This reflects the problem. . . . If the state protects the physical, mental and moral health of minors and it guarantees their right to food, health, education. . . why doesn't it invest more than 2.6 percent of GNP in health and education? . . . It 'protects' certain children, but through their internment in a special center.[20]

Contradictions: *The Minor's Code, juvenile justice, and the child's best interest*

The schizophrenic nature of public policy aimed at protecting children, on one hand, and locking them away, on the other, has historical roots in Guatemala. Legislation safeguarding the rights of children as well as institutions reforming their behavior have existed in the country since at least the 1830's. Ostensibly, the legal treatment of minors has improved over time, with most liberal developments occurring in the 1930's, when governments throughout Latin America established separate tribunals to treat, teach, and essentially "save" juveniles from vice, illegal activity and other dangers.[21] The underlying philosophy of juvenile programs has survived, however, remaining basically unchanged until the present day.

The Minor's Code adopted by Guatemala in 1979 (hereafter, the Code) provides a striking example of how government's dual functions vis-a-vis juveniles can become tragically inseparable. Under the Code, internment for both juvenile offenders and "at risk" children substituted for more appropriate and complex social interventions. Worse, the Code actually facilitated the government's mistreatment of children, especially street children, in various ways. First, it clothed the government's present wholly inappropriate, highly punitive response to "delinquent," and even neglected and abused, children in liberal terminology. Euphemisms such as *institute* instead of *jail* and *protection* in place of *repression* have helped to disguise the state's actions *on behalf of society* as interventions *on behalf of children*.[22]

Similar to the Constitution, the Code defined juveniles who committed crimes as unindictable, either because of their insufficient capacity to reason (if under twelve), or because of their underdeveloped mental or moral state. The Code prohibited police or court proceedings against children younger than twelve and forbade punitive treatment for all those under eighteen, as a result.[23] On the surface these stipulations may seem benevolent, but when children are assumed incompetent or inadequately developed they easily become mere *objects of the state* rather than full citizens[24] and their rights become dangerously open to trampling. Such misconceptions in Guatemala have facilitated a "sweeping under the rug" of children and have permitted the government to breach its obligations under national and international law to guarantee fundamental rights to all, without regard to age.

Second, because the Code assigned jurisdiction to juvenile justices not only in those cases involving delinquents, but also in those related to children in need (those in the "irregular situations" of abandonment or endangerment), it confused punitive issues with primarily social welfare concerns. The same outcomes were prescribed by the Code for both groups of children (fines, probation, or internment in a juvenile center).[25] Article 49 of the law required court officials to investigate all reports of abandonment and endangerment involving children and to report their findings to Guatemala's juvenile justices. The judges, in turn, would consider endangered any child whose parent(s) engaged in prostitution or other "viceful or immoral" practices, any child exploited by adult family members, or any child who for *whatever reason* was *at risk* of adopting "irregular" behavior. The judges then most often placed "endangered" children in state custody, sending them to the same juvenile centers used to detain delinquents.

Deeply troubling was the Code's classification as endangered any minor who for *whatever reason* was *at risk* of adopting viceful behavior. The broad language used left judges with extraordinary discretionary powers. It allowed them to legally deprive a child's liberty based solely on the *probability* (calculated by the judges) that he or she would behave immorally in the future. At a minimum, this violates well-founded principles of law. Article 17 of the Constitution, for example, recognizes as non-punishable any act or omission not classified as an offense and

penalized by law.[26] Since judges obviously could not predict any *specific*
future action of a minor, they had no legal grounds to impose sanctions,
yet they did under the 1979 Code.

Article 43 of the Code violated this same constitutional principle by
leaving the release of minors to the discretion of reformatory directors.
Directors could release minors only when they deemed their reinsertion
into society as plausible. This also raised the possibility of indefinite
internment, for the Code instructed directors to hold at their discretion
even those juveniles turning eighteen while in state centers.[27] Thus we
saw directors, not judges and not the law, defining the terms of a minor's
internment. As Paz and Ramirez reason, constitutional Article 17 establishes that "only a law can define an action as illegal and only a law can
impose a penalty. . . . The punishment, therefore, must be set by the leg-
islature and include minimum and maximum duration."[28] Under the
1979 policy, a minor who broke the law, and even the judge who ordered
internment, had no way of determining the duration of the penalty.

Equally problematic were the legal procedures employed in juvenile
courts. Article 12 of the Constitution guarantees to all Guatemalans the
right to defense. In order to exercise this right, though, minors would
have to fully understand the charges against them and actively participate in court proceedings.[29] Because few children possess adequate
knowledge to defend themselves, Article 37 of the Convention mandates
their access to prompt legal assistance. Nonetheless, in Guatemala, a
child most often faced a judge alone in his or her first hearing. A lawyer
from the Attorney General's Office on Minors would assist the child only
if the judge ordered a second hearing for the presentation of evidence.[30]
Even then, neither minors nor their families could request a substitution
if dissatisfied with their lawyer's performance. The lawyer's affiliation
with the Attorney General, moreover, required his or her protection of
the interests of society, as well as those of the minor; this had the potential of compromising the impartiality so necessary for adequate defense.[31]

Underscoring, of course, all of these concerns are Claudia and
Carolina's assertions that they *never* appeared before a judge in relation to
their many arrests. Carol states "[The police] only took our prints and
they frisked our whole body, and they brought us from there to the jail."
Similarly, Claudia indicates "they took you, but to the police, from there

they told you where they would take you." Whether or not judges later
heard their cases, Carol and Claudia clearly had no knowledge of the
proceedings.

The Code furthered this inappropriate treatment of minors by deny-
ing them the right to equal justice. Article 36 instructed judges to consider *not only the facts* surrounding each case, but also the *lifestyle, socio-
economic circumstances*, and *personality* (as determined by a team of
experts) of the minor. Article 41, in fact, identified these concerns as *more*
important than even the gravity of the offense in determining the appropriate treatment for a minor.[32] A rich child and poor child, then, never
would receive the same treatment by the courts even when committing
the same offense. An obvious bias toward depriving poor children of
their freedom has occurred, then, in Guatemala. Of all children in the
government's institutions, 96 percent came from either poor neighborhoods (31 percent), marginal settlements (42 percent), or the streets (23
percent), as compared to roughly 80 percent for the overall population.[33]
Ninety percent of the boys and 76 percent of the girls in detention centers for stealing came from families (which include small groups of street
children) with monthly incomes of $1 to $100, and the remaining 10 percent and 24 percent, respectively, from those with incomes of $101 to
$200. Even more striking, among girls detained for prostitution 100 per-
cent come from families earning less than $100 monthly.[34] These eco-
nomic circumstances, in addition to revealing the courts' biases toward
detaining poor children, suggest that the majority of incarcerated minors
engage in illegal activity for survival, and that once again a penal answer
has substituted for social policy. The same social order that leads minors
to steal and prostitute then sanctions them for this activity.

The courts have discriminated specifically against street children in
an additional manner. When deciding whether or not to intern minors,
judges often consider familial situation. In a recent survey, Guatemala's
juvenile justices indicated that they regularly deprive minors of their liberty when no evidence of familial support exists.[35] This obviously places
street children, who have broken family ties, at a disadvantage.
Moreover, reformatory directors often release minors only after peti-
tioned by parents or guardians. Although TOM recommends that
minors remain in its "observation centers" no more than forty-five

days—long enough to complete the court ordered evaluations—when adults do not request their release, children often remain much longer. Several of the girls detained at TOM's observation center for girls had already spent more than three months there when I first went to visit. In fact, one young woman was in her *eighth* month of internment for *vagrancy*. When I questioned the center's director about this case, she explained that the girl's mother would not assume responsibility for her. If the girl were released, she might return to vagrancy and perhaps more serious forms of delinquency in the streets.[36] Thus, it appears that the government had locked away the child because of her mother's indifference.

The 1979 Minor's Code, therefore, rather than emphasizing support for children in need, encouraged their mistreatment by the state. In response to the diverse social problems confronting destitute children, it provided predominantly a penal answer, internment. Juvenile justices, rather than considering alternative interventions more appropriate to the needs of minors, frequently made decisions without so much as consulting them. While inexcusable, this negligence may, in part, have stemmed from the scant human resources dedicated to the juvenile courts. Up until a new code (discussed below) passed Guatemala's Congress in late 1996, only six judges heard all cases concerning minors nationwide. In 1993, the national police had only four staff members in their minor's section, and the Attorney General's office only three.[37] In a country of ten million inhabitants, half of them children, any true effort to adequately promote minors' rights and provide for their integral development would demand a much larger governmental commitment.

Treatment within institutions

Since Guatemalan judges so often impose internment on minors, the government morally, as well as legally, has an obligation to ensure the "integral development" of children detained in its facilities. Again, however, as the interviews in chapter two reveal, appalling conditions exist within these institutions. Ruth twice "escaped" the Ayau because she felt locked up there, the older kids trafficked drugs, and the staff hit children. Claudia confirmed "It's a jail there. . . . They hit you there, abused you. I escaped from there." Ines also felt endangered in the shelter because of the government's mixing of girls and boys together. Interestingly, the government lists Rafael Ayau as an open shelter, where children leave and enter freely.[38] Yet, Ruth relates that on at least one occasion when she tried to leave with her brother, staff members returned them against their will.

Besides the Ayau, TOM operates five detention centers within the Guatemalan metropolitan area, and a new *escuela juvenil*, discussed later in this chapter. At TOM's Diagnostic and Placement Center, staff members evaluate "at risk" children and place them in longer term treatment programs or reunite them with their families. At its two "observation centers," one each for boys and girls, a team of psychologists, physicians, and other professionals examines the detained minors and recommends either their release or placement in one of the agency's two "reeducation centers." Finally, at the reeducation centers, children receive classes and learn good health and hygiene habits, and *discipline*.

Carol explains the nature of this discipline: "one would bathe, like, naked in front of the police . . . for a rude answer they gave you a really hard punishment. . . . They hit *me* several times, they isolated me, and. . . they stripped us in front of the men." When the police returned her to the center after she escaped once, staff members submerged her in a storage sink, hit her, and placed her in solitary confinement. Claudia lists many of the same hardships encountered in government rehabilitation centers: "Lesbianism, they treated you like an animal . . . there was a pig there and they'd make you clean there. Or sweep, do sit-ups . . . or they put you in a dark room. Horrible."

In October 1994, Casa Alianza initiated an investigation of the security firm, hired by the Guatemalan government, that ran the Gaviotas Detention Center for Boys. Several street children held at the facility tried to escape on the eighth day of that month. When the guards caught them, one beat sixteen-year-old Luis Felipe Pop with an iron bar. The Attorney General's office also, eventually, pursued the case and interviewed the center's guards. Several of these admitted to the authorities that they regularly placed children in *solitary confinement* cells within the center. Still, even with this evidence neither the guard who beat Pop, nor any other, has received punishment.[39]

By permitting such barbaric treatment within its centers, the state
blatantly violates its legal responsibilities under national and international mandates. Article 37 of the Convention stipulates "States parties
shall ensure that . . . no child shall be subjected to torture or other cruel,
inhuman, or degrading treatment or punishment. . . . Every child
deprived of liberty shall be treated with humanity and respect for the
inherent dignity of the human person. . . ." Likewise, Article 6 of the
Code and Article 20 of the Constitution prohibit punitive treatment of
minors while in detention. More fundamentally, however, the abusive
environment within government centers violates the mental and moral
integrity of the children detained there against their will.

Sociologist Vieira Arruda noted similar discrepancies between the
proposed "integral development" of children in Brazilian rehabilitation
centers and actual circumstances. He writes:

> The way children are treated in the state run institutions is
> highly divergent from the treatment manuals produced by
> their governing bodies. When a child enters the reception area,
> he removes his personal clothing, hands over all personal items
> . . . has his head shaved, and goes through an identification
> process that includes fingerprinting, photographing, from
> front and sides. They are treated just as prisoners and the
> mentally ill. . . . Also there is a great shortage of staff. One offi-
> cial estimates that in order to attend to minors as indicated in
> instruction manuals and policies, institutions would need five
> times the staff they have.[40]

Lesbia de García, director of TOM's observation center for girls, identified her program's greatest problem as a lack of funding and resources
from the government.[41] When I visited the center in mid-July 1994 I
found its facilities physically deteriorated. There were no bars on the
windows, but these were sufficiently elevated to prevent easy escape,
and armed, uniformed police guarded the doors. On the first floor, three
small rooms held ten bunk beds each, where the girls slept. When Lesbia
de García showed me the rooms, a disagreeable odor escaped from them
because they lacked ventilation and remained shut all day. Two larger,
more cheerful rooms occupied the second floor, where the girls received
classes and practiced arts and crafts and sewing. Two teachers arrived

each day to instruct the children, but found their work difficult with no blackboards and few other implements.

Despite this want for supplies in Lesbia de García's center and TOM's solicitation of international funding from UNICEF and the European Economic Community (EEC), a recent study of the agency's expenditures revealed that it under-spent its budgeted resources. Of the nearly Q.2 million allocated to it in 1992, TOM spent only 77 percent, or roughly Q.1.5 million. The majority of this shortage stems from salaries that TOM would have paid workers had its administrators promptly filled staff openings.[42] Instead, the centers remained understaffed for long periods and the agency wasted even the scant resources that it did attract. In a related problem, bureaucratic procedures prevented needed supplies from reaching the centers on a timely basis. A typical request took five months to fill, and only 37 percent of the total requests ended in the successful distribution of funds.[43]

The dreary facilities, abuse from staff and other children, and enclosed environment, so difficult to accept for street children accustomed to the unstructured outdoors, all cause an overwhelming desire among interned children, like Luis Felipe Pop and his friends, to break out of government rehabilitation centers. Indeed 81 percent of minors sent to the centers escape.[44] ACA's Bruce Harris also relates this figure to the indifference of those working with the juveniles: "The staff is not motivated," he says, "it is easier to leave the door open than have to worry yourself."[45] Of all those who escape or are released, 37 percent are interned for a second time, and thus, as Paz and Ramirez conclude, "The system captures them, lets them leave, and then selects them again, which accentuates the vicious circle. This has jail as the only outcome upon becoming an adult."[46]

Finally, one must not forget that some minors are incarcerated prematurely in adult prisons and suffer even worse treatment than those in juvenile centers. Carolina's testimony illustrates both the possibility of incarceration for minors and the unbearable conditions within Guatemala's adult prisons. She indicates that she told her arresting officers her age before they sent her to an adult jail, but that they did not believe her; this posed a striking deviation from the Code's requirement that police and court personnel assume minority when it cannot be proven.[47] Franklin Azuldia, the director of TOM, explained that cases such as Carol's involve system-wise teenagers who often declare themselves adults when arrested for minor offenses. The reasoning: for such offenses they can pay a fine and secure a speedy release from adult prisons, while they would spend at least forty-five days in juvenile centers for any offense, unless they escaped.[48] ACA attorney Hector Dionicio suggests that this is uncommon, though, and points to several of his cases in which police have sent minors to adult facilities against their will.[49]

Steps in the right direction?

Shortly after Guatemala signed the Convention on the Rights of the Child in 1990, lawmakers there began the process of reconciling the country's existing, problematic domestic policies with its new enlightened international commitments. The national Attorney for Human Rights created a special subdivision, the Defender of the Rights of the Child, and expressly charged it with receiving and investigating complaints of children's rights violations, monitoring governmental protection and assistance to children, and raising awareness of children's rights throughout the country.[50] In addition, the Defender became an active member of another public body, the Pro-Convention Commission on the Rights of the Child (Commission, hereafter), which began the work of analyzing Guatemala's juvenile justice system in 1991 in order to draft new child-oriented legislation.[51] This Commission recommended a replacement of the flawed 1979 Minor's Code with a new one that it proposed, the Code for Childhood and Adolescence.

The Commission's proposal addressed many of the legal and social principles violated by the 1979 law. First and foremost, it identified children as *subjects of rights* "capable of expressing their own opinions and contributing to the country's democratic system."[52] It underlined the need for judges and others involved in the juvenile system to consider children's opinions in all matters affecting them, and established the internment of children as a last recourse in any case involving separation from the home. The proposed code also called for a restructuring of the juvenile court system to provide for procedural guarantees, such as adequate defense, historically subverted.[53] Finally, the code defined, in specific language, the categories of children considered in need or "at risk" and, according to Commission member Gloria de Castro, in its final form was to advocate the separation of these cases from juvenile delinquency cases.[54] Under this system, judges would hear exclusively one type of case or the other.

The Commission labored commendably in drafting and generating support for the new code. Innumerable modifications from the Guatemalan Congress based on both principle and political in-fighting, however, diminished the potency of the Commission's original proposal. Certain pro-family groups, along with the conservative, evangelical-oriented FRG party that won a majority of congressional seats in the 1994 elections, objected to clauses bolstering children's rights to denounce their parents and choose their own religion.[55] Some of the country's juvenile justices also resisted the proposed changes, firmly defending the utility of the 1979 Code, which they had upheld for the past fifteen years.[56]

At the same time, other prominent political leaders lent support to the new legislation, either believing in its merits or recognizing the public relations benefits for themselves and their parties in favoring progressive change for children. Thus, the Guatemalan Congress finally approved, in September 1996, the new Code for Children and Adolescents. Even though a diluted form of the Commission's work, this law realizes certain key changes, including a bolstering of the juvenile system with additional judges and a more pronounced separation of protective and penal matters within the courts.[57] Ultimately, it is these courts and these judges who will determine the success or failure of the new legislation, for the mere formulation of a new code cannot guarantee substantive change. Modifying the mindset of the old guard, unfortunately, may prove more difficult than simply reforming laws.

In terms of programmatic change, within the past few years UNICEF and the EEC have begun channeling funds to Guatemala, specifically to address its juvenile rehabilitation system. Utilizing these funds, in August 1993 TOM inaugurated the first phase of its *escuela juvenil*, a reformatory on the grounds of the San José Pinula Reeducation Center. The project aims to break with the punitive orientation of other TOM facilities by fortifying children's self-respect, granting them greater liberty within the center, and training them in trades such as breadmaking, carpentry, welding, and agriculture.[58] The program currently is available only to boys that have broken the law and who now demonstrate a willingness to change. TOM's diagnostic center, not the boys, however, decides who may participate in the program. Phase II of the project calls for the conversion of part of the school to an open center for first-time offenders and abandoned children. While positive, the *escuela juvenil* leaves unaddressed the problems that children continue to suffer in already existing TOM facilities, and it provides for girls no new option to confinement within these dreary centers.

With the spur of additional international funding, TOM began addressing, at last, the needs of children still in the street. In July 1994, the organization initiated its "integral services" project, a voluntary daytime drop-in center for working street children. Following the lead of programs such as Casa Alianza and CEDIC, TOM hoped to attract children to the center through the presence of street promoters in *focos*. Staff members within the center would then conduct trade-related and recreational activities for the children and run special Sunday and night classes.[59] A second innovative program, *libertad asistida*, aimed to give judges a new option for juveniles violating the law for the first time or participating in minor offenses, such as drinking or taking part in student protests. Rather than the old routine of internment, judges could opt to sentence these children to community service or participation in special ngo youth programs.[60] Because both of these programs began only a short time ago, though, their success and actual implementation may not yet be evaluated.

A third public effort oriented toward street children has developed under the auspices of the Defender of the Rights of the Child. Begun in March 1994, the U.S. Aid in Development (USAID)-backed "Support for Street Children" project focuses on preventive intervention as a means of curbing the growth of the street child population. Under this program, the Defender's office, along with Casa Alianza and Programa Materno-Infantil (PAMI), promotes a grassroots understanding of children's rights in the departments, as well as the capital, and has begun training departmental committees to facilitate the denouncement process in outlying areas, necessary for quick and effective assistance to children in need.[61]

Despite its name, however, the program provides little assistance to the children who slip through prevention efforts and land on the streets.

The government aimed to improve its interactions with *these* children through a proposed national police juvenile unit. Officers serving in the unit would receive special training and handle only those cases pertaining to juveniles. According to program advocates, the unit's work would standardize the treatment of street children by police officers and prevent a continuation of the present excesses of force and intimidation. Many who work with street children were skeptical about its potential, however, as it would have left unaddressed the corruption and other motivations behind the current abuse of street children. Police intimidation tactics, therefore, would likely continue with or without the unit. Second, as ACA's Marvin Castillo noted, to the street child who has suffered police persecution, "a cop is a cop." No basis existed for the street child to trust police officers, no matter what their affiliation.[62] Third, as exemplified by similar programs in the Philippines, even those officers receiving special training often find it difficult to change their attitudes toward street children, whom they have learned to regard as trash. Evaluating the Manila Child and Youth Relations Units, ChildHope Asia director, Teresita Silva still considers "the Filipino police as 'enemies' rather than 'partners' of children. Low pay, the crime-busting culture and macho self-image of the police made change difficult."[63] In Guatemala, in fact, despite its international backing, the proposed juvenile unit never formed. ACA's Dionicio attributes the failure of this plan to a general lack of enthusiasm from within the national police.[64]

Thus, while the public sector in Guatemala recently has progressed in acknowledging the needs of street children, largely at the prodding of the international community, and while some public employees have worked intensively for improvements, the programs now in place still leave thousands of children unprotected, both on the streets and within institutions. Until the government eschews its current piecemeal approach for one more firmly rooted in respect for the dignity of children, street kids will continue to suffer the same ghastly abuses that have thrust Guatemala periodically into the forefront of international scrutiny.

Human Rights and
the Guatemalan Street Child

*An angry agent steps from the fog; with the
point of his boot he tries to wake the tattered,
sleeping children, who, with little desire to return
to the hostility of the asphalt, take some time to
emerge from the mountain of papers that covers
them. And then the barbaric representative of
authority, the protector of society, the same
 society that hasn't known how to give a cloak to
these children and permits that hundreds of them
sleep in the streets, lights the papers on fire. . . .*

1920's newspaper clip from Bogotá's *El Tiempo*, as
reprinted in Muñoz and Pachón, *La niñez en el siglo XX*
(Bogotá: Planeta, 1991), 285.

*02:55 . . . I fire repeatedly, without remorse,
satisfied that another street child, alone and
malnourished since birth, abused by his
companions, another child at whom no one
smiles, no one hugs, no one protects, no one
comforts, no one loves, never again will have the
opportunity to stain the society that gave birth to
him.*

Fictitious diary of a city police officer, as appears in
"Prisioneros de la calle," *Siglo Veintiuno* special report,
Guatemala. 9 March 1992.

The brutal treatment of children on Guatemala's streets began receiving international attention in 1989 through the persistent work of ChildHope, an international children's rights organization, and Casa Alianza. ChildHope first reported on the gruesome October discovery of the bodies of seventeen-year-old street child René Giovani Soto (eighteen in some sources) and his twenty-two-year-old friend, Edgar Patzán, near the University of San Carlos. The bodies were found with single bullet holes through their skulls and obvious signs of torture (cigarette burns, scalds, feet and hands bound).[1] ChildHope's Mark Connolly recounted that months before the murder, national police officers had detained Giovani in the Zone 18 adult prison, where older prisoners repeatedly raped him and carved their names into his skin with rusty nails.[2]

Five months after Giovanni's death, a second graphic incident received international attention. In March 1990, four national police officers so severely beat thirteen-year-old Nahamán Carmona that they ruptured his liver, broke six of his ribs, and fractured two of his fingers. Bruises, including a ten-centimeter gash on the back, covered 70 percent of his body.[3] After ten days of lapsing in and out of a coma, Nahamán died in Guatemala's public San Juan de Dios Hospital. Just three months later, in perhaps the most heinous of all of Guatemala's abuses involving street children, a group of plain-clothed assailants, including two off-duty national police officers, abducted six teenagers from a busy street in the city's center. The bodies of four appeared several days later with grotesque signs of torture; their eyes and tongues had been removed, their fingernails ripped out, and large burns covered parts of their corpses.

Amnesty International (AI) and Guatemalan rights groups have publicized most extensively these three cases. Unfortunately, they merely symbolize the frequent abuse and almost daily harrassment that Guatemalan street children suffer. Many governments have condemned Guatemala's treatment of its street children and they have pressured its leaders to curb abuses. A report on international cooperation commissioned by the Guatemalan presidency in 1991 indicates that the violent treatment of these children factored second only to the country's overall human rights record in the decline of foreign assistance.[4] Since 1990, the

U.S. Department of State has referred consistently to cases involving street children in its annual human rights country report to the congressional foreign relations bodies. Its 1990 briefing states, for example:

> In 1990 there were credible reports that policemen and private security guards tortured and killed street children. . . . Four policemen were arrested for the murder of thirteen-year-old Nahamán Carmona López, who was kicked to death. . . . The Police were investigating several other reports of torture of street children.[5]

The following year the State Department reported:

> In 1991 the military, civil patrols, and the police continued to commit a majority of human rights abuses, including extrajudicial killings, torture, and disappearances of, among others, human rights activists, unionists, indigenous people, and street children.[6]

The report also brought to congressional attention the case of seventeen-year-old Walter Federico Flores, in which two police cadets severely beat Flores, "leaving him in the street unconscious, when [he] objected to turning over his identification papers. The Minister of the Interior promised to look into the matter but, as of the end of the year, no result had been announced."[7]

Feeling pressure from the international community, the Guatemalan government began paying lip service to street children's rights. Immediately after the announcement of democratic elections in 1985, international assistance for Guatemala greatly increased. U.S. economic aid, alone, rose from the 1977-84 levels between $10 million and $30 million annually to approximately $100 million in 1985.[8] Moreover, during Marco Vinicio Cerezo Arévalo's presidency, the Guatemalan army had won the battle for reinstatement of U.S. military funding. In 1990, arms shipments ceased, once again, and perhaps wishing to avoid any further endangerment of assistance, the administration of then-President Jorge Antonio Serrano Elías began pledging, among other promises, to curb the violence directed at street children and to prosecute police officers involved in cases of abuse. In late 1991, the Minister of the Interior reportedly stated that during that year no complaints of abuse involving street children had been filed, a blatant misrepresentation of the gruesome reality, as Casa Alianza alone filed at least seventeen formal denouncements.[9] Further, addressing the nation after his first year in office, President Serrano insisted that the situation for street children had improved significantly during 1991, and that instead of receiving letters criticizing his inaction, he had begun to receive mail thanking him for his work (a statement to which ACA Director for Latin America Bruce Harris later quipped "I don't know from whom, perhaps his wife").[10]

The State Department acknowledged the Guatemalan government's increased attention to the issue of street children's rights in its country reports, but did not lend full credence to Serrano's or his administration's statements. The 1992 report indicates,

> The government, especially the Attorney General's office, dedicated additional personnel and undertook increased efforts to end police abuse of street children in coordination with Casa Alianza . . . Casa Alianza reported no extrajudicial killings of street children in 1992. There were, however, numerous reports of policemen beating or illegally detaining street children.

The 1993 briefing relates the new police chief's promises to punish officers abusing street children, but also reports the March detention and torture of Julio César Reyes and the April shootings of Henry Yubani Alvarez and Francisco Tziac.[11] In the face of such international attention, persistent communications from AI, and mounting pressures from rights groups within the country, why has the government of Guatemala allowed such abuse of street children to continue? More fundamentally, why would these children, mere children, not subversives or activists, continually suffer gross mistreatment?

The actual cases of human rights violations involving street children provide many of the clues necessary to understand both the government's inaction and the abusers' motives. In 1989, as a growing number of cases came to light, ACA and other rights groups in Guatemala alerted AI to the emerging patterns of violence directed at street children. AI published a special report, in July 1990, documenting the street children's situation. The same year, ACA opened a legal aid office and began assisting street children to legally redress their abuse. The office soon held almost exclusive responsibility for the investigation and prosecution of human rights violations against street children, as the Attorney General's office and the National Police Minors' Division remained uncommitted to resolving such cases, and, in fact, often impeded ACA's work.

During its first four years of operation, the legal aid office pursued 126 cases of abuse. These 126, as current legal director Hector Dionicio asserts, include only those for which sufficient evidence existed to make formal complaints. Often children report abuses to Casa Alianza weeks or months after they occur; this lapse in time hampers successful investigations. Other times, witnesses will not come forward or investigators uncover only limited physical evidence. In still many other instances, children choose to remain silent, fearing violent reprisal from their attackers if they speak out.

Besides Amnesty International and Casa Alianza, Guatemalan newspapers also have reported acts of violence against street children. These three sources, taken together, provide a good record of known human rights cases involving street children in Guatemala over the past five years. Brief descriptions of many of these cases appear below. With these descriptions, I have attempted to highlight those points necessary for understanding patterns and possible motives behind reported abuses. All information, unless otherwise noted, comes from an unpublished report of ACA legal aid office files, updated as of July 1994, and/or the *Report to the UN Committee Against Torture on the Torture of Guatemalan Street Children*, printed by ACA in Novermber 1995. The italicized quotes are excerpts from the street children's testimonies appearing in chapter two.

Human Rights Abuses of Guatemalan Street Children

1989-90

'Take me,' he said, 'don't leave me here alone,
take me with you'
and I didn't take him, and I left.
'Don't leave,' he said to me,
'I know, I know why I'm telling you not to go.'

In its July 1990 publication, Amnesty International reported several disturbing incidents which occurred during the last few months of 1989. According to this publication, on 6 September 1989 national police officers surrounded a thirteen-year-old street child in Guatemala City's Zone 1 as he inhaled glue from a plastic bag. The officers began insulting the boy, confiscated his glue, and then poured it over his head. AI reported two similar abuses, in which police in Zone 1 poured glue on children's heads, on 13 February and 16 May 1990, and a more severe case on 9 April, in which officers forced two street children to swallow their bags of glue. Four days later, Casa Alianza learned of an incident in Zone 11, where police forced a boy to swallow his glue directly, without the bag. The child suffered burns in his stomach and developed severe bronchitis as a result of the attack.

The 4 March 1990 beating which resulted in the death of Ruth's brother, Nahamán Carmona, also began when national police approached a group of children inhaling glue. At about 12:30 am police spotted the group in front of the Centro Capitol, a busy shopping center and movie theater in Zone 1, two blocks from ACA's crisis center, the *refugio*. Several children escaped as they saw the police heading toward them, but Nahamán and a few others were not as lucky. The officers, four in total, began dousing the kids with their glue. When Nahamán resisted they became enraged, kicking and beating him into unconsciousness. As the other children fled, the police left Nahamán to die. He lost control of his bladder and bowels, but managed to crawl half a block, into a doorway. Someone there placed a white sheet and paper flowers over his body—a customary act in Guatemala when children die.[12]

> *When I heard about my brother's death . . . I didn't believe,*
> *and they told me 'take it, read it,' they told me.*
> *When I read it I believed,*
> *and I said 'It can't be my brother, no. . . .'*

The injustice of Nahamán's beating did not end on the street. AI reports that when the boy arrived in an ambulance at the San Juan de Dios Hospital, no accident report was filed by the police, as required by law. Hospital workers admitted Nahamán as "XX" (identity unknown), an act which began ten days of neglect and mistreatment. Although Nahamán suffered repeated convulsions, doctors performed no brain-scan or x-ray of his skull. Also, despite the large quantities of blood in Nahamán's urine, doctors ordered no diagnostic tests or surgery for more than 30 hours, when a Casa Alianza worker coincidentally saw Nahamán and demanded that the doctor on duty help the boy. Although hospital staff then operated on his liver and removed more than 1.6 liters of blood from his abdomen, Nahamán died several days later from liver failure. Those at his bedside report his last words: "I only wanted to be a child; they didn't let me."[13] Casa Alianza arranged for his burial in the organization's mausoleum in Ciudad Vieja. Hundreds of street children attended the funeral.

No more than two months after Nahamán's burial, AI reports, police once again brutalized a street child, when an officer fatally shot twelve-year-old Marvin de la Cruz in the head as he ran from the scene where he had robbed a tourist. Further, on 23 May, four private security guards illegally detained two street children, forcing them into the basement of the Centro Capitol, where they beat and threatened the boys, and one of the guard's dogs attacked them. In a similar incident on 13 August, two guards from the same company forced two street children, again into the basement of the Capitol, demanded money, and held the boys there until national police arrived and released them.

The Bosques de San Nicolás case was the third reported homicide of street children in 1990 and the one mentioned so frequently by the children. It involved the abduction, torture, and execution of four boys, ranging in age from fifteen to twenty years old. During the second week of June, a group of plainclothes individuals, including two off-duty national police officers, drove to Eighteenth Street, a popular hang-out for street children, and forced six youths into the back of their four-wheel-drive vehicle. One of the abducted youths, a fourteen-year-old girl, survived to tell a ghastly tale of what happened that night. In a video about the case produced by Judy Jackson for the BBC and narrated by Bruce Harris (*They Shoot Children Don't They?*), the survivor tells how she regained consciousness in the back of the vehicle and, looking out, saw that they were in a cemetery. One of the abducted boys was still alive also and told her to run, that he was too weak to escape, and that only she and God could save them.

> One's name was 'el Catracho,' he wasn't from here,
> another 'el Soruyo,'the brother of Jorge Luis, my daughter's father,
> his brother was there.
> Luis was there. There were about six and they turned up tortured.

The girl noticed that the captors tied another of the boys to a tree and beat him severely, demanding that he "tell the truth." She then fled and reached safety. Her last words on this poignant tape warn other children not to leave their homes, because in the streets they would only find "the life of a dog." She knows this, she says, because while still only fourteen, she has endured more than most adults.

Four of the bodies in this case appeared between 16 and 17 June in the Bosques de San Nicolás neighborhood of Zone 4. The fifth never surfaced. At the time of the discovery, no one identified the bodies, and so police photographed and registered them as "XX." A month later, according to AI's report, Casa Alianza workers reviewed a book of police photographs and recognized the missing youths. Although the pictures clearly showed that the boys' eyes had been gouged or burned, and their tongues and ears removed, the accompanying police reports made no mention of these atrocities. According to ACA's legal aid office, in a related incident on 25 June the same national police officers were accused of shooting and killing seventeen-year-old Anstraun Villagran, a friend of the victims. Eyewitnesses testify that the police called to Anstraun, who, after talking with them for a few minutes, began running away from them down Eighteenth Street. The officers then opened fire at the youth's back and fatally wounded him.

> *Whenever they kill like that, a group, kill several, everyone leaves.*
> *They don't stay in the street, fear that they'll kill them too.*

As 1990 came to a close, other disturbing incidents occurred. Six separate beatings of twelve- to sixteen-year-old children by national police officers occurred in close succession. In one case three police officers detained sixteen-year-old Abraham Moran and, although never charging him with a crime, handcuffed him and forced him into a police vehicle. The police then drove Moran around the city, beat him, threatened him, and eventually left him at the edge of a ditch in Zone 18. A photographer captured this detention on film, but national police administrators never took measures to discipline the officers. Two days after Moran's abduction, police made yet another chilling discovery; the body of an eight-year-old boy, beaten and strangled, was found under Olympic Bridge in Zone 5 of the city. Although faulty handling of evidence by the police prevented prosecution, the Minors' Division pointed to the boy's father as the chief suspect.

> *I cursed him. And the more I cursed him, the more he beat me.*

On 26 November an unknown male apprehended thirteen-year-old Juan Linares and brought him to where two national police officers held fourteen-year-old Antonio Franco. The officers handcuffed and beat the boys and also permitted the man to beat them. *[T]he police officer . . . continued beating me. With the handcuffs he gave it to me. . . . He drew blood, he broke my head.* Similarly two officers beat fifteen-year-old Victor Manuel Salguero on 3 December inside an Eighteenth Street market. Although photographs taken of the assault provided sufficient evidence for prosecution, the national police's internal review board claimed that the officers were impostors.

1991

How often would the police approach you?
Ay, they stopped you almost every day on Ninth. For papers, why were you
drugged, anything. . . .

Notwithstanding the Serrano administration's assertions about improving respect for street children's human rights, Casa Alianza's case files clearly show that 1991 proved just as morbid as the 1989-90 period. Attacks began on the very first day of the year, when two inebriated military police officers brutally beat two street children. The guards were still assaulting the boys when ACA employees, alerted by another child, arrived on the scene to intervene. On 18 February, an unidentified individual shot sixteen-year-old William Salguero in the vicinity of Eighteenth Street and Fifth Avenue. Police detained and beat a fifteen-year-old street girl several blocks from there on 14 March. Then just twelve days later, unidentified men abducted street children William Chalin and Francisco Paz as they rested in front of the *refugio*. The abductors held the children for several hours, deeply intimidating them before releasing them. *And they forced him into that car. They forced him into that car, and they forced me in too.* Abductors also tracked down Franciso Tziac, a sixteen-year-old who was with Nahamán Carmona the night of his assault, one block from the *refugio*. On 26 May, he was forced into a car, driven through the city, beaten, and then abandoned in a peripheral neighborhood of Zone 19.

Even though you can be in the street for a long time, know everyone, there are always police, people that want to hurt you . . .they've beaten our own friends, they've taken them to prison, some have shown up dead. The majority now are dead. . . . In late April, Francisco Chacón Torres, a fifteen-year-old boy, died on Guatemala's streets after a private security guard for a synagogue shot him through the head. The National Police Minors' Division later discovered that the security company that employed the guard operated clandestinely, without license from the Interior Ministry. In this case, one of Casa Alianza's few legal successes, a judge sentenced the guard to ten years in prison and a Q. 10,000. fine for the murder (still unpaid). A second street child, Gustavo Adolfo Concaba ("Toby"), died twelve days later when he fought with another youth, Carlos Moreno. *Corina cried when she spoke of Toby. It seems he had been a great friend to her. She remembered that before he died they had spent much time together. When she felt cold, she said, Toby would give her his jacket, when she needed money, he would obtain it for her . . . when she heard of his death . . . [s]he would sit for hours in the same places they had frequented, waiting for his return.*

National police continued assaulting street children in the same fashion that they had in 1989 and 1990. On 30 April a uniformed officer entered the Cine Bolivar, a popular movie theater, where sixteen-year-old Juan Manuel López sat watching the feature. The officer accosted the minor, struck him violently and poured glue over his head, then forced him to leave the theater. In mid-June, when a drunken man beat thirteen-year-old Felipe Gonzalez Barrios, outside of the *refugio*, police detained both the boy and his attacker . When the police sent the case to court, Felipe appeared as the defendant, however, and the drunken man as the injured party.

> *And they grabbed me by the hair and . . . I told them that*
> *they shouldn't grab me like that because. . .*
> *he didn't know what punishment God could give him.*

A particularly disturbing attack, reminiscent of the Bosques de San Nicolás case, occurred on 1 August 1991, when three unidentified men forced sixteen-year-old Edwin Esteban Garcia into a pickup truck near Eighteenth Street. Shortly after the abduction, the vehicle stopped and two national police officers boarded. Although the officers soon left the vehicle, they allowed the three men to continue holding the minor. *And I was really afraid to be there, but there was a friend who told me . . . to just think about God, and that He was going to help me.* The captors bound Edwin's hands and feet and blindfolded him. After driving him around the city for roughly four hours, they stripped him, lead him on a leash to a wooded area, tied him to a tree, burned various parts of his body with cigarettes and, finally, threw him down a ditch. When Edwin regained consciousness he walked to a farm on the outskirts of the capital, where the caretakers gave him clothing and drove him back into the city.

They cut out their eyes, their, their, their eyes. They branded names on them with hot irons. . . . A similar abduction occurred on 23 September, when a group of unidentified men approached Abraham Moran and Geovanny Chonay as they sat in front of the *refugio*. The men beat and threatened the minors, asking the whereabouts of Ronaldo Moreno, another witness in the Nahamán Carmona case. When the aggressors forced the two youths into their car, *refugio* staff members immediately called the police. After a long search, police in one of the dispatched cruisers located the vehicle, with the minors still on board, but they made no arrest.

Other serious assaults on street children in 1991 included the 13 August shooting of Walter Rodriguez, who recognized his attacker as a guard for a local women's apparel store, the 19 October brutal beating of Mayra Carranza by two unidentified individuals and the attack on Walter Federico Flores, mentioned by the U.S. State Department in its country report. When Flores refused his identification papers to two national police cadets, they struck him in the head and face with their batons. After he fell to the ground, the cadets continued by kicking him into unconsciousness. Approximately an hour later Flores came to and struggled to the state-run Rafael Ayau shelter, where workers refused to admit him or extend medical attention. *They transferred me to Rafael Ayau. And what's it like there? It's a jail also. They hit you there, abused you.* Flores did attain help several blocks away, at the *refugio*.

1992

The pattern of abuses involving street children began shifting in 1992. Not only did the reported beatings and abductions of children increase, but also the harassment and intimidation of Casa Alianza employees that had begun in 1989. The year began in typical fashion, when street child Felipe Gonzalez Barrios suffered three separate brutal attacks in a ten-day period. On 11 January, five unknown individuals grabbed him, beat him, and accused him of burglarizing their car. The following day the same individuals beat him again, requiring his treatment at San Juan de Dios Hospital. He was attacked a third time, four blocks from the original assault, when two armed men beat him so severely that he once more required hospital treatment. *They left me black and blue in all this part here, here and here, see.* On 2 February, fifteen-year-old Luis Antonio Roldan boarded a city bus without paying his fare. The driver stopped, took out a pistol and shot Luis in the leg, then calmly restarted the bus and left the scene.

Two police officers and two private individuals abducted seventeen-year-old Karlo Contreras on 25 February as he rested in the Barajuste neighborhood. The four men approached Karlo, accused him of stealing a pair of sunglasses, and began beating him. Other street children came to Karlo's aid, but one of the officers threatened them with his gun, and forced the youth into an unmarked car. The captors drove Karlo to the Zone 3 cemetery, beat him and eventually abandoned him. *And it seems that, last, they shot him three times in the forehead. And she saw, and with that she says that they were in . . . the public cemetery.*

A long series of nearly constant abuses involving street children and ACA workers began on 6 March 1992, coincident with the formation of the *hunapú* ("hunters") security force, a special corps created by the Minister of the Interior to combat urban crime and comprised of military, national, and transit police officers. On that day, between 12:30 and 1:30 pm, a group of approximately thirty-five mobile military policemen rounded up sixteen youths in a five-block area known for its presence of street children. When ACA employees reminded the officers that by law they could not handcuff minors, one replied that they had "orders to follow." They then transported the youths to a nearby police precinct.

A deeply disturbing event, which also involved military police, occurred on 15 March, in the Barajuste neighborhood. On that occasion, five military policemen surrounded sixteen-year-old Juan Antonio Hernández and demanded his identification papers. When the minor complied and handed over his birth certificate, one of the officers noticed the ACA seal on the paper and became furious, shouting that all Casa Alianza kids were thieves. Another officer struck Juan Antonio with his baton and a third destroyed the boy's birth certificate. The officers then ordered the youth to remove his shoelaces, with which they tied his hands behind his back, and began parading him through the city's busiest streets. As they started out, one officer ordered Juan Antonio to hold his head high, so that the citizenry of the capital would realize that the military police were capturing thieves.

Arriving at the Centro Capitol with Juan Antonio, the officers stopped for a few moments, during which time a large crowd gathered and started staring at Juan Antonio, "as if he were a rare animal."[14] From there, the officers paraded the boy back to the plaza where they had detained him, threw him to the ground, and held him motionless for roughly two hours. Finally, one of the men dragged Juan Antonio to a nearby alley, kicked him and told him to "disappear filth."

We are not garbage, animals, or anything. We are people.

Four days after that attack members of the *hunapú* force continued their campaign against street children. *She said she knew what it was like to be tracked, hunted by the police.* On that day, five separate abuses were reported to Casa Alianza. In one case, four officers abducted four street children, ages thirteen to seventeen, beat them, and threw them out of a moving vehicle at the Zone 3 garbage dump. In a second incident, two officers, who earlier had detained and hit a boy in front of the *refugio*, returned to the scene, frisked two youths, then assaulted them and con-fiscated their glue. In a third case that day, two Barajuste market ven-dors attacked fifteen-year-olds Edwin Antonio Mux and Carlos Amilcar Gomez, beating the youths with a tube and indicating that it was street children's fault that sales had declined, and that if the cops had not yet killed them, the vendors would.

On 5 April, six uniformed *hunapú* officers surrounded Ludwin Gutierrez and Carlos Coy, destroyed their identification papers, and poured glue over their heads, an act which one officer said might "take care of" the boys' "whim." *With that, they threw a bottle, you know, of glue at us, at our head. A little more and they would have hit us in the head with that jar, because it was a jar, and I don't know how, I turned around and I just managed to duck. And we started running. . . .* Exhibiting the typically aggressive behavior of inhalant abusers, the youth who had murdered "Toby," Carlos Moreno, fatally stabbed a second boy, Francisco Paz on 24 March. Carlos apparently became violent after Francisco refused him a bag of glue.

On July 31st, in one of the few cases of abuse *reported* by girls (street educators and children, alike, indicate that boys receive harsher *physical* mistreatment on the street, but girls more prominent *sexual* mistreatment; this may make them more reluctant to report), two national police officers approached Yessica Villatorio, a resident of an ACA home, as she and a group of friends left night school. The officers detained and drove Yessica and one of the boys to a deserted area saying they would go free if Yessica gave them "something" in return. When she refused, the officers abandoned her, intimidated her friend, and returned twenty minutes later in an effort to "convince" her. *He wanted to try to rape me, and I began to scream. And I told him 'Let me go! Let me go!' I said. 'But I want you, son of a bitch' he said to me. . . . And he had a pistol. 'If you move, I'll kill you.'*

On 4 August, police attacked fourteen-year-old Byron Geovanny Castillo and fifteen-year-old José Chicaju as they sat outside a clothing store on Eighteenth Street. Two other boys that had been inhaling glue in the same locale fled, leaving their glue behind, as the cops approached. The officers began beating and kicking Geovanny and José, calling them pieces of shit, sons of bitches, animals and thieves. *We were there by the Presidenta and, there were several of us. They only kicked me in the stomach. And with the rest, they really gave it to them.* Noticing the abandoned glue of the other boys, the officers dragged the two minors into a nearby market, poured the glue on their heads, beat and kicked them again, and then ordered them never to be seen again in the neighborhood. The next time, the police warned, they would kill the boys.

Two unidentified individuals made threats of a similar nature to Felipe Gonzalez Barrios on 6 August as he rested in the Hipódramo del Norte, Zone 2. The individuals asked Felipe who had broken into their car, accused him of stealing sunglasses from the dashboard, and assaulted him with the butt of a gun. Before leaving, the two men told the minor that this time he had been lucky, the next time they would kill him. Four days later two armed individuals again attacked Felipe, when they forced him into their car with polarized windows, kicked and punched him, and abandoned him in a neighboring municipality.

A private security guard brutally beat street child Mario René Hernández on 22 August, in front of the Club Guatemala, one block from the *refugio*. The attack produced serious wounds requiring treatment at the San Juan de Dios Hospital. Police officers arriving on the scene, intervened and arrested the security guard. On 9 September a large group of men, wielding bottles, angrily approached the *refugio* and began beating two youths. When ACA employees tried to stop the men, one angrily shouted that the *refugio* was a refuge of thieves, then all began the beating once again until the boys lost consciousness.

When you were on the street, how frequently would the police approach you? You know, when I was consuming glue, stealing, or we were having a fight, or they simply grabbed us for being there.... The next day, four national police officers boarded a city bus on which an ACA employee traveled with two residents of the *Comunidad*. The officers drew their guns and ordered the two youths off the bus and against the wall. When the employee complained, the cops released the boys, but warned them not to be seen in the neighborhood.

National police also attacked a group of street children on a city bus the afternoon of 20 September. After the officers demanded money, the youths attempted to exit the bus. *If one gave them their share of what one stole, they grabbed it. But if one didn't give them anything, that's when they got angry.* One agent drew his gun, shot sixteen-year-old Daniel Balam in the leg, and then beat him severely with the butt of the gun. The other kids then gave the officer Q. 50, screaming that they would report him to the ACA office. The officer replied that he feared no one. Five days later, an unidentified man fired a BB gun from his car and hit two minors in front of the *refugio*. *And you know, you always have problems on the street. And without realizing that those problems can even bring you death.*

Other shootings occurred in November. On the 7th José Olindo Corado was shot in the back by an unknown attacker; on the 26th Daniel Balam was shot and killed in a violent altercation with an unidentified female. Closing out the long, trying year, two employees of Guatel severely beat fourteen-year-old José Luis Gonzalez with a telephone cable on 4 December, one block from the *refugio* and, finally, on 7 December, two national policemen boarded a city bus on which five street children rode, ordered the bus driver to detour past the third precinct, then arrested all five youths. The officers later explained that they had detained the street children for "being suspicious."

1993

Although street children reported fewer violations in 1993 than in the devastating prior year, the gruesome nature of their abuse continued unabated. On 15 January, two unidentified men chased a group of street children through Concordia Park, in Zone 1. When one of the youths, fourteen-year-old Mynor Vasquez, tripped and fell, the two men severely beat him and threw him against a food stand in the park. Mynor's impact against the metal structure produced four gashes on his left arm. Receiving treatment later at the *refugio*, the boy told staff members that he had seen his attackers on other occasions dressed in police uniform.

On 18 March, two individuals identifying themselves as the police woke eighteen-year-old José Antonio Higueros as he slept in a park near the Barajuste market. The men indicated that they had come for a gold chain, but José Antonio had nothing for them. The officers then kicked and beat the youth, hoping to extract something of value, but when José Antonio still could not comply, they forced him into a vehicle and, before abandoning him, warned that the next time they saw him in Zone 1 they would arrest him.

> *When my* compañeros *saw a police officer and they had money, they would give us the money right away, because they stop you, they search you, and everything . . . if you have money they let you free, and if not they take you to jail, or they hit you. . . . They only search you for money or some object of value, something you are wearing, jackets, like that.*

Two additonal, deeply disturbing incidents of the same nature occurred in March. In the first, two uniformed national police officers corralled fifteen-year-old Heriberto Méndez Herrera and two other street children on Eighteenth Street and demanded their identification papers. The officers also made the children hand over their only valuable possessions at the time, a pair of Fila sneakers and Q. 45. Shortly afterwards, the officers forced all three boys into a patrol car, handcuffed and blindfolded them, and drove them to the Zone 3 cemetery. At the cemetery, they burned Heriberto four times with a cigarette, then abandoned them. *And they forced us out there by the Zone 3 ditch. They let us go and told us that they were going to throw us from the ditch.*

In the second incident, two days after the attack on Heriberto, two men abducted a group of four street children at gunpoint. Seventeen-year-old Diego Chouza escaped, but the men drove the others around the city for three hours, demanding money, gold objects, and Ray Ban sunglasses. As the minors possessed nothing, their captors forced them to reveal where they could find Diego. *And . . . we were really scared. . . . We went to a hotel. I don't even know what was wrong with me. . . .* At the Hotel Xelaju, near Eighteenth Street, they located and abducted Diego for a second time, then drove him to a remote neighborhood and finally extracted Q. 175 and a gold chain from him. Reporting the abuse to Casa Alianza, Diego stated that the same men had demanded money from him in the past and that they worked with the National Police Department of Criminal Investigations.

That man laughed and he said that at last he had us, and that there were many more left still, and that, little by little, they were going to die. The widely publicized torture case involving fifteen-year-old Julio César Reyes occurred 14 March 1993, when two plainclothes detectives stopped the youth and another street child outside Concordia Park and demanded their identification papers. The boys had no identification and the two men began aggressively leading them to a nearby police station. Before arriving, however, one of the two pulled Julio César aside and burned his left arm and fingers with a cigarette, nineteen times in total. Recounting the story later, the boy told how one of the men lamented that he had no salt to throw in the wounds, and how the other scratched each of the burns that he produced.[15] The two men also threatened to take the boys to prison if they were seen again in the neighborhood. Fearing for his life, Julio César fled to Honduras, but by the time he arrived, his wounds had become deeply infected.

> Now, you mentioned before that you have known several
> that have died on the street . . . *Yes.*
> or that have been abused . . . *that they have killed.*

On 17 April a private security guard responsible for policing several stores on or around Nineteenth Street suddenly approached and shot eighteen-year-old Henry Yubani Alvarez. Although the youth died several hours later in San Juan de Dios Hospital, his attacker remains free. A second shooting occurred just five days later, when two unknown men parked their car in front of the *refugio* and fired upon Francisco Tziac. Terrorized, Francisco fled the scene collapsing after twelve blocks amidst a group of street friends. The two men also fled the scene but soon returned, identifying themselves as military commisioners to the *refugio* guard on duty. They said they would be back for Francisco. Indeed, he was attacked again on 7 August, as he slept outside the *refugio* with two friends. In that instance, three police officers snatched the boys' glue and poured it over their heads.

> *And they were going to kill 'Cheni' also. And Bruce left with her.*
> They left the country or what?
> *They got her out of the county in time. They later brought her back and they were going around looking for where she was. The men were looking for her.*

The shootings continued. On 29 September the owner of a hair salon near the Centro Capitol shot seventeen-year-old Ronaldo Moreno (like Tziac, a key witness in the Carmona case). Ronaldo noticed that the man followed him and had his hand tucked inside his jacket. He became deeply frightened. The man calmly told Ronaldo to walk, that he would not do anything to him. Four steps later he turned and shot.

A second incident occurred on the first of October as nineteen-year-old Rigoberto Caal walked along Eighteenth Street. Noticing a police officer beating a fellow street child, Rigoberto went to observe what happened. Coincidentally, the owner of a restaurant at the scene took out a gun and fired a shot into the air. Hearing this shot, the restaurant's security guard believed Rigoberto had fired and shot the youth in the chest. Fortunately, Rigoberto recuperated. October 5th held a different fate for nineteen-year-old Marvin Monterrosso, mortally wounded by the shotgun blast of a private security guard near Concordia Park.

Still another brutal attack widely publicized by Casa Alianza occurred on 22 May, when two uniformed national police officers approached sixteen-year-old Esvin Noe Flores in the Plazuela Bolivar on Eighteenth Street. One of the officers, in a drunken state, asked Esvin if

he had "gotten anything" for him yet. When Esvin responded negatively, the officer forced the boy to accompany him and his partner to the
nearby Amate Bridge. He began visciously beating Esvin with the butt
of his gun and, more maliciously, poured a potent acid on the boy's head
and chest.

With the intense burning produced by the acid, Esvin struggled back
to the Plazuela and sought help from vendors. Arriving by ambulance at
the crowded San Juan de Dios Hospital, Esvin waited a long period for
medical assistance. Giving up, he left the hospital and headed for a Zone
1 hotel frequented by street children. The hotel attendant, alarmed by
Esvin's screams of pain, however, called an ambulance to bring the boy
back to San Juan de Dios. This time, the registering nurse said that Esvin
would not be seen at all, since he left unattended the first time. The boy
finally went to a relative's house and was taken to a different hospital,
where doctors treated him for burns to the throat and face. According to
one report on the case, "out of fear of the authorities, the minor did not
want to be hospitalized, even though his wounds required it," and, thus,
five weeks after the attack Esvin sought medical help at the *refugio*.[16]   By
that time, his burns had become severely infected.

In a perhaps related event, designed to intimidate Esvin, the driver of
a car pulled up next to him the morning of 9 October, as he walked near
the Plazuela Bolivar. The individual rolled down his car window and,
without saying a word, pointed a gun at the boy, held it there for several seconds, then drove away slowly. The incident frightened Esvin
immensely and he quickly requested the help of ACA legal aid office.

A final tragic development in 1993 involved the growing violence
among street children, themselves. *They stab each other . . . and they
fight . . . There have been many boys killed there, among . . . among the same
gang.* The children always have fought over drugs, betrayals and jeal-
ousies, but the level of this violence escalated in 1993. On 23 May, Edwin
Mux stabbed and killed eighteen-year-old Hugo Rolando, while both
were under the influence of glue. "Vagabonds" in the streets of Zone 7
raped a fifteen-year-old street child on 11 September. The following day
three street youths murdered Ana Elizabeth Cisneros by stabbing her in
the throat after an altercation with her boyfriend. Finally, on 27
November, a group of street children approached seventeen-year-old José

Moises Diaz as he slept, poured flammable liquid on his leg and set him on fire. Fortunately, the youth survived the attack.

1994

Life in the street is really sad, its really hard.
The one who learns to survive lives, and the one that doesn't,
doesn't live.

Because Casa Alianza is still investigating most of the rights violations occurring between 1994 and the present, the legal aid office has not as yet generated reports on these cases. Information on several abuses have appeared in the press and human rights bulletins, however. Five national police officers reportedly beat street youths Francisco Tziac, Luis Antonio Roldan, and Myriam Eugenia Fuentes in Guatemala's Central Park on 4 March 1994. According to witnesses, one of the officers approached the three youths as they argued and began beating Roldan with a night stick, the force of the blows so severe that the stick broke in half. A second officer "took off his badge, handcuffed Roldan and continued the beating."[17] When Fuentes attempted to intervene the first officer beat her with his club and severely bruised her elbow.[18]

On 14 March, national police officers also severely wounded eighteen-year-old Luis Arolodo Vasquez. The agents reportedly stopped Vasquez and some friends in Zone 1 and demanded money. When Vasquez refused, one of the policemen hit him in the face with a pistol, then shot him as he attempted to flee the scene.[19] On 10 April unidentified individuals savagely attacked eleven-year-old Carlos René Gomez as he slept in Central Park. According to other children in the park, a group of men approached Gomez and poured a flammable liquid on his legs, then set him on fire. The minor sustained a burn twelve centimeters by fifteen centimeters on his right leg before extinguishing the flames.[20]

At least thirteen street children lost their lives through gruesome homicides in 1994, according to ACA legal aid director, Hector Dionicio. On July 20th sixteen-year-old Cecilio Yash and nineteen-year-old Juan Humberto Ramos disappeared. Several days later, their bodies turned up in a city garbage dump showing signs of severe torture and riddled with bullets, seventeen in total. Although witnesses originally implicated national police officers, the details surrounding the case remain unclear.

On 7 September, a private policeman patrolling a busy marketplace fatally shot seventeen-year-old Sergio Miguel Chavez, through the head, after he stole a pair of sunglasses. The many witnesses to the incident hopefully will facilitate justice in this case. In late September a twelve-year-old street child, Fidel, died when a bomb exploded in his hands. An unidentified individual reportedly handed the bomb to Fidel in a local fast food restaurant bag. This barbaric act provoked demands from politicians and a Q. 100,000 reward for information leading to the arrest of the responsible "terrorists."[21]   Also in late September, two heavily armed private security guards opened fire on a group of street children trying to sleep outside a bus terminal. A ten-year-old and fourteen-year-old died, and a third (twelve-year-old) child required hospitalization.[22]

Intimidation of street educators and ACA staff members

We were talking when a car wtih polarized windows passed by . . .
it stopped in front of the refugio, *and they began insulting us.*
And . . . they just lowered the window, they began firing at us. And
there were some educators upstairs, and they shot at them, too.
They knocked down the sign that was there.

Guatemala's campaign of terror against street children has extended to those few people trying to assist them. Intimidation of ACA employees and threats to its facilities began in earnest in 1989, but intensified greatly during 1992 and 1993. On 25 April 1992, the driver of a vehicle stopped suddenly outside the *refugio* and shouted into the lobby that he would plant a bomb to "put an end to" all of the kids. The driver also tried to attack two minors in the entrance to the building, but fled when an ACA employee intervened. Two days later, two plainclothes police suspiciously watched Eileen Ovalle, a secretary for ACA's legal aid office, as she talked with several street kids in downtown's Central Park. Ovalle became alarmed and decided to photograph the men, an act which apparently upset them. The next day, the same individuals surrounded one of the boys present during the incident and said that they would break his and the *"señorita's"* asses. Two uniformed cops also went to Ovalle's home and extracted personal information about her from her housekeeper.

Another ACA employee, Londy Urizar, received a call at work on 8 May, indicating that she was "sentenced," that if she did not leave ACA she would be killed. The next day she noticed a strange vehicle parked outside of her home during two periods of one-and-a-half hours each. Similarly, on 19 August, José Mariano Girón, an attorney with the legal aid office, noticed an unknown individual standing outside his home signalling several times to a near-by pickup truck with polarized windows. When Girón looked toward the truck, he saw that several of the passengers had large guns and one carried a two-way radio. After a period of three hours, the pickup and the individual disappeared.

Two other incidents of intimidation occurred that same morning, August 19th. At 8 am a strange car with polarized windows and three men aboard parked outside the ACA group home CEE. From inside the car, one of the passengers revealed his .38 caliber gun to a staff member. Another of the home's employees recognized the individual as a national police officer. Later, at 9:15 am, an unknown individual stood outside the group home San Francisco for more than an hour. The same individual returned, accompanied by another, at 10:45 am, this time in a vehicle with polarized windows.

Employees at several ACA homes also reported receiving bomb threats during this period of intensified activity. On 7 May someone called the Flor Bella home to say that a bomb was about to explode in the building. Five days later, a similar call was made to the *refugio*. On 7 July, the driver of a pickup with polarized windows braked suddenly in front of the *refugio* and shouted "sons of bitches, why do you run this den of thieves? I'm going to kill these kids one by one." Then, two months later, a pickup stopped again in front of the *refugio* and a man riding in the back fired a shot into the air. The *refugio* for girls received various bomb threats on 8 July, then on 4 October two armed men scaled the walls of the home, cut the telephone wires and fired shots into the air. Finally on 15 December employees at the *refugio* for boys once again received various phone calls indicating that a bomb would explode in the building "at any moment."

Heavy intimidation of Casa Alianza employees continued into and throughout 1993. On 6 January, José Mariano Girón once again fell victim. He noticed two unknown individuals on his street that morning, looking under the hood of a pickup. He thought nothing of the two men until a third approached him downtown, asking when Bruce (Harris) would next be in town. When the attorney replied that he did not know Bruce's plans, the individual insisted that he must know, that he knew but did not want to say. Moving away, Girón boarded a bus and, looking back, saw that the man signaled a few blocks up to a pickup, the same one parked earlier at his house. The pickup followed Girón's bus for several blocks until he nervously abandoned it and entered a nearby national police building, calling friends for assistance.

The former coordinator of the ACA legal aid office, Edgar Raúl Toledo, also received threats. Between 5 and 8 February a female caller left numerous messages on the answering machine in Toledo's private office. The content of the messages ranged from lude sexual fantasies to death threats against Toledo and his family. In one message the caller warned that she would denounce Toledo to the police because he did not work, he only represented "those thieves that like to take money from people." In late August, the attorney received a second series of calls in his private office. This time, a male caller, distorting his voice, left a message asking "Why are you still in the country, big-time lawyer?" Five minutes later the same caller left a second message in more threatening tone: "You want to die." The next day the man spoke directly to Toledo, identifying himself as "with the Attorney General's office." He warned Toledo that his office had information on corruption in Casa Alianza and stated that the sooner Toledo left the organization the better.

On 14 February 1993, three unknown individuals arrived at the *refugio* for girls, asking for educator Anabella Cordón. When co-worker Marlene de León informed the men that Anabella was off-duty, they left this message: "Tell her that she has three days left." De León, herself, also suffered intimidation and harassment. In mid-February two men tried to grab her as she left work, but she escaped, calling on a nearby policeman for assistance. Then on 4 May, a few blocks from the *refugio*, a man cornered her and kicked her in the groin area. De León again ran for help from the police, but the officer responding indicated that he could not arrest her attacker because "it was her word against his."

Beginning in early 1990 *refugio* educator Axel Mejía and his family received numerous threats and warnings, including the abduction and beating of his brother David in March 1992. In September 1993 the series of intimidations continued when a man called the *refugio* and asked for Mejia's schedule. The social worker who attended the call said that she did not know when Mejía would be working next. The caller left a message: Mejía should take good care of himself, from one moment to the next "they" would get to him. He interfered in matters that did not pertain to him.

Analysis of human rights cases

The cases of human rights violations against street children evidence clear shifts between 1989 and the present. The number of reported cases increased drastically between 1989-90 and 1992. Part of this increase, naturally, may have resulted from greater knowledge of and trust among the street child population in ACA's legal aid office, which began operating only in 1990. Aside from disparities in the number of cases, however, one also sees contextual changes during the same period. In late 1989 and 1990, the great majority of abuses were committed by uniformed state security officers, or individuals later identified as such. In 1991 this proportion dropped when children reported growing numbers of abuses by private or unknown individuals. Both the total number of violations and those committed by private or unknown individuals grew in 1992. In 1993 reported violations fell from 1992, but the number of abuses committed by unknown or private individuals compared to those perpetrated by state security forces remained roughly the same.

With the exception of the few cases in which violence directed at street children occurred as an immediate response to a foiled robbery, however, one cannot eliminate the possibility that the unidentified individuals committing the growing number of human rights violations against street kids do, in fact, pertain to state security forces. While many street children do steal sunglasses and burglarize cars as survival tactics, the frequency and similarity of incidents in which unidentified men, almost always in groups of two or three, approached street children, vaguely accusing them of these acts, supports the possibility that at least some of these "private" individuals were, in reality, state-sponsored agents acting in collusion. That the perpetrators of these abuses also frequently abducted street children, warned them "not to be seen again," and drove them to cemeteries, garbage dumps, and other remote areas—all typical tactics of state-sponsored intimidation—also casts doubt on the "private" nature of the acts.

According to the Guatemalan Archbishop's Office for Human Rights, a coincident shift from overt to "private" (or clandestine) rights violations occurred in the larger context of Guatemala City, as well, adding weight to the possible link between street children's abuse and "established" sources of terror.[23] Comparing human rights cases across the country, the Archbishop's office found clandestine sources of violence much more predominant in urban zones than rural areas. Abuses of a clandestine nature occurred in only two rural cases, involving a doctor and a priest, leading office staff to hypothesize that as the likelihood or ability of a victim to denounce increases, so too does the preoccupation with secrecy by the repressive apparatus.[24] The increased numbers of formal denouncements made through Casa Alianza's legal aid office in 1992 and 1993, then, may have factored into the observed shift away from the open, obvious police brutality in 1989 and 1990 to the more frequent "private" abuses beginning in 1991.

The reliance on intimidation and threats against ACA workers and facilities also fits the larger pattern of human rights violations in Guatemala City. According to the Archbishop's office, the "language" of state-sponsored terrorism has moved toward the "psycho-physical" sphere, in which "intents" and "lightning" abductions assume new importance.[25] Such violence, while often leaving the victim physically unharmed, deeply disturbs and demoralizes him or her. As a result, if successful, it convinces victims to limit their participation in activist organizations or opposition parties.[26] The intimidation and threats directed at ACA employees since the opening of the legal aid office, fit the "psycho-physical" pattern of violence directed at other urban targets, as elaborated by the Archbishop's Office. Common characteristics of this intimidation include:

a) The victim receives notices (telephone calls, hang-ups, obvious surveillance at his/her home and place of work).

b) There is a program of following the victim, that may extend to various weeks or months; also it may recur (return after one or two years).

c) The victim is surprised in the street, either when traveling alone or accompanied, and also there is no typical schedule (which shows that the surveillance is quasi-permanent).

d) The victimizers form teams of at least two people up to four. They may be organized into two units, foreseeing backups in case of emergency.

e) The victimizers speak little and perhaps only one of them. They do not always physically appear in front of the victim.

f) They utilize large vehicles with polarized windows, without plates, in good condition, suitable for highways. . . . [27]

The Injustice System

You didn't feel that you could complain or denounce?
No, because for nothing, because denunciations here, in Guatemala are worthless. . . . And everyone in Casa Alianza knows that.

The individuals who have violated street children's human rights, in almost all cases, have acted with complete impunity. This impunity, coupled with the Guatemalan government's inaction and, at times, seemingly blatant obstruction of justice when addressing street children's abuses, further point to the systemic nature of the violations. Over the past four years ACA's legal aid office has acted almost exclusively in investigating the abuses reported by street children. According to Hector

Dionicio, Casa Alianza used to process all of its cases through the National Police Minor's Division and the Attorney General's office. Because these organizations constantly avoided their professional responsibilities, however, the legal aid office now presents all cases direct-ly before a judge. It still routinely forwards its denouncements to the law enforcement agencies, though, and to the quasi-state human rights bodies (the Presidential Commission on Human Rights and the Defender of Human Rights) in order to solicit support in cases where the courts have acted inappropriately or in excessively untimely manner.

Since ACA acts as legal guardian to all participants in its programs, it may initiate court proceedings without first going through the Attorney General's office. Even in by-passing the Attorney General, how-ever, Casa Alianza has encountered widespread negligence and delays in the institutional handling of its cases. The national police has continu-ously assumed a non-cooperative stance in investigating street children's abuses. Blatant examples of police incompetence, indifference, and out-right interference have occurred at all stages of the investigatory process. First, at the actual crime scene, the police have failed to detain street chil-dren's aggressors, even those individuals caught with abducted children in their cars. They have allowed private individuals to beat street chil-dren in their presence and they have "mishandled" evidence on numerous occasions, stalling or preventing the filing of formal denouncements.

More often, police obstruct justice after ACA has filed its complaints with the appropriate judicial bodies. The courts generally order the police to gather information on the complaints it receives, but frequent-ly, even after this order comes, police fail to initiate even rudimentary investigations of street children's cases.[28] This failure to cooperate, of course, stems in large part from police interest in blocking hearings of precisely these cases; police and other security officers form the chief sus-pects in roughly one-half of ACA's complaints.

Convincing the courts to order, let alone enforce, these police inves-tigations also proves, in and of itself, a long, difficult task. ACA's Regional Director, Bruce Harris, explains the taxing judicial process:

> There is an incident. The child reports it to the Legal Aid Office of Casa Alianza. The Office investigates it and, having

sufficient evidence, makes a denouncement before the justice of the peace. This process can take two days or an hour. The justice of the peace has three days to pass it to a penal judge, and there he has a week to assign it to an official. And an official, with everything else he has, if you are lucky, within three months he'll call you to ratify the denouncement. Afterwards, if he is very fast, within a month he sends an investigation order to the police. So, it is already five months.[29]

Realizing how quickly evidence disappears, Harris asks "What are they going to investigate after six months?"[30]

The history of interactions between Casa Alianza and the judicial system has left what newspaper analyst Carlos Rafael Soto describes as "a tense relationship [between the two], not very cordial and of absolute disparity in criteria on the treatment of the problems personified in the activities of [street] children."[31] The majority of Casa Alianza's cases have never been tried. Judges have stalled in almost all of these cases. Of seventeen denouncements made by ACA through judicial bodies in 1993, for example, none has reached the trial stage yet. According to ACA's case files, eight of the seventeen still await ratification, including the 12 September murder of Ana Elizabeth Cisneros and the 4 October shooting of Rigoberto Caal. Court officials have ratified the remaining nine cases, and five have provoked investigations by the Attorney General's office, the National Police's Minors' Division, or both. Yet, even in the 14 March torture of Julio César Reyes, the 17 April murder of Henry Yubani Alvarez and the 22 April shooting of Francisco Tziac, in which cases significant evidence has existed, the possibility of court proceedings remains nebulous.

In several instances court officers, themselves, have acted openly hostile while on ACA cases. In the August 1991 abduction and torture of Edwin García, the police's Minors Division collaborated with ACA and determined the registration number of the vehicle used by the perpetrators. They also located the exact site of the torture and found physical evidence still present. The owners of the farm where Edwin obtained clothing after recovering consciousness also verified the event. Despite this clear evidence, though, the officer assigned to the case has refused to act. Furthermore, even though ACA has filed two complaints with the

General Supervisor of Courts, the officer's posture has remained unchanged. As of July 1993, ACA had filed similar complaints against court personnel in sixteen other cases, all unanswered.[32]

Other cases have failed because the street children involved will not cooperate. In approximately fifteen of ACA's cases, minors have expressed fear of testifying. At times the minor acts in such a way to avoid reprisal, and at others to avoid implicating him or herself in an unlawful act relating to the rights violations (e.g. the abuse occurs during an attempted robbery by the minor). In still other instances, judges bar minors from testifying because they lack identification papers, because they have lapsed into "instability," or because they have gone into hiding.

In total, fewer than ten cases of human rights abuses involving street children have ever reached their conclusion. The first of these was the landmark Carmona case, in which a criminal court found the four officers who had beaten Nahamán guilty of homicide. The sentencing judge ordered one of the agents to fifteen years in prison, two others to twelve years and the fourth to ten years. ACA appealed the sentence, on the basis of Article 28 of the penal code, which indicates that penalties should be doubled for police officers commiting homicide while on active duty. On 5 August 1991, however, the appellate court ruled the original sentence void, apparently because while listing the crimes charged to the four police officers, the sentencing judge incorrectly stated the time of the beating as 2:30 am, instead of the actual 12:30 am.

Many delays and apparent attempts at obstructing justice stalled the second sentencing. In August 1991, for example, already seventeen months after Nahamán's murder, the original sentencing judge removed himself from the case because of a defendant's note which said: "Study the case well, judge." The judge believed he no longer could act impartially in the case. A chief witness for the prosecution also received threats and relocated in Canada, fearing for her life. A long series of changes in representation for the defendants further delayed sentencing, but finally, in April 1992, a new judge increased the sentence of the first officer from fifteen to eighteen years, nine months, and that of the other three to twelve and a half years each. The judge also ordered each of the officers to pay Q. 5000 in civil damages.

Although pleased with the increases, Casa Alianza again appealed the sentence, believing the twelve-and-a-half-year terms still too small. On appeal this time, however, the organization lost ground when the presiding judge held the officers guilty only of homicide "by omission," and sentenced each to just twelve years in prison, plus a Q. 10,000 fine. These four police agents currently are serving their sentences but have never paid the civil damages. Despite this and the reduced sentences, the final outcome in Nahamán's case has proven monumental, marking the first case in Guatemala in which state security officers received jail time for the abuse of a street child.

In the shooting death of Marvin de la Cruz, a judge found two police agents guilty, giving the murderer only three years and his partner only a one-year suspended sentence. Neither of the officers actually served time, however, as the courts permitted them to pay off their sentences with a mere Q. 300 in damages to the boy's father.

In the Bosques de San Nicolás case—involving the abduction, torture and assassination of four street children, and the murder of a fifth (Anstraun Villagran)—the sentencing judge, after a long series of delays, found the two police officers and the private individual charged in the case, not guilty. The Attorney General's office immediately appealed the decision, but in March 1992, the appellate judge upheld the original verdict. Taking the last possible legal step in Guatemala, the Attorney General employed *casación*, under which the Supreme Court reviewed the appellate court's decision, but to no avail. Given the severity of the rights violations in this case, the existence of ballistic and testimonial evidence, and the exhaustion of all legal recourse within Guatemala, rights groups working with Casa Alianza recently brought the case before the Inter-American Commission on Human Rights of the Organization of American States. The outcome of this action is still pending.

In the October 1990 cases in which national police officers assaulted William Chalin and Moises Díaz, and abducted, beat and threatened Abraham Moran, two agents posted bond and avoided serving any jail time. In the Moran case, the court ordered several arrest warrants for a third officer, but the national police ignored all of them. Additionally, courts convicted the military police officer implicated in the 1 January 1991 beating of Victor Manuel Castellanos and Walter Chapetón and sentenced him to a year in prison. He escaped serving jail time, however, as the two agents in the de la Cruz case had, by paying a fine of only fifty centavos (about ten U.S. cents) a day to each of the two boys for the same period. Casa Alianza has criticized and appealed the levity of the fine, but considers the conviction of a military police officer a triumph, in and of itself.

The national police ignored numerous orders to detain the officer charged with brutally beating a street girl in March 1991. After more than two years the officer was finally indicted, but posted bail. Finally, on 26 March 1992, a judge sentenced the private security guard charged with killing Francisco Chacón to ten years in prison and Q. 10,000 in civil damages. The partial justice served in these few cases, however, while significant, in no way redresses the years of systematic abuse suffered by children on the streets.

Discerning Motives

The frequency of attacks on street children, the reported use of tactics, such as torture, abduction, and surveillance, normally associated with state-sponsored terrorism, and the impunity with which the aggressors have acted all seem to indicate that government officials have sanctioned the use of violence against street children in Guatemala. Certainly, some individuals have acted independently in brutalizing street children, or in relation to their duties as private security guards, but the majority of cases fit already established patterns of organized violence.

Several factors may be at play in the institutionalization of violence directed at street children. First, during the past decade the growth in common crime, such as assault, petty theft, and non-politically motivated murders within the capital, has sparked fear and discontent among city residents, who condemn the government's failure to control such crime. The recent violent outbursts among city residents demanding better protection for their children, protection from kidnappers and organ stealers, are only one expression of this discontent. In 1990, Amnesty International reported that the "spiraling crime rate" in

Guatemala City led, in part, to the United States government's re-issuing of a travel advisory for Guatemala. Further, AI indicates that "[t]he police maintain that, in Guatemala City, at least, groups of street children (called *maras* [gangs]) are responsible for high levels of crime, and in an apparent effort to convince U.S. and other critics that a serious effort is being made to combat crime in the capital, there has been a noticeable crackdown on street children there. . . ."[33]

Most groups working with street kids or youth gangs in Guatemala City (see Levenson's study, for example) affirm that street children generally do not form gangs, but rather groups of three or four. Perhaps because both street children and gang members steal and consume drugs on the streets, however, an obvious difficulty or disinterest exists among police and politicians when separating the two groups. A 1993 newspaper article on the lives of street children, for example, states "the national police assured that bands of street children known as *maras* are those responsible for the high rate of delinquency. The police, in an effort to convince the United States and other critics that they are carrying out great efforts to combat delinquency in the capital have detained gang members and street children."[34] Similarly with a bribe and a promise of anonymity one city cop spoke to a *Siglo Veintiuno* reporter about the rising crime rate: "'Every day there are more and more gangs of street children that cause many problems. They are bad for investment, for tourism, bad for our 'national image.' . . . We do what we can and obey orders.'"[35]

Thus, that commanding officers within the police hierarchy have targeted street children for repression and have given special orders along those lines to police on their beats seems more than a remote possibility. In fact, the March 1992 "sweeps" of street children illustrate that this, precisely, has been the case. Recall that when the Mobile Military Police arrested sixteen street youths within a few block radius on 6 March, one of the officers stated that he placed handcuffs on the minors in the group, even though technically illegal, because he had "orders to follow." Similarly on 15 March when five military policemen paraded street child Juan Hernández through the streets of Zone 1, they ordered him to hold his head high so that the "citizenry would realize that the military police were capturing thieves."

Argentine anthropologist Laura Gingold found that similar episodes of police brutality in Buenos Aires coincided with a transition from dictatorship to a more democratic form of government. In this process, the police mission changed from ensuring citizens safety (from insurgency) to preserving public order (from delinquency). She notes that between 1983 and 1987, the period of political transition, "non-politicized" youths in Buenos Aires were ten times more likely to be murdered by police than their New York City counterparts.[36] Police and media often reported slain youths there as delinquents, she writes, regardless of their identities:

> In these versions, the victims are presented in abstract and stereotypical form, not as individuals . . . the victim already has been condemned—by the police who act as judges and by public opinion supporting police action—not as a result of any transgression of norms, but rather as a result of their suspicious appearance. [37]

In Guatemala this stereotype of all street children as criminals seemingly factored into a number of reported violations, as well. Responding to questions after his arrest for beating a street child in the Centro Capitol, one private securtiy guard told reporters, "the problem with street children in the Centro Capitol occurs every day when they band together and cause a scandal. They even have broken windows at times."[38] The driver who rode by the *refugio* on 7 July 1992 screamed into the entranceway, "sons of bitches, why do you run a den of thieves? I'm going to kill these kids one by one." On 4 August that same year, the cops who beat two street children called them "pieces of shit," "sons of bitches," "animals," and "thieves." Similarly, the owner of a car broken into on 9 September 1992 beat two minors in front of the *refugio* and accused Casa Alianza of harboring thieves. The police officers who detoured an urban bus past the third precinct arrested the street children on board, they claimed, for looking "suspicious." Finally, the restaurant security guard shot, of all the people in the vicinity, street child Rigoberto Caal, when he heard a gun fired and became alarmed.

A few cases of seemingly non-systematic violence directed at street children appear to stem more directly from the kids' actual behavior. At least some of the numerous attacks on Felipe Gonzalez occurred while car owners surprised him in the act of extracting articles from their cars. The Barajuste market vendors who assaulted two street youths threatened that they would kill the boys if police did not because street kids "were the reason" why sales had declined, presumably because they frequent the area to pickpocket and, thus, make customers reluctant to return. Additionally, some of the cases in which private guards have attacked street children may have occurred in connection with attempted robberies.

> *'Breathe on me,' I told him. And he had the odor of glue.*
> *And I cracked his face. I told him 'You idiot boy!'*

The cases described throughout this chapter also evidence a second, related motive for the abuse of street children in Guatemala. Police officers and other state actors must confront every day the results of the social system's inability or unwillingness to adequately care for abandoned and runaway children, to say nothing of the inequalities generated by the larger economic order. The fundamental flaws in social welfare and juvenile justice programs, addressed in chapter three, often lead these children into a cycle of violence and delinquency. The void in drug treatment programs for street children (or for any children) often prevents them from obtaining the counseling they need to end their dependence on glue, solvents, and other addictive substances. Police officers, obviously, do not like to see children inhaling glue on street corners. The barbaric acts in which officers have confiscated glue, then poured it over kids' heads or forced them to swallow whole bags of it, illustrate that the cops are frustrated by the continual presence of child addicts on the streets. The police have directed their anger or disgust at the street children, themselves, instead of the system which fails to treat their addictions. Perhaps some officers believe that punishing street children in this way really will "take away" their "whim," but perhaps also they feel anger at their powerlessness to change the depressing reality that they witness every day on the streets.

Similarly, Guatemala City's beat cops continually confront the failings of the nation's juvenile justice system. Two days after these cops arrest a child for stealing or prostitution, they may see the same child back on the street because she or he escaped or had a parent intervene. In another case, a juvenile judge may send a minor to a detention center for three or six months, but after that time, police may see the same minor consuming drugs or stealing again, in other words, completely "unrehabilitated." Thus, cops frequently opt to overstep the system, by meting out the child's "punishment" directly and immediately, on the streets. When this occurs, however, "[t]he human cost . . . becomes out of all proportion to the damage suffered by society, such as a minor theft."[39] The motive behind many of the attacks on street children, then, may be as Bruce Harris suggests: "The authorities do not know what to do with them . . . historically, in the last three years, the government has used political repression in order to resolve social problems."[40]   A Brazilian "death squad" member explained in more cold-blooded terms this "rationale" for violently treating street children. "It is better to kill a street kid than let him grow into a dangerous criminal. They should all be eliminated. . . ."[41]

A third set of motives behind the frequent abuse of Guatemalan street children relates to the unbridled corruption within the ranks of the national police. The officer who allegedly shot Daniel Balam in September 1992, did so when the youth refused to give him money. After the shooting, the officer heartlessly extracted Q. 50 from Daniel's friends. His response to the kids' threat to report him to ACA ("I'm not afraid of anyone") illustrates the brazen attitude, cultivated by impunity, of the police that exploit street children in this way for their personal gain.

The March 1993 beating and abduction of José Antonio Higueros also occurred because the youth could not comply with an off-duty police officer's "request" for a gold chain. The abduction and torture of Heriberto Mendez and the abduction of Diego Chouza later that same month similarly involved demands by police for money, gold chains, sunglasses and other expensive items. Furthermore, the May 1993 incident in which a police officer beat and threw acid on Esvin Noe Flores demonstrates the consequences for street children when they break "arrangements" with corrupt cops. The testimonials in chapter two of this work further evidence the widespread practice of extortion by Guatemala

City's beat cops. Ironically, instead of patrolling the streets to prevent crime, then, some officers actually encourage and profit from increased illicit activity by street children.

> *They almost always searched you for money.*
> *Do they take money away from the person?*
> *From the majority.*

National police administrators periodically acknowledge the existence of corruption among their agents. (These admissions, however, never jeopardize the administrators' positions, as too many Guatemalans already know the situation). In 1990-91, approximately 400 police officers lost their jobs because of corruption or other abuses. Yet, illegal practices among cops still commonly occur. As recently as September 1994, the current director of the national police, Salvador Figueroa, stated that within the organization "too much corruption exists, where everyone covers himself under the same mantle. I am conscious of it and it is something that we try to eradicate or minimize."[42]

A final motive that may be discerned from the actual abuses street children have suffered in Guatemala, reprisal, has most likely been primary in many of Guatemala's darkest cases. Regarding the Bosques de San Nicolás case, the Attorney General's office admitted to Amnesty International that the mutilations of the four boys' bodies "are consistent with the treatment the police normally mete out to those that inform against them. Mutilation of the ears, eyes and tongue signifies that the person had heard or seen something and then talked about it."[43] Another source indicates that mutilation of the victims' tongues, here, warns witnesses to the abduction, not to talk.[44] Two of the key witnesses, in fact, have been killed, one in a stabbing, and one in a hit-and-run accident. Furthermore Casa Alianza maintains that the assassination of Anstraun Villagran shortly after the youths' disappearance relates directly to knowledge he had of the case.

> *Stay like that, stay quiet, because if not, at times they took you in.*
> *It depends, they kill you sometimes, they do different things.*

Reprisal or intimidation also appears to have played a role in the persecution of Francisco Tziac, one of the chief witnesses in the Nahamán Carmona case. The first incident involving Tziac occurred on 26 May 1991, when two unidentified men abducted and beat him. From there, incidents occurred in April 1992, April 1993, and August 1993, which suggests a long-term or repetitive surveillance of the youth. The September 1991 abduction of Abraham Moran and Geovanny Chonay also related to the Nahamán Carmona case, as the perpetrators sought information about Ronaldo Moreno, a second key witness. It was Moreno who the owner of a beauty shop at the Centro Capitol, the site of Nahamán's beating, shot in September 1993.

Moreover, the twenty-five to thirty reported cases of threats and intimidation involving ACA employees and facilities clearly signal the unhappiness of some group or groups within Guatemala over the organization's activist role. Bruce Harris, in fact, worries about the recent decline of such activity, only half-jokingly indicating that during the periods of strongest intimidation, at least he knew that Casa Alianza "was doing something right."[45]

Easy Targets

The persecution of Guatemala's street children, of course, has never proven difficult for those groups involved in their abuse. Where can these children go when they need to protect themselves, beside back to often equally abusive homes or into institutions which try to "rehabilitate" them? Street children are generally easy to locate, for they spend virtually all night and day on the open streets, almost always in the presence of other street children. Every day they congregate in the same areas: in front of the *refugio*, Eighteenth Street, the Centro Capitol, the Barajuste and Presidenta markets, the Central, Concordia, Colon and Amate Parks, the Zone 4 terminal, the Hipódramo del Norte, or the Zone 3 landfill. Sixty-eight of the attacks on street children in Casa Alianza's case file reportedly occurred in the vicinity of these areas. Those "hunting" for street children know where to find them.

Most importantly, with the exception of a few rights activists, nobody protests when police or death squads beat street children—or pour glue over their heads, or murder or mutilate them. Who cares about these children? Who will risk their own security to protect them? Thus, "the problem of violence against destitute children cannot be reduced to the mere actions of the actual killers . . . the finger on the trigger is ultimately pulled by societal indifference and apathy. . . ."[46]

CHAPTER FIVE

The Construction
of Social Indifference:
Shaping Images of Street Children

*It occurs that the other world first thinks
(because the society of classes generates this way
of thinking) of transforming the world of the
street children, and not society. When we intend
to change only the street child's situation, it is
because we start from the following assumption:
We are better off, 'the people,' are better,
otherwise there would be no need to transform
the world of the street children.*

Paulo Freire, "And the Street Educators," No. 1 of *UNICEF
CEDC Methodological Series*. (Bogotá: UNICEF, 1987), 20.

*According to the needs and the interests each
person defends . . . he selects facts from reality in
order to defend his way of seeing things . . .
There is no way to see reality 'objectively.'
'Objective descriptions' are a myth.*

Basílica Espínola, *et. al., In the Streets. Working Children in
Asunción.* (Bogotá: UNICEF, 1987), 12.

M ost Guatemalans have reacted to the nearly surreal brutalization of their country's street children with seeming indifference. As noted in chapter one, the efforts to redress the grave
injustices of street children's abuse mostly have involved internationally
funded rights groups operating inside Guatemala. An exploration of this
failure to respond to street children, found among so many Guatemalans,
follows.

Historical Concepts of Childhood

As in any society, a barrage of images shapes the way Guatemalans
perceive and interact with children. The predominant model of childhood in Latin America has evolved over time to mirror that held in the
Western industrialized nations. Up until the 1800's, adults generally
regarded children as smaller versions of themselves and made few dis-
tinctions about their treatment. Mexican paintings dating from the
1700's, for example, depict children as miniature adults.[1] Similarly, scholar Guillermo Páez notes that in Colombia, "[h]istorical documentation
on children is limited, since adults generally seemed to view them as having little to bear on their reality. When children are mentioned, it is to
explain their eventual behaviour as adults."[2] These images began to give
way, however, in the nineteenth century to a new view of childhood as
a separate stage of life. Reflecting an emerging "appreciation of the difference in knowledge possessed by children and adults," education gained
in importance, adults began dressing their children distinctly from themselves, and games for the two generations began to differ.[3]

Also in the mid-1800's, families began to recognize their role as
socializers of children, accepting them as dependents for more than just
physical sustenance. Images of children remained predominantly negative, though. According to Elizabeth Kuznesof, Brazilian society viewed
children as "mischievous and irresponsible; that was their nature. It was
their parents' responsibility to raise . . . them so that they would act with
respect, consideration, and shame. . . . These are qualities that it was
hoped children acquired within their household and family and for
which they must show gratitude to their parents."[4] The present con-

cepts of childhood, as requiring special protection and assistance, fully emerged only in the mid-twentieth century. Following the lead of the International Union for Child Protection, which promoted children's rights at the global level beginning in the 1920's, Latin American governments adopted pro-child legislation at home. Progressive codes governing the treatment of children became law in Brazil in 1927, Costa Rica in 1932, Mexico in 1936, Venezuela in 1939, Colombia in 1946, and, as indicated in chapter three, Guatemala in the 1930's.[5]

The predominant model of childhood as a protected stage of life, brought to Latin America chiefly through elites "who stay abreast of progress in the United States and West Europe and try to apply it at home,"[6] reflects little the reality of poor families, however. In Guatemala, where poverty encompasses roughly 80 percent of the population, the majority of children still face dangers from malnutrition and sickness, poor medical attention, lack of schooling, limited play time, and adult work from an early age. Thus, the model propagated by the elite remains applicable only to the elite. Studying different household arrangements in the Latin American region, Susan De Vos, indeed, found significant variations from one socioeconomic class to the next. Non-formalized or "consensual" unions, often considered a "second class type of marriage," occur more commonly among poor than middle- or upper-class families. Members of the upper class, moreover, emphasize legally recognized marriage, for in their vigilance of their dominant position in society the elite often expand and fortify familial alliances through bonds of matrimony. This emphasis on legality has had important social and psychological influences on the poor, De Vos notes, but "it is doubtful that many people could actually live up to it . . . the ideal required greater financial resources than were available to most people."[7]

Even given the devastating economic circumstances of most Guatemalans that prevent conformity with this ideal version of family life, however, adult members of society generally do try to protect children from harm. Their recent outcries against foreigners and nationals, alike, believed to endanger children, and their subsequent calls for greater police presence in their communities, reveal the overpowering desire of adult Guatemalans to fulfill their socially defined roles as protectors of children. Yet, they make no similar commitment to street children, even knowing of their gruesome treatment. The factors behind this apparent indifference to the needs of children on the street are discussed in the remainder of this and the next chapter. Although one may observe in any society some of the conditions described, it is their combination in Guatemala that particularly damns street children.

Religious teachings

Within Guatemala, the Roman Catholic Church (hereafter, the Church) plays arguably the largest role in propagating moral concepts among the populace. Under great siege from Protestant evangelical groups since the 1960's, the Church has labored to make its doctrine, and the need for conformity, more explicit in Guatemala over the past several decades. New communication between priests and parishioners has occurred through community scripture classes and retreats, and special committees have formed to clarify Church teachings. Overall, Church outreach has become more oriented toward the grassroots level.

Traditional practices of Catholics reveal an often overwhelming religious devotion among Guatemalans. Each Friday during Lent (the forty days of preparation for Easter Sunday), for example, processions of chanting believers, some carrying life-sized statues of Jesus and Mary, leave their parishes and parade through town and city streets, stopping at private homes along the way to simulate the stations of the Cross (different moments of sorrow on Jesus' path toward crucifixion). The processions vividly remind observers about Christ's sacrifice and the need to follow His way. Moreover, during Holy Week (the week prior to Easter Sunday), the processions become daily, much larger, and more elaborate. Virtually the whole community participates in these events. On Good Friday, the day commemorating Jesus' death, parishioners alternate carrying large platforms with, again, life-sized images of Christ crucified or Mary weeping, her heart pierced with swords. Other marchers play the role of Romans or Jews, and those community members not directly involved make elaborate "carpets" of colored sawdust along the route. Guatemalans often stay working on these carpets through the night, creating masterpieces later trampled within thirty seconds of the marchers' arrival. The solemn events of Holy Week and other Church celebrations throughout the year generate an outpouring of religious fervor.

The work of evangelical groups also has brought religious concepts to the forefront of Guatemalan mentality in recent years. Preachers with large amplifiers and powerful messages of damnation and salvation address crowds gathered around them in parks and public plazas. They make frequent visits to private homes, also, in order to deliver the same "good news." *"Jesús es mi Señor"* (Jesus is Lord) and *"Confío en Cristo"* (I trust in Christ) stickers have become ubiquitous, both in the capital and the countryside. Informal estimates grant that evangelicals now have converted as much as 35 to 40 percent of the population.

Several years before his death, slain Jesuit psychologist Ignacio Martín-Baró wrote of the significance of this massive religious conversion in Latin America, particularly in countries experiencing intense civil strife. He asserted that the "striking growth of evangelical churches in a traditionally Catholic country [offered] . . . not only a way for certain individuals and groups to satisfy their psychological ('spiritual') needs, but also a political instrument for those who hold power, and more specifically, an element of psychological warfare."[8] Martín-Baró recognized, further, that the main and most prolific thrust in Latin America's evangelical movement began only a short time after the emergence of Catholicism's "liberation theology," viewed by many, correctly or not, as fueling the region's populist insurgencies. The early targeting of grassroots-oriented clergy and lay theologians by repressive military regimes revealed that the political elite, indeed, perceived a threat in the new movement. Since a sustained use of force to combat the liberationists would have risked a widespread condemnation of the government by the masses and, perhaps worse, risked the making of martyrs

> early on a decision was made to substitute as much as possible a psychological war of conversion for the dirty war of repression. . . . The recourse to pentecostal fundamentalism, frequently imbued with intense anticommunism, was logical, since it entailed a religious world view that postulated direct intervention of the Holy Ghost in the solution of human problems. More or less explicit governmental invitations were accepted gladly by various North American evangelical

churches, which greatly intensified their missionary efforts in the nations of the south.[9]

The key to understanding fundamentalism's link to a diminished threat of social disruption may lie in its teachings on the relationship between individuals and God and between individuals and the social order. A survey of the meanings attached to both religious and sociopolitical concepts by fundamentalist and liberationist communities in El Salvador highlights some dramatic differences. While liberationists viewed "salvation" as "to *create* the Kingdom of God through *work*," fundamentalists defined it as "to *achieve* the eternal life promised by God." Similarly, liberationists saw El Salvador's social system as an "unjust system; corrupt, alienating, and unfair to the poor," while fundamentalists viewed it "an evil system due to man's sins." Finally, regarding civil strife in El Salvador, liberationists claimed: "the war is due to consciousness of structural injustice. It will end as people organize, enter a dialogue . . ." but fundamentalists contended that "only God can end it; man can only pray and ask for mercy."[10]

In her study of youth groups, Levenson touches upon some aspects of fundamentalism's appeal in Guatemala. By accepting an all-powerful God, she says,

> the individual understands it is useless to try to change the world. Rather, one must endure it. It is oneself, not society, that one can and must transform to prepare for the Second Coming; this involves desisting from anger, fighting, jealousy, drugs, alcohol, laziness, tobacco, illicit sex and crime. . . In a society characterized by immense distrust (who is a government spy, who is a subversive?) a pamphlet written for young people asks, 'who is your best friend?' and replies 'God.' . . .
>
> Positing the overriding importance of this one relationship— the individual before God—and appealing to the real fear Guatemalans have of one another after years of a repressive apparatus that gathered information through neighborhood and even familial networks, Evangelicalism downplays ties of class, community, and ethnicity. . . . Their vision makes class solidarity meaningless.[11]

Martín-Baró, citing an analysis by Carrasco (1988), also focuses on the convert's rejection of politics. He notes that because of their intense emphasis on religion above almost all else, fundamentalists often become isolated and "dependent on the sociopolitical analyses of their religious leaders."[12] These leaders in Guatemala, lest we forget, have included Efraín Ríos Montt and Jorge Serrano Elías, both of whom called for and implemented severe repression campaigns against street children and other common delinquents.

While undeniably successful in conversion, promotion of religious concepts, and downplay of social suffering in Guatemala, evangelical groups are highly splintered and present no single doctrine to their believers, as with Catholicism. In a telling analysis of fundamentalism in Brazil, Berryman found that between 1990 and 1992, 710 new churches formed in the greater Rio de Janeiro area alone, but of these only one was a new Catholic parish.[13] The multitude of churches, moreover, was "by no means all cut from the same cloth . . . there is great diversity within the Pentecostal sector of the Protestant church."[14] Thus, the numerous fundamentalist denominations in Latin America, although formidable, play a *less uniform* role than the Catholic Church in shaping moral thought in the region.

In an atmosphere of intense religiosity, such as Guatemala's, the Church, naturally, penetrates the private sphere of the household, influencing the way Guatemalans behave and view appropriate behavior within it. In previous epochs in Latin America, the Holy Family of Jesus, Mary and Joseph represented the model of familial interaction. The father, like Joseph, would work to support his family and partake of community life. The mother, like Mary, would embody the virtue of humility and would sacrifice all for her family. Similarly, children, like Jesus, would be all obedient.[15] In Northeast Brazil, Nancy Scheper-Hughes observed that families had "an intense devotion to the Virgin Mary and to São Antônio, the patron saint of mothers and children," but that poor women, especially, revered a particular image of Mary, that of *Nossa Senhora das Dores*, Our Lady of Sorrows. This "mature Mary, the widow standing tearfully at the foot of the cross or sitting in its shadow while cradling the dead adult Jesus in her arms . . ." loomed over the shantytown where Scheper-Hughes worked, as if to cue women on their roles in accepting loss and grief in motherhood.[16]

In a June 1994 pastoral letter, reprinted in parish bulletins through-out Guatemala, the bishops of Latin America reaffirmed the Church's position on the sanctity of the family. Contributing to the increased international dialogue on family life surrounding the Cairo Conference on Population and Development held later that year, the bishops wrote:

> The family is a treasure pertaining to the patrimony of human-ity. It is founded upon matrimony, that intimate union of life, the complement between a man and a woman that is consti-tuted in the indissoluble, freely consolidated, publicly affirmed marriage that is open to the transmission of life.[17]

The church conceives of children as "the most precious gift from God . . . an immense good that should be received with joy, thankfulness, and responsibility."[18] At the same time, in his February 1994 "Letter to Families," Pope John Paul II idealizes the *all obedient* child symbolized in Jesus' interactions with the Holy Family. "It is known," he writes,

> that the Redeemer spent a large part of his life hidden away in Nazareth: 'subject' as the 'Son of man' to Mary, his Mother, and Joseph, the Carpenter. Is not this filial 'obedience' already the first expression of his obedience to the Father 'until death' . . . ?[19]

The Church uses equally strong moral terminology to encourage or influence the commitment of couples to one another, through fidelity and the sacrament of marriage. Throughout his letter, the Pope refers to families as "domestic churches." With regard to consensual unions, he laments that:

> At times it even seems that . . . situations which are in reality 'irregular' are presented as 'regular' and 'attractive.'. . . In effect such situations contradict 'truth and love' [for in them]. . . . Moral conscience becomes obscured, that which is truly good and beautiful becomes supplanted by an actual enslavement.[20]

How would proponents of these views respond to the one in seven

Guatemalan women who is a single mother?[21] While expressing sympathy for her situation, they might see her, if not a widow, as John Paul II describes: a participant in "a concrete form of 'anticivilization,' destroying love . . . with inevitable repercussions for the whole of social life."[22] They might deem her irresponsible, disrespectful of the "patrimony of humanity," giving birth to unholy children through a union not indissoluble, not publicly affirmed, in short, not sanctified.

Anthropologist Emilio Willems, like De Vos, found this view prevalent in Latin America, despite the high incidence of common law marriage in the region. He writes of the "chasm between ideal and real pattern, between Christian precepts and actual behavior . . . Consensual unions are glossed over or merely seen as deviations from 'normal' marriage, and references to the mating habits of the lower class are often referred to in terms of sexual 'chaos,' 'anarchy,' or 'promiscuity.'"[23] Milne and Ennew note, further, that:

> Mother-headed families are always described in terms of what they lack—a husband or father figure. Evidence of the economic and affective strengths of women . . . to rear children successfully on their own is ignored in favor of a pathological approach.[24]

Within Guatemala, policymakers consistently blame marital instability and poor familial guidance for spawning anti-social behavior in children. As Levenson asserts: "Adult critics employ the concept of 'disintegrated family' to explain delinquency and as a synonym for 'familial crisis.'"[25] Even those groups most "enlightened" about children's issues demonstrate this tendency. Back in the 1960's, a conference held by the Inter American Institute for the Child generated a list of factors contributing to anti-social behavior among Latin American youths. "Deterioration of the nuclear family" topped the list, followed by the "greater infiltration of alcoholism and gambling in society."[26] Thirty years later, regrettably, little has changed; experts still couch delinquency in the same terms. A report from the February 1993 UNICEF conference on street and working children, for example, indicates: "The causes and nature of delinquency also led to considerable—if inconclusive—debate.

The question was: Are children in conflict with the law themselves delinquent or does the real delinquency lie with their families?"[27]

Explanations of delinquency which focus on deviations from the sanctified, "indissoluble," "publicly affirmed" union of the Church, however, only obscure the deeper, structural, factors contributing to family breakup and "socially unacceptable" behavior in children. According to a 1993 report of the UN Economic Commission on Latin America (ECLA), unemployment and emigration (to look for work) among male heads of house increase the responsibilities of poor women and, sometimes, children in maintaining their homes. When this *economically necessary* shift conflicts with the traditional, widely revered model of male dominance, familial strain and personal stress often result, with breakup and dysfunction soon following.[28] The ECLA report also finds that the poor's historical reluctance to enter into formalized commitments stems primarily from socioeconomic factors, a "constellation of circumstances" stacked against them, rather than any type of "sexual chaos," promiscuity, or anarchy.[29]

The use of such morally charged terminology to explain familial breakup and deviations from the ideal model of childhood deeply divides the poor. Schibotto asserts that:

> The incomprehension, covering up, and denial [of social causes surrounding these phenomena] . . . does not seem ideologically neutral, but rather responds to a precise class interest. . . . The different forms of being a child . . . are hierarchically ordered, valuing only the model pertaining to the dominant classes. In the end, the life and identity of the very population are devalued in so much as they fail to conform, precisely, to these stereotypes.[30]

Argentine anthropologist Laura Gingold reports, similarly, that when authorities in Buenos Aires use the label "delinquent" to describe certain youths, they "introduce a cleavage that divides social actors within the subordinate sector."[31]

Exploring familial arrangements and circumstances within this "subordinate sector" in the Dominican Republic, sociologist Marina Ariza Castillo found clear differences in the household structures of street and working children. She highlights that among street children, 75 percent come from single-parent or "reconstructed" families, while among those youths who work but return home each day, a full 53 percent live in intact nuclear families.[32] Thus, even in a context where the majority of households cannot conform to the ideal model of family life because of their economic situations, those from which street children emerge break most completely with the model. They become vilified, even by the poor, themselves. Freire writes: "There is no substantial difference between them [in their economic conditions]. However it is dramatic to perceive how the oppressed introject the oppressor within [them]. On occasions, what actually occurs is that the oppressed subject attacks the oppressor in the body of the oppressed."[33] Therefore, in so much as religious doctrine and elite propaganda, widely diffused among the poor, recognize only one family form as appropriate, they erode unity and foster a harsh response, a condemnation of street children and their families. Worse, they provide a moral justification for the condemnation.

The Media

The press in Guatemala compounds this damage to street children. Media sources generally portray street children on two levels: as delinquents and drug users, or as society's troubled victims. Both images, for distinct reasons, prove highly dangerous for street children in terms of their treatment by the larger society. If articles depicting street children and their life circumstances in these ways appeared only occasionally, their damage would remain limited. In reality, in just the year and a half period that I have studied (between January 1993 and July 1994), at least 100 stories on street children made editions of local newspapers and regional digests. Naturally, the more Guatemalans receive images of street children as either vandals or victims, the more likely they are to internalize those notions. Moreover, many times photographs of young people inhaling glue from plastic bags, or strewn across the sidewalks, accompany press stories and reinforce the negative portraitures communicated by the texts.

Depictions of street youths as delinquents and drug addicts often appear in articles seemingly sympathetic to the plight of the kids. Yet the authors' proposals to improve the street children's situation almost invariably call for changes in the behavior of the children, themselves, rather than in social or institutional behaviors. These articles often show such little comprehension of street children's realities that one wonders whether their authors, too, have not dared get too close to these kids that they claim to portray. The authors of other articles on this population clearly demonstrate malicious intent. I have selected a few examples of each type to illustrate in which direction the Guatemalan press has molded public opinion of street children. All italics indicate my emphasis.

■ 24 July 1993 *Siglo Veintiuno,* "Torturados por la sociedad," [Tortured by Society]: "Street children have their lives determined within a world of violence, physical discomfort, with no defined future, because of this *they soon become bitter and completely anti-social.*"

■ 12 April 1994 *La República,* "García Laguardia demanda efectiva pro-tección para los niños de la calle" [García Laguardia (Human Rights Ombudsman) demands effective protection for street children]:

> It is necessary for the government, by means of the institutions it counts on to such effect to adopt a deter-mined attitude of support for these children, because they have the right to conditions in which they can grow in harmony and become *useful* people for our country.

■ 8 March 1993 *El Nuevo Diario,* "Niños de la calle, entre maltrato y mendicidad" [Street children, between abuse and begging]: "National police assured that those responsible for the high index of delinquent acts are the bands of street children known as *maras.*"

■ 10 December 1993 *Siglo Veintiuno,* "Policías privados propinan golpiza a niño de la calle" [Private police beat street child]: "The *problem* with street children in the Centro Capitol *occurs* every day when they band together and create a scandal. At times they have even broken windows."

- 23 March 1993 *El Gráfico*, "Víctimas de fuerzas de seguridad" [Victims of security forces]:

    As *victims* or *delinquents*, street children certainly need attention. But apart from providing shelter and food, what is really urgent is the elaboration and execution of plans for reorientation, formation and social reinsertion, to *rescue them and make them useful to society*.

- 23 March 1993 *El Gráfico*, "El problema de los niños de la calle" [The problem of street children]:

    These children with irregular conduct, legally cannot be indicted or treated as delinquents, our legal system considers them 'transgressors,' the reason why they lack all responsibility for the actions they commit, including crimes and armed assaults. Thanks to this, if they are captured, they are freed almost immediately: and back to the same! . . . Much modern legislation is lacking, that permits judges to impose upon them the penalty of attending juvenile rehabilitation centers and not let them free to return to crime.

- 10 August 1993 *La República*, "Pegamento con aceite de mostaza (II Parte)" [Glue with oil of mustard (Part 2)]: "Helping street children is not easy, nor simple, nor cheap. *They are the fruit of a complex sickness* that has profound roots of diverse classes. . . ."

- 17 December 1993 *La Hora*, "'Niño de la calle' agredido por policías particulares" [Street child assaulted by private police]:

    The problem of street children is one that for many years has been unaddressed in Guatemala, above all, because the institutions that would have to watch over these minors do nothing to maintain control over them.

*It is common to see 'street children' being delinquent and caus-
ing problems,* principally when they are under the influence of some drug (glue).

- 3 October 1993 *El Gráfico*, "Los niños olvidados" [Forgotten children]:

  Those that are abandoned commonly end up inhaling
  shoe glue, stealing in markets, and loitering in the
  streets. The other group that begs, grows accustomed
  to not realizing any activity that will benefit them in
  the future, to the contrary, as is typical, they enclose
  themselves in the electronic game parlors that abound
  in the city and there they learn idleness.

- 24 July 1993 *Siglo Veintiuno*, "La sociedad los crea y los rechaza"
  [Society creates then rejects them]:

  Even though the majority scorns them, because *all said
  and done they are little delinquents, and a risk for society,* no
  one can take away what they are: children who in order
  to have grown *usefully* would have had to receive moral
  values, and above all, love.

- 24 July 1993 *Siglo Veintiuno*, "Los niños de la calle necesitan una
  oportunidad para reincorporarse" [Street children need an opportunity to reincorporate themselves]: "From the mid-80's, the theme of
  street children has held the public's attention, especially because of
  their supposed link with juvenile gangs, classified as *maras*."

After reading articles such as these, the person who has never known
or spent time with Guatemalan street children might easily conceive of
them as armed, highly dangerous criminals with no hope, no desire to
change their lives in the future, and of no use to society. Guatemala's
street children, in reality, deviate greatly from such expectations. First
while many do engage in petty theft, most do not carry arms, rather they
snatch purses, chains or sunglasses from unexpecting passersby, then flee
rapidly, or, like Claudia and her friends, they burglarize unattended cars

with no intention of encountering anyone, much less stabbing or shooting them. Far from hardened criminals, street children express fear,
apprehension, and guilt over robbing and most often drug themselves in
order to overcome these feelings. The countless times that police have
beaten and humiliated whole groups of street children reveal that most
neither carry arms nor pose real threats to anyone's physical wellbeing.
Attorney Mary Ana Beloff notes a similar paradox in Buenos Aires,
where, in fatal confrontations between police and youths, the alleged
instigators of the attacks, the youths, almost always are the victims.[34]

Secondly, depictions of street children as "anti-social" are, at best,
misleading. Certainly, street children break many norms established by
the larger society; they must, merely to survive. But street children
replace these norms with others that allow for their survival. Always
forming small groups, they create the family structure lacking in their
homes, and they determine means for fairly distributing their resources.
As revealed in chapter two, within their small groups they demonstrate
a strong sense of solidarity, a value waning in the larger society, and
always struggle to find ways to help a *compañero* in need. Claudia's testimony of friends that helped her so that she would not have to prostitute herself, and her tales of countless times when she and other street
kids rallied to post bail for detained friends, evidences this solidarity. So,
too, does Carolina's haunting recollection of words interchanged
between herself and other youths during moments of intense fear and
danger. On one occasion, she says,

> They let us go and told us that they were going to throw us
> from the ditch . . . he asked that they at least let me go. That
> at least, if they wanted, that they harm him but that they not
> harm me. And I . . . I had him by the hand and I said to that
> man that if they were going to throw us off, that they throw
> both of us . . .

In a different incident with another street child she recalls:

> I saw that, that they wanted to open the door, and I spoke to
> him and he told me to calm down . . . he told me 'if they kill
> us here, they're going to kill both of us here. We just have to

entrust ourselves to God.' . . . And he said to me that if I was
going to die, he was going to die with me.

Nahamán Carmona, whom police kicked to death for posing as a menace
to society, also possessed these values, as his sister, Ruth, recalls: "my little brother helped me. When I said to him 'Look Nahamán, I haven't
eaten,' he went quickly to look for food. Or I said to him, 'Look
Nahamán I've got problems,' and he helped me."

Finally, when journalists depict street children as in need of re-for-
mation or reinsertion into society, they foster the idea of *the children's*
inadequacy, of *their* need to change. As chapter six will reveal, this allows
others to distance themselves from the suffering of street children. More
damaging, as with religious doctrine, it prevents people from connecting
the presence of children on the street to the inadequacies of overwhelmingly damaging social policy.

This represents the danger of the second type of depiction by
Guatemala's media, of street children as the poor, hapless victims of soci-
ety. Titles such as "Forgotten Children" (*El Gráfico*, 3 October 1993),
"Children, Our Eternal Scars" (*Siglo Veintiuno*, 30 May 1994), "The
Shoeshine Boys' Way of the Cross" (*Prensa Libre*, 2 October 1993),
"Childhood Clamors for Attention" (*La República*, 4 August 1993), and
"Let the Children Live" (*La República*, 1 October 1993), often set the tone
for articles portraying the lives of street kids and child laborers. These
articles generally make heartfelt calls for intervention on behalf of the
children living and working in Guatemala's streets. In fact, they usually
call for some heroic "rescue" of these children from the sordid street environment, and come heavily clothed in ideological language and idealism.
A 1 October 1993 *La República* article illustrates. "Why celebrate
International Children's Day," writes columnist Gonzalo Marroquin,
pondering the day's holiday. "I believe that the most important [reason]
is BECAUSE CHILDREN REPRESENT THE FUTURE. . . . Children are a
blessing from God for this, our world." On 30 May 1994 *Siglo Veintiuno*
printed a full page story ("Los niños, nuestras eternas cicatrices," or
"Children, our eternal scars") based on the precept "aggression, sadness,
bitterness, reproach, and sorrow are the scars of Guatemalan infancy and
childhood," while an earlier several page supplement on street children in

the same paper ("La sociedad los crea y los rechaza") states: "Something should be clear: they [street children] have the constitutional right to be helped and rescued, instead of exterminated."

Observing the same language of victimization in local press coverage of Peruvian juvenile workers, children's rights advocate Giangi Schibotto asserts:

> The newspaper headlines express well the scandalous tonality and the morally exclusive tonality with which we often approach the phenomenon. It is not that that is bad. . . . But all this is insufficient and even can become mystifying if we do not understand that the criticism of child labor is the criticism of the social system which produces it.[35]

He adds:

> We are always thinking about what it means for a child to work. But we also must learn to ask what 'not to work' means for the poor child . . . well the alternative to working is not insertion into the lifestyle of the middle and upper class members of his age group, rather it is poverty without work, violence and desertion without work.[36]

Thus, efforts to "rehabilitate" street children, to "rescue" them, without also modifying the social forces which drew them into the streets (the need to supplement family income, parental alcoholism and abuse, overcrowded and inadequate housing) only leave the children as vulnerable, perhaps more so, than when on the streets. Sociologist Rinaldo Vieira Arruda, who spent several years living with children in the streets of Brazil and studying that country's child welfare system, acutely observes that such "rehabilitation" programs end with children "developing submissive behaviors, a necessary condition for the formation, without threatening the social order, of the role of 'worker' in a society where being a worker does not guarantee to individuals the minimum conditions for a dignified existence."[37]

Very few newspaper accounts effectively link the presence of street children to the larger socio-economic structure. Some, as the *República* article on International Children's Day, recognize inconsistencies within society. "What is happening with Guatemalans?" the author asks, "Our economy grows but the health of the people, in general, does not improve and of course, neither do life expectations and opportunities for our children. . . ." But, here, as in most cases, the author misses the next logical step, that pro-growth policies may cause health conditions, in general, to remain poor and life expectations abysmally low.

A second, much more contemptible, article nearly exonerates Guatemalan society for the presence of its street children by pinning the blame on foreigners. In the 10 March 1993 article "El rostro de la vergüenza (II)," Carlos Rafael Soto writes:

> I don't know if you, friendly reader, might have noticed this, but have you realized by now how many street children, with Asiatic traits there are in the city? I began to think about this and finally I realized that it had to do with a logical derivation from the poverty of the masses and from the uncontrollable form in which foreigners coming illegally to the country exploit and abuse our co-nationals. Many of those children, with their torn eyes, are products of the quasi-rape by the restaurant owner of one of his employees.

Thus, for Soto, foreign restaurant owners become the villains, rather than national business and land owners who so over-exploit laborers that they make impossible children's survival within poor households.

A 3 May 1993 *Prensa Libre* article ("Destacan explotación de niños trabajadores"), while laden with the language of idealism, begins to link children's conditions in Guatemala directly to the socio-economic order. It indicates: "In Guatemala close to one million two hundred thousand child laborers, who like exploited and depressed heroes contribute their sweat to the development of a nation where they survive as innocent victims of social marginalization." Yet this article, like the others, misses the point that the sweat of child labor has contributed only to small pockets of development, not *national* development, as claimed. When poor families, reeling from the strains of structural adjustment, sent their children to work in ever larger numbers during the 1980's, inequalities increased. Between 1980 and 1989, the share of national income captured by the wealthiest tenth of Guatemala's population rose from 41 to 44 percent, while that of the poorest tenth sank from 2.4 percent to just 0.5 percent.[38]   The reliance on child labor, thus, enabled *capital* to improve its economic position, but not the remainder of society, and in this way contributed to the social marginalization condemned in the article. Moreover, the same article later glosses over this classist nature of child exploitation by quoting a Coordinadora Interinstitucional de Promoción por los Derechos del Niño (CIPRODENI) message proclaiming the child laborer a "'hero of Guatemala for whose situation we are all a bit responsible.'"

Interestingly, a second CIPRODENI message, published as a half-page advertisement in *La República* (6 July 1994), unquestionably links the issue of child-snatching to socio-economic policy. The disappearance of children, it states

> is a phenomenon that cannot be seen at the margin of the eco-
> nomic, social, and cultural problems of poor countries: A sys-
> tem that condemns the dispossessed to misery, lack of oppor-
> tunities and mere survival, and a state that does not give pri-
> ority to children in aspects such as education, health and recre-
> ation in an integral form, convert Guatemala into fertile
> ground for the existence of thousands of children, victims of
> mistreatment, abuse, exploitation, drug addiction, alcoholism.
> This situation has been aggravated by the disappearance and
> traffic of boys and girls with such diverse purposes as prostitu-
> tion, illegal adoption, kidnapping and the undocumented but
> publicized . . . traffic of children's organs.

The advertisement ends positively by exhorting the government to investigate cases of child disappearance and increase the coverage of social welfare programs. Additionally, one article from the 16 August 1993 edition of *La República*, which summarizes a newly released International Labor Organization report, also clearly, although conserva-tively, elaborates the connection between children's misery and socio-economic policy:

> If it were not for the work of minors, the levels of poverty . . .
> would be higher. In this sense, it can be affirmed that the
> reduction in the poverty gap, a task which should be the

responsibility of the whole society, is being assumed in certain measure by children.[39]

CIPRODENI's *República* ad asserted that governmental policy has made Guatemala "fertile ground for the existence of thousands of children, victims of mistreatment, abandonment, abuse, exploitation, drug addiction, alcoholism." Generally, though, press accounts, like the statements of policymakers and analysts, condemn behavior and values within families for these social phenomena, rather than going deeper to the impossible situations in which families find themselves. As a result, readers of the news may all too easily blame street children and their parents for their difficult situations rather than rallying to their aid and demanding change. A reporter for *La República*, for example, blatantly associates street children with "delinquent" parents:

> The lack of responsibility, the freedom of vices, little education and familial orientation that exist in our environment are some of the causes of the breakup of a home or the luck of a child who comes to the world carrying a cross since birth, responsible for the sins of that mother, that father without scruples.[40]

Another writes: "What values can we speak of when on street corners we find tattered and barefoot children that ask for a quetzal for a box of gum or a rose, while the mother is taking her *siesta* in the grass with the father or stepfather?"[41]

Here we see how destructive the media's use of idealism to clothe the issues of child exploitation and neglect has become. The headlines and excerpts make what is fundamentally a class struggle appear as an encounter between the normal and the pathological, the pattern and the divergence, or order and disorder.[42] Yes, Guatemalan street children emerge from abusive and "broken" homes. But, "[a]re the poor naturally more violent, *machista*, authoritarian?" asks Schibotto.

> Are they naturally negligent with their children, irresponsible with their families, dominated by base sexual instincts, etc., etc.? Or is it precisely not their life situation, of destitution, of

fatigue, of suffering, many times of desperation, is it not their class marginalization which also originates behavioral phenomena?[43]

The diffusion of upper-class ideals through the mass media, the Church, and the state has resulted in a moral devaluation of Guatemala's reality, "what is observed every day on the streets."[44]

In his study of the Brazilian child welfare system, Vieira noted the same covering of connections between the presence of street children and the capitalist growth process. He argues that just as the Brazilian government created the school snack to combat children's nutritional deficiencies rather than guaranteeing higher salaries for parents to provide, themselves, for the dietary needs of their children, so too the government has created national child welfare policy in order to diffuse, in seemingly humanitarian and Christian terms, a concept of "the juvenile problem" that faults juveniles, themselves, and not the social order which "generates the juvenile delinquent."[45] Pedro Pellegrino, a Brazilian psychologist who has worked in the Rio de Janeiro FEEM, the national juvenile rehabilitation system, similarly interprets the country's child welfare policy. Referring to FEEM's work, he indicates:

> we are talking about a political question that can never be disassociated from the whole society. Because it is an illusion for you to think you are going to work with the juvenile. It is an illusion because work with the juvenile exists in order to camouflage the social contradictions of the class struggle. You observe that the majority of the personnel who 'work' with the juvenile have the function of 'helping' society, but cannot 'think about' society, they depart from the ideological presupposition that . . . society is perfect . . . it is one, without contradictions.[46]

Vieira concludes by condemning this whole generation of images of street children as pathological and divergent, and criminal. The real crime, he asserts, occurs when "in defense of private property (the 'common good,' paradoxically private) one can kill, arrest, depersonalize, void an individual or, as also the case, stigmatize the majority of the population."[47]

Mayan Concepts of Childhood

Running counter to this predominant model of childhood which encourages the stigmatization of street children and their families are the customs and views of the Maya. In her powerful testimony of Mayan culture and resistance, Nobel laureate Rigoberta Menchú Tum recounts that for her people, "From the very first day [a] baby belongs to the community, not only to the parents. . . ."[48] Elaborate rules and ceremonies surrounding the birth of children highlight their significance within the culture.

> When [a] baby is born . . . [t]he people present should be the husband, the village leaders, and the couple's parents. Three couples. The parents are often away in other places, so if they can't be there, the husband's father and wife's mother can perhaps make one pair. If one of the village leaders can't come, one of them should be there to make up a couple with one of the parents. If none of the parents can come, some aunts and uncles should come to represent the family on both sides, because the child is to be part of the community . . . that's why three couples (but not just anybody) must be there to receive it. They explain that this child is the fruit of communal love.
>
> Candles will be lit for him and his candle becomes part of the candle of the whole community, which now has one more person, one more member.[49]

A study of Mexico's Zincanteco Maya describes similar practices:

> Immediately after the birth, elaborate rituals are performed.... Prayers and incantations by the mid-wife exhort the gods to bestow on the child all the manly or womanly attributes for success in the *Zincanteco* world [my emphasis]. . . . The result of their handling of babies seems to be to set up a mode . . . adopted to the culture's emphasis on equality and interdependence.[50]

Further highlighting the differences between Guatemala's indigenous and non-indigenous family structures, a third study indicates that:

> The Mayan family is totally distinct from the ladino family....
> The Mayan family is extensive, the problems that affect one
> element of the family impact the rest of the family's members
> and the Maya population. The Mayan family has been
> thought of since time immemorial as unified with the com-
> munity or town where it is established. . . .[51]

Menchú provides a key explanation for the special place of children within her community: they offer continuity for the Maya, their traditions
and lifestyles, under brutal attack since the days of the conquest. "The
child will multiply our race, he will replace all those who have died," she
says. "This is part of the reserve that we've maintained to defend our
customs and culture."[52] Thus, special practices at birth remind the Maya
that they should welcome and accept children into their community,
rather than reject, void, kill, or stigmatize them, as Vieira asserts of the
predominant model.

> So, a mother, on her first day of pregnancy goes with her hus-
> band to tell [the] elected leaders. . . . The leaders then pledge
> the support of the community and say 'We will help you, we
> will be the child's second parents.' They are known as *abuelos*,
> 'grandparents,' or 'forefathers.' The parents then ask the
> 'grandparents' to help them find the child some godparents, so
> that if he's orphaned, he shouldn't be tempted by any of the
> bad habits our people sometimes fall into.[53]

Children also have obligations to the community and these obligations strengthen their sense of belonging and commitment to Mayan
ways. Eight days after a child is born:

> Four candles are placed on the corners of the bed to represent
> the four corners of the house and show him that this will be
> his home. They symbolize the respect the child must have for
> the community, and the responsibility he must feel towards it
> as a member of a household. The candles are lit and give off an
> incense which incorporates the child into the real world he
> must live in.[54]

Furthermore, during the eight days prior, members of the community arrive and present gifts to the parents and at the end of this time

> the family counts up how many visitors the mother had. . . . If,
> during the eight days, most of the community has called, this
> is very important, because it means that this child will have a
> lot of responsibility towards the community when he grows
> up.[55]

Unlike in the non-indigenous view of childhood, the Maya accept from the outset the need for and the value of their children's work. This, again, prevents the stigmatization within the community of children and their families who must detract from education and play time. Among the Zincantecos, "A child is expected to assume adult tasks and responsibilities by the sixth or seventh year and is given increasingly difficult chores from infancy."[56] Menchú astutely observes the nuances between the two cultures' views. Of her community she says:

> the baby must learn from all of us. . . . in fact, we behave just
> like bourgeois families in that, as soon as the baby is born,
> we're thinking of his education, of his wellbeing. But our peo-
> ple feel that the baby's school must be the community itself.[57]

She also indicates that parents explain well to their children why they must perform their assigned tasks, and that children perform them well, for if not, fathers have the "right" to scold or beat them.[58]

Carlos Mansón, who assists working children in the indigenous capital of Xela, Guatemala's second largest city, attests that he has encountered children with signs of physical abuse and that those children generally accept their mistreatment as normal.[59] Lately, he says, growing tensions have developed within Xela's indigenous families stemming from the increasing economic burdens of the "crisis" and the increasing attraction of younger household members to Western culture. Parents and grandparents, like so many of their ancestors, fear for the survival of their traditions and beliefs.

The role that the younger generation plays in maintaining those traditions and beliefs perhaps has sped the re-absorption of the war's orphans and displaced children into indigenous communities.

Testimonies in Ricardo Falla's moving work *Massacres in the Jungle* verify this process. Survivors of the army's massacres who went from house to house searching for others still alive, gave the following accounts:

> We arrived at a house where there were three children around seven or eight years old. They started running away from us. We followed them. They were frightened. They thought we were the army. We asked them where their mother and father were. 'They went out to market, they went to church,' they answered. We said they wouldn't return home, as the army had killed them. We told them that they could stay with a widower who was in his home.

> We found an eight-year-old girl. She was alone in the jungle. . . I talked to her. Her parents and brothers and sisters had gone to market. She began to cry. We sent her to the widower and they took her to the jungle.

> The children were aged four, six, and eight . . . alone for exactly eight days. They gave the orphans to my brother. My brother had four orphans: the boy from La Nueva Concepción who escaped while his parents were being burned to death and these three from the Maravilla center.[60]

Falla concludes from these testimonies that "weeping also gave way to solidarity and love: the orphans became the children of new parents and family boundaries opened up."[61]

As commented in the introductory chapter of this book, very few of Guatemala's street children come from Mayan families. Moreover, Carlos Mansón estimates that fewer than twenty children live on the streets of Xela and that they receive little physical abuse. The human rights cases involving Xela's street children relate more often to their forced military conscription than to the scorn of the community.[62]

CHAPTER SIX

The Silent Majority:
The Response of Private Citizens to
Street Children

Instead of helping them, they destroyed them.
And I don't think it should be like that because
being in the street you have rights, because you're
still a human. And if others deserve respect, we
also deserve respect. Because we are not
garbage, animals, or anything. We are people
and, just like the rest of people in society deserve
respect, we also deserve respect.

Carol

What if the disappearances, the piling up of
civilians in common graves, the anonymity, and
the routinization of violence and indifference were
not in fact an aberration? What if the social
spaces before and after such seemingly chaotic
and inexplicable acts were filled with rumors
and whisperings, with hints and allegations of
what could happen, especially to those thought of
by agents of the social consensus as neither
persons nor individuals?

Nancy Scheper-Hughes, *Death Without Weeping*. (Berkeley:
University of California Press, 1992), 219.

C orroborating the stigmatization of street children at the societal level, discussed in the previous chapter, deeper, more personal motives held by private citizens in Guatemala may prevent the effective protest of abuse against kids on the street there. These motives encourage Guatemalans who might otherwise act to protect street children, as they have for other children in their community, to remain silent.

Making the visible invisible

In his studies of homeless families in New York, author Jonathan Kozol observed that many members of the larger community tried to distance themselves from the realities of those on the street. Perhaps finding the tragedy of homelessness too overpowering, perceiving the possibility that they, too, could lose everything just as the homeless had, city dwellers mentally remove themselves from the sadness and pain they see on the streets. Confronted by the deeply disturbing images of men, women, and now children sleeping in parks, pleading for help on every street corner, or slowly withering away from hunger, sickness, and depression, people respond, Kozol suggests, by seeking ways to "safely" explain homelessness, by finding qualities within the homeless, themselves, that somehow differentiate them from the rest of society.[1] By pinning the responsibility for the tragedies of homelessness on the homeless, themselves, the larger society frees itself of anxiety and guilt for not responding to others so desperately in need. Thus, a young woman's numerous illegitimate children, a young man's drug use, a veteran's mental trauma, or a family's failure to plan for the future all become viewed as factors causing homelessness, while the changing political and economic landscape that spawned the rise of homelessness becomes lost.[2]

Applying these ideas to Guatemala, one may begin to discern, albeit only in part, why so many Guatemalans remain silent while street children continue to suffer abuse. Walking through the nation's capital, Guatemalans witness a barrage of ghastly visions which surely assaults their ideals of innocent and protected childhood. In Central Park or in abandoned alleyways, groups of homeless children sleep huddled together in order to protect themselves from the cold and dampness of the streets. Under bridges or in markets children sit among fetid waste inhaling glue or solvent. Young girls walk the strip back behind Eighteenth Street looking for sex-craving customers or wait for them in filthy hotels in Zone 4's *El Hoyo*. Police violently haul children along sidewalks, cursing them and kicking them into patrol cars. That Guatemalans would want to avoid these distressing images, in the same way that New Yorkers avoid their city's homeless, is not surprising.

The same distancing process that Kozol observes in New York, then, may also take place in Guatemala, promoting indifference toward street children. In order to assuage feelings of guilt and fear, Guatemalans may find ways to blame street children for their own destitution, their own tragic abuse. When seeing a police officer beat a street child, a city resident may first respond by thinking "that child has stolen something" rather than "that child needs assistance." Similarly, Guatemalans may become angry or disgusted when seeing a child inhale solvent or sell her body, or may simply avert their eyes to her tragedy, rather than understand that, already at such a tender age, she is an addict, that she sells her body because she has no other way to earn enough to buy food. A special report on street children in the local paper *Siglo Veintiuno* documents this cold response:

> For the great majority of individuals, it is unpleasant to see a street child. This sensation changes when the latter approaches, becoming a nervous chill produced by a fear that the youth will, with some weapon, bring about an assault. Obviously, a child that lives in the street is dirty, has rumpled clothes and smells bad, moreover he is generally on drugs. . . . In order to survive day to day he begs for money or food and most frequently: he robs or assaults.[3]

Carolina testifies to the prevalence of such attitudes when she describes her treatment on the streets:

> people on the street feel sickened by you, they feel afraid, they feel . . . it's like they can't look at you because they are talking, they're whispering, they're moving away from you. And you

feel bad. And if you approach a person, that person moves away, plugs his nose.

Claudia relates these same attitudes in her testimony:

> I worried because imagine at times you didn't have anything to eat, or anything, you had to see how you made do. Go back to your house or whatever because if you don't know how to rob, don't know anything, you die of hunger. The humiliations that they gave you . . . they looked at you funny, they insulted you, they hit you. . . . At times you were dirty, you didn't have anyone on your side. Instead of helping you, they pushed you aside.

This impulse to push aside street kids has become so marked, perhaps, because the children, of their own accord, refuse to remain hidden. For their protection and livelihood, they spill out into the most public, and busiest, places—plazas, shopping districts, and parks. Scheper-Hughes and Hoffman reason that

> A street child is, like our definition of dirt, soil that is out of place. Soil in the ground is clean, a potential garden; soil under the fingernails is filth. Likewise, a poor, ragged kid running along an unpaved road in a *favela* or playing in a field of sugar cane is just a kid. That same child, transposed to the main streets and plazas of town, is a threat . . . about which 'something must be done.'[4]

In a second study of destitute children in New York, Kozol touches further upon this concept of displacement. One fifteen-year-old he interviewed in the South Bronx ("the poorest congressional district in the nation") describes her place in society in the following terms: "It's not like being in jail . . . it's more like being 'hidden.' It's as if you have been put in a garage, where, if they don't have room for something but aren't sure if they should throw it out, they put it where they don't need to think of it again."[5] The same girl's sister, reinforcing Carolina's assessment of her own situation in Guatemala, poignantly adds:

If you go downtown to a nice store . . . they look at you sometimes as if your body is disgusting. You can be dressed in your
best dress but you feel you are not welcome. They follow you
sometimes but they do not want to touch you. You pay for
something—she pulls back her hand—like that! as if my hand
is dirty.[6]

Working among child laborers in Brazil's informal economy, analysts
Vera da Silva and Helena Abramo noted the "contrast between the public visibility acquired by 'street children' and the invisibility . . ." assigned
to their private struggles.[7] With few exceptions, the contact between
Guatemala City residents and a street child ends with the shoeshine, the
purchase of gum or cigarettes. As a young boy boards a bus and sadly
sings of his life on the streets, a handful of passengers reach perfunctori-
ly into their pockets, looking for spare coins to drop into his hand as he
leaves. How many will remember his story five minutes later, as he
boards the next bus in line? How many will recall his face, his voice, as
he stretches across the barren sidewalk to fall asleep? His personal drama
becomes quickly "lost in invisibility."[8]

Through a process of social distancing, then, Guatemalans are able to
relegate the street child to the status of "other," and the very real abduction of the street child becomes separated from the rumored abduction of
the neighborhood child. Scheper-Hughes noted that in the shantytowns
of Brazil

the rumors of the 'medically disappeared' and mutilated bodies
continue unabated, coexisting, of course, with actual cases of
politically motivated abduction and mutilations of . . . men
and young boys, about which people are too afraid to speak, so
that when touching on *this* subject *moradores* [inhabitants] are
suddenly struck mute.[9]

Moreover, Laura Gingold found that when police murdered poor
youths in Buenos Aires, the "bonds of solidarity" felt by members of the
community for the victim nearly always determined the level of public
outcry over his or her death. Factors which promoted those bonds of
solidarity included steady work, long-term relationships, and participa-

tion in community activities.[10]   Street children, obviously, have little or
no access to these. The most pronounced examples of citizen outrage
that Gingold found, in fact, came in response to police attacks on known
"honest," "working" juveniles *mischaracterized* by officers as
"wrongdoers."[11]

Overt Hostility

Guatemalans' attempts to remove themselves from the painful realities of their city's street children may also lead to attitudes potentially
much more dangerous than the indifference documented by Kozol.
Sociologist Richard Sennett theorizes that during their formative years
people adopt a world view, "a clear and articulated image of themselves
and their place in the world."[12]   Any serious affronts to this world view
produce sharp discord within most individuals. As a result, Sennett suggests, people learn to filter out diversity by "insulating" themselves, asso-
ciating with others holding similar world views or projecting similarities
onto those who surround them.[13]   When dissonances do surface, people
may perceive them as "less than real" or attempt to repress them, as
acknowledgment of discord might require painful changes in the way
one conceives of the world and produce a frightening sense of insecurity.
Thus, when a person who previously held idealistic notions of childhood
as innocent and protected sees a child rummaging through a garbage
dump or passed out on a street corner, or when the same person is robbed
by a street child, he or she will likely not seek to understand that child's
reality immediately. Rather, he or she may attempt to filter out the disturbing images through isolation or calling for repression of the child.
    Sennett asserts that "the eruption of social tension becomes a situa-
tion in which the ultimate methods of aggression, violent force and
reprisal, seem to become not only justified, but life preserving . . . in this
way some communities, through such tools as the police, respond totally out of proportion to the provocations they receive."[14]   In July 1993,
when military police massacred eight Brazilian street children as they
slept on the steps of Rio de Janeiro's Candelaria cathedral, many Rio res-

idents applauded the officers' actions. Of eighty-six phone calls made to a local radio station covering the massacre, sixty accused street children of being delinquents and criticized the mass media for treating them like little angels.[15] A Rio taxi driver working the area of the massacre reacted jubilantly. "It's something beautiful," he exclaimed. A vendor in a nearby shopping center replied "the whole city is more relaxed now," and a public relations woman said "they're eight less. . . . The *pivetes* [a common, derogatory term for street children] make me uncomfortable and I prefer to live without them."[16]

Hearing similar comments during her fieldwork, Scheper-Hughes writes:

> It is curious to note how the official discourse about street children has changed in Brazil (and more widely in Latin America, as well) over the past two decades. In the 1960's street urchins were accepted as a fairly permanent feature of the urban landscape, and they were referred to affectionately as *moleques*, that is 'ragamuffins.' . . . They are now either referred to either as 'abandoned' children or as marginals . . . both labels justify radical interventions and the removal of these all too public 'pests.' . . .[17]

ChildHope's Mark Connolly also has witnessed "increasingly negative public perceptions" of street children. In a 1993 interview, he forecast the consequences of these attitudes in grizzly terms: "more kids will be killed, definitely. It's what's acceptable now."[18] Despite the *international* outcry over the Candelaria massacre in Brazil, for example, and the arrest of four officers accused in the crime, the murder of children on Rio's streets continued unabated and even increased in the bloody event's aftermath. In that same year, 1993, 1152 Rio youths died violently—more than twice the 1992 figure of 450. In 1994 the number rose again to 1226.[19]

Calls to rid Guatemala of the dissonant presence of street children surface periodically. The language used during several of the attacks described in chapter four demonstrates an overt desire on the part of perpetrators to annihilate street children. One individual screamed into the *refugio* doorway that he would plant a bomb to "put an end to all of these kids." Another threatened to "kill these kids one by one." Carol recalled also that one of her attackers laughed as he said that little by little all of Guatemala's street children were going to die. In July 1993, the same month as the Rio massacre, a *Siglo Veintiuno* report in Guatemala affirmed these attitudes:

> What is certain is that those who work to rescue them assert that [the children] are not responsible for their misfortune. It may be that this notion is shocking for the many who consider these children social stains that deserve all of the punishment in the world for intimidating passersby, for being thieves, and at times murderers. They have a right to think that way.[20]

A letter to the editor, written by a man who had witnessed a street child attempt to rob a middle-aged woman, appeared in the 24 May 1994 edition of the *Prensa Libre*. The child's actions so affronted the man's sensibilities that, he writes, he wanted to give him a beating. The man did not act, though, because he reasoned "I would have gone to jail for beating a street child and he would have been protected and supported by organizations dedicated to them and even by Human Rights." In the letter he condemns Casa Alianza for harboring criminals and argues, "The truth is that for this type of individual institutions like Casa Alianza and other shelters should not exist . . . I think that in reality there should be centers where this type of subject is concentrated. . . ."[21] He ends the letter with a warning: "Careful with this street garbage."

A second *Prensa Libre* reader sent a similar letter that appeared in the 11 April 1994 edition just a few pages behind an article on the torching of twelve-year-old Carlos René Gomez. After observing the same group of children, all under age thirteen, regularly rob and harass passersby on his city block, the letter's author solicited help from a pair of police officers. The officers replied, "'Sorry mister, but we can't do anything. . . . If they complain, human rights send us to jail, they defend delinquents.'" Hence, the author concludes, "in our dear country, everything is backwards, 'the delinquents,' because that's what street children are, can offend, hit, steal, rob, insult people and everything remains unchanged.

If street children are not controlled and educated, they'll be the criminals of the future."[22]

18 calle: the interaction of street children and child-users

Private citizens may also remain silent to the abuse of street children if they directly benefit from their exploitation. While social institutions stigmatize street children, protecting the system of privileges and the structure of social and economic dominance in Guatemala, a smaller group of individuals gains more directly from their presence on the street. The experiences of Ines and Elida evidence how certain wealthy families prey on young girls in unstable or abusive domestic situations. Elida, referring to the colonel's wife with whom she lived for two years after becoming an orphan, relates

> when I met her she took me away . . . she offered me school-ing, and everything. And when the moment came, well, I went, and at the last minute she didn't give it to me. . . . She treated me like, I could say like, a servant girl. And the day that I left, well, she . . . didn't pay me one cent . . . the day that they came for me they told me that I wasn't going to be a ser-vant in their house, that I was going to be like a daughter, like their daughter.

Ines similarly tells how after she went to live with her grandmother on a Southern coast plantation in order to escape the life-threatening abuses of her step-mother, a wealthy woman from the capital arrived and promised to buy her many of the things that her grandmother could not afford. She escaped and rode back to the capital with the rich woman, only to find that she received none of the things promised and that the same woman treated her as a slave. In both girls' cases, periods of great instability followed, in which they moved from home to home or landed on the streets.

Once on the streets, children find multiple forms of exploitation, as revealed in chapter two. Adult members of society use both boys and girls for sexual gratification. ACA street educator Marvin Castillo, in his work assisting children before they make it to the *refugio*, observes how homosexual men loiter in Concordia Park nightly and frequently proposition homeless boys there, offering them meals or cash in return for sexual favors. Prostitution usually begins, he says, at age nine or ten for boys and twelve or thirteen for girls.[23] A recent study by three ngos reveals that 101 out of 143 surveyed street children admitted to having one or two sexual partners a day, six to having three or four a day, and thirty-six (three boys, thirity-three girls) to having more than four partners each day. Additionally, 75 percent of those surveyed said that they, like Alba, Brenda, and Vicente, engaged in bi-sexual behavior.[24] The same study reports a logical consequence of this promiscuity, 78 percent of the 143 children had contracted genital herpes and 46 percent gonorrhea.[25] In interviewing teenage prostitutes for a newspaper feature, reporter Manolo García spoke with one fifteen-year-old who works Eighteenth Street and *El Hoyo*, who revealed her thoughts on her activity: "busying yourself with whomever . . . without love . . . Uuuhhh, how disgusting! It is not pleasant . . . but you have to eat, clothe yourself, pay room and buy drugs in order to get up the courage. . . ."[26]

Those that produce and traffic the glue and paint thinner that most kids buy to "get up the courage" also directly exploit Guatemalan street children. A North American company, H.B. Fuller, produces the majority of industrial glue sold on the Guatemalan market. In the United States, federal law prohibits the company from selling the same solvent-based glues it produces and markets to consumers throughout Latin America because of their high flammability—they border on explosive.[27] Commonly used by shoemakers in Guatemala, these glues contain toluene, a chemical that makes them highly addictive. Bonnie Hayskar explains the effects of toluene when inhaled:

> Just as it effectively dissolves plastics, it also dissolves brain cells and other organ tissue. Reacting to this damage, the brain becomes flooded with soothing endorphins and, for a brief time, children actually feel no hunger, no cold and no discomfort. When the period passes, they experience desperation and crave more glue for relief. . . .[28]

Another analyst explains that "Resistol [a Fuller glue] turns off the brain's connection to reality, neutralizing stress, pain and fear, taking the place of parental affection."[29]

Fuller's questionable business practices drew more widespread notoriety in mid-1992, when, in order to avoid exposure on the U.S. television news show *Dateline NBC*, executives announced a decision to halt sales of solvent-based adhesives in places like Guatemala, where their abuse is a matter of common knowledge. Critics learned that by October of that year, however, Fuller had not stopped selling Resistol in Central America and, in fact, had no intention of doing so.[30] The company, since then, repeatedly has stated its current position, that inhalant abuse in Central America is a "social problem, not a product problem."[31] Others remove focus from the company by noting that even if no glue products existed, street children would find other cheap highs in order to escape their dreary situations.

Editors at Minneapolis/St. Paul's *StarTribune* effectively counter these arguments, however, in a succinct 3 May 1996 piece. They write:

> The issue at hand is not the judgment of a poor Third World child but the ethical obligations of a First World corporation. Confronted with a harm in which one's product plays a part, and conceding that a harm not done by one firm will be done by another, it is still possible for a corporation to decide: Then let someone else do it; we won't be part of it. . . . Fuller should reconsider the moral questions involved in profiting—even unintentionally, even unwillingly—from the bad judgment of desperate children.[32]

No Guatemalan law effectively regulates the sale or production of solvent adhesives or paint thinners and, as indicated in chapter three, the government historically has done nothing to control their sale and distribution. Adults easily purchase large quantities of glue and other toxic substances, such as paint thinner, in hardware stores and then distribute smaller "doses" to street children for profit, sometimes directly—often through other children. As one *La República* columnist points out, these adults sell each ounce "at a cost to the neurons and precious cerebral fiber of hundreds of children and adolescents. Irreversibly damaged. In every breath, a noxious invasion of toxic chemicals that extract, like an invading demon, the mental clarity and potentiality of these children."[33]

In Medellín, Colombia, another of the "Gang of Three" perpetrating violence against young people, powerful drug dealers have used their vast wealth and influence to socialize virtually a whole generation into a criminal way of life. In order to keep the wheels of their vice machines well-oiled, dealers use youths "as cannon fodder in their confrontations with each other and with state authorities."[34] Analyzing the impact of this environment of force on the city, journalist Alonzo Salazar underlines that:

> For the boys of Medellín . . . drug trafficking has marked them for life. It brought them the fantasy of wealth and the reality of death. First it became normal to witness killing and dying: then to kill and to die.[35]

Many of Guatemala's beat cops, as noted throughout chapter four, do little or nothing to prevent the tragedies of child exploitation from occurring. Nor do they inhibit the socialization of young people into a "criminal way of life." Rather, some actually encourage the environment of illegality surrounding street kids by "utilizing" them for personal profit. Casa Alianza has documented numerous cases of police corruption, in which officers force children to supply cash, "Ray Bans," gold jewelry, and other valuables, such as U.S. brand tennis shoes and jackets. Carolina described a less documented, but perhaps equally common, form of exploitation of street girls, from whom police demand sexual favors. She relates how she "landed" in jail for the first of six times while living on the streets:

> We were going to break into a car [when] they grabbed me by the hair. . . . Then that cop said to me . . . 'if you give yourself to us we'll let you go, if not we'll take you in.' So I preferred that they take me in . . . because I would rather be in jail and not give myself to them. . . . I was there six months, six months I was detained.

A *Siglo Veintiuno* article narrates the similar events leading to a thirteen-year-old girl's initiation into prostitution. One of the precipitating factors, which prompted the child's almost complete loss of self-esteem, occurred when a police officer caught her stealing, dragged her to a back street and repeatedly raped her. She was ten years old then.[36]

In Claudia's testimony, still another group emerges that profits from the presence of street children in Guatemala City, the owners of the hotels and restaurants frequented by the kids. As she mentions, street children often sleep together in groups, pooling their resources between them to obtain a room for the night. Several places around Eighteenth Street, Avenue Bolivar, and *El Hoyo*, in Zone 4, open their doors to the kids, no questions asked, and also allow them to use rooms for sexual transactions. Claudia recalls:

> They were good people. They knew us already. But there were people in the hotel that didn't care about you, perhaps, because if they would have wanted to help you . . . they would have told you 'don't do that,' or whatever. But at times they saw us drugging ourselves and they wouldn't say anything. It was like nothing to them, they never supported us like that, directly.

Likewise the vendors in such places as Zone 1's Presidenta market who buy stolen goods from street children for profitable re-sale. On any given day, one observes vendors and street kids coexisting in the tight quarters of the Presidenta. Vendors see these youths inhaling glue from seven o'clock in the morning to closing time, right beside them. Still, they say nothing, preferring to see a child destroy his life rather than break their profitable arrangements. Observing the scene, one begins to understand what ACA legal expert Raúl Toledo asserts: "behind a child there is always an adult."[37]

A History of Terror

Finally, any attempt to understand the limited reaction to the abuse of street children from within Guatemala must comprehend, without question, the terrorizing effects of the massive state-sponsored violence practiced there since the mid-1950's. Guatemalan scholar Carlos Figueroa-Ibarra has documented the development of the government's repressive machine in his work *El Recurso del Miedo*. I will summarize here the main tenets of his work for the purpose of illustrating how state-sponsored terrorism in Guatemala has traumatized the people and weakened their ability to respond to gross injustices, such as those currently occurring with street children. According to Figueroa, the government's use of terrorism against its own people has its roots in the colonial period and the long years of oligarchic rule following independence from Spain. The utilization of state terror became a "permanent" fact in Guatemalan political life only after the 1954 United States-assisted overthrow of Arbenz, however, with the restoration of the "capitalist model" and the "constant popular agitation and moments of social explosion" resulting from the inequalities inherent in that model.[38]

The state's weakness, measured in its inability to pacify armed resistance in the countryside and circumvent labor and other popular unrest in the cities, reached its crisis point during the mid-1970's under the ineffectual rule of Kjell Eugenio Laugerud García. Strikes and labor stoppages had plagued the previous two administrations, with 51 such manifestations involving 42,000 workers and 441,200 lost labor days occurring during Julio César Mendez Montenegro's four-year presidency and 74 involving nearly 72,000 workers and 887,500 lost labor days occurring during Carlos Manuel Arana Osorio's. But under Laugerud these numbers soared beyond tolerable levels, to 119 strikes and stoppages encompassing more than 100,000 workers and more than 1.2 million lost labor days during his four-year rule.[39] These protests, naturally, had a devastating impact on the morale of business leaders.

The state's inability to control labor and offset other, by then widespread, demands for social change, according to Figueroa, demonstrated clearly to the bourgeois establishment that bases for political domination via popular consensus simply did not exist within the country. Hence, after the fraudulent election of Fernando Romeo Lucas García in October 1978, the state's approach to social control became much more crude and overt. The strategies included first raising the level of repression significantly in order to eliminate opposition, fostering a form of "passive consensus;" and second employing propaganda to gain a wider base of support, fomenting "active consensus."[40] The first of these tactics proved deadly for the Guatemalan people. The campaigns of mass persecution that had marked periods of the Mendez Montenegro and Arana Osorio administrations now became commonplace—the defining characteristics of the Lucas García (*luquista*) regime. Newspaper accounts alone report 879 political murders and disappearances for 1978; 1371 for 1979; 2264 and 3426 for 1981.[41]

These numerous murders, writes Figueroa, must not be interpreted as casual, but as "symptoms of the *fundamental object* of state terrorism, which is the annihilation, in the heart of the population, of the *will for transformation*."[42] Statistics on the number of popular protests during Lucas García's first years in power show the regime's success in quelling at least open signs of discontent. While forty separate actions were registered in 1978, only twenty occurred in 1979, and even fewer, sixteen, in 1980.[43]

Perhaps the most significant characteristic of state repression under Lucas García, though, involved not the sheer numbers of assassinations and disappearances, but the manner in which these atrocities occurred. The dictator had constructed a complex terror machine. Ultra-rightist groups, supposedly unrelated to the state, would first announce their intention to begin an "extermination campaign" by publishing "death lists" in local papers, placing phone calls to their chosen targets, or sending notifications through the mail. These tactics were then "complemented with photographs published every day about discoveries of brutally tortured bodies . . . ."[44]

The state also found it convenient to show that workers, intellectuals, peasants and students not only would risk losing their lives through continued opposition activity, but risk losing them "by means of the most atrocious suffering."[45] Bodies of kidnapped friends or leaders would appear with horrible signs of torture, including holes in their tongues, feet and testicles, drillings through the skull, electric shocks, hammering of the hands, and asphyxiation by water immersion (the *pila*).[46] Furthermore, the actual disposal of the victims' bodies sent chilling messages to activists, as many males were discovered with their testicles in their eye sockets, females with brutal signs of sexual violence, and both sexes buried up to their heads, decapitated, or hung from trees and electric posts.[47]

Parallel to this terrifying unleashing of the repressive machine, however, emerged Lucas García's second strategy of projecting the state's inculpability. Figueroa describes this as an effort by the state to "abandon the unilateralization of terror" by forging consensus.[48] To this end the *luquista* dictatorship attempted to balance its bloody subjugation of dissent with a multi-faceted approach to boosting its national and international image. In the city, the dictator relied heavily on death squads to handle the filth of repression, rather than on uniformed security forces. In this way, he could claim, even if unbelievably, that "extremists" (i.e. ultra-rightists and guerrillas) rather than the state were responsible for the tortures, assassinations, and abductions occurring within Guatemala.

According to Amnesty International's Michael McClintock, Lucas García also used murders of common criminals to conceal his administration's role in political killings. "Portrayal of the 'death squad' murders as 'vigilante' acts cleansing the society of vicious criminal elements," McClintock writes, "distracted domestic and international public opinion from the government's policy of systematic political murders."[49] Additionally, Lucas García, even while "placing emphasis on the most perverse forms of the coercive function of the state, always maintained the whole framework of the bourgeois democracy."[50] Thus, his government continued to recognize in word many of the rights that it actively violated. Likewise, public officials lauded the autonomy of the national university (USAC), at the same time assassinations of teachers, administrators, and students and bombings of facilities nearly dismantled the institution.[51]

Propaganda portraying local entrepreneurs as "good Guatemalans" who invest in their country's growth also became salient at this time, along with depictions of the guerrilla movement as "a frightening evil that corrodes Guatemalan society," and exposes "the cancer of communism."[52] None of this propaganda, however, consolidated bourgeois support for the state because of the heightened armed conflict. The brutal repression had pushed even moderates underground and, thus, augmented support for the revolution. In the western *altiplano*, "the guerrilla movement was growing, particularly as a result of the impetus from the

Sandinista revolution (19 July 1979) in Nicaragua. The generalization of guerrilla warfare began in the Ixil highlands . . . and in the Ixcán, the rebels concentrated forces."[53]

By 1982, therefore, the threat of a guerrilla victory had become more plausible than ever. Local press coverage illustrated the growing danger for the state. In 1979, newspapers reported the number of guerrilla assaults (including confrontations with the army, bombings and propaganda drops) at 113 or roughly one every three to four days. In 1980 this number rose to 500 attacks and in 1981 to 932 attacks. For just the first three months of 1982 (before the *luquista* period came to a speedy close), guerrilla forces carried out 432 assaults. Had this rate continued after the March coup, the year's attacks would have topped an astonishing 1700— or four to five *per day*.[54]

This intensified revolutionary activity, along with the government's waning international image stemming from its bloodletting, and a building economic crisis at the time, all combined to fracture the already weak bonds of the bourgeois state. The Ríos Montt regime that assumed the dictatorship after Lucas Garcia's fall, however, only intensified terror within the country and enhanced its predecessor's drive to expand consensus. The incoming general promised to halt death squad activity but, as McClintock notes:

> in his first television address to the nation, Ríos Montt [declared] . . . 'There will be no more dead bodies on the road sides, we will execute by firing squad whoever goes against the law. But no more murders.'[55]

In August of 1982, the dictator referred to this policy as "killing people legally."[56]

In the countryside, attempts to discredit the revolutionary movement took on new, horrifying form. Posing as guerrillas, army soldiers would enter a village and virtually destroy it. Several days later the troops, now uniformed, would return and reconstruct the village, accusing the guerrillas of having executed the massacre, or would redistribute the land among supporters of the regime, thus driving the country's indigenous people to increasingly marginalized areas.[57] Two hundred-fifty massacres of this type—eighty alone in the El Quiché highlands and sixty-nine in the department of Huehuetenango—had traumatized the countryside by the end of 1982, only nine months after Ríos' assumption of power.[58] Anthropologist Ricardo Falla describes the scene behind this scorched-earth campaign:

> In 1982 and 1983, blood flowed like water . . . as the population grew in solidarity and became more antagonistic toward the army, torture became increasingly ineffective as a way of providing information. . . . The information obtained was more adulterated, more people were beaten up and tortured who had nothing to do with the rebels, and discontent and hatred of the army grew. This became a vicious circle, as the local inhabitants increasingly closed ranks against the army. It is not surprising, therefore, that the outcome of this process resulted in selective and then indiscriminate massacres. Why lose time abducting and torturing? It is far more effective to simply wipe out entire sections of the population.[59]

Manuel Uribe and Andrés Segovia, also analyzing state terrorism in Guatemala, indicate that Ríos Montt reduced the indigenous population "to the category of subhuman . . . the concept of guilt and crime biologically transmitted underlies the razing of entire villages. . . ."[60] Falla believes that the stereotype of the Indian as vile and despicable, treacherous and cunning, childlike and gullible, heightened the atrocities in the countryside, although he cautions that "racism is a specific trait of counterinsurgency in Guatemala, but it is not the main motivation for it."[61] He describes one army officer's frustration over the evasion tactics of indigenous villagers:

> How could a child or a vile and despicable being trick him? His hurt pride and frustration gave way to great anger, which motivated him to exterminate not just one person but the whole community. I can't control you? Well, you'll see; I'll wipe you off the face of the earth. The officers in charge of counterinsurgency were probably influenced by the [same] psychological and social need to overcome their sense of humiliation.[62]

Ríos Montt further accelerated devastation in the highlands by turning the indigenous against themselves through the installment of civil
defense patrols (PACs) whose members, conscripted forcefully, all came
from the villages and had the task of eliminating "subversives" within
their own communities. The earliest activities of these patrols included
identifying areas of the jungle used by their fellow villagers for hiding
and storing crops, naming insurgents and their sympathizers from
among those leaving the forest, and spreading propaganda to convince
others, still fleeing persecution, to return.[63]

Utilizing such tactics, the government gained significant ground on
the revolutionary front, but the dictator's sheer excesses, his religious
fanaticism, and his inability to achieve economic recovery eventually
split the bourgeoisie once more and sparked a second coup in less than a
year and a half. Although the Mejía Víctores administration, which followed, greatly stabilized the state through the establishment of free and
fair elections and through the subduing of Ríos Montt's terror monster,
it also amplified the state's social control tactics in the countryside. In
addition to institutionalizing the PACs, Mejía Víctores continued building the "model villages" begun under Ríos Montt, in which indigenous
peasants re-settled in return for state provisions of housing, services and,
sometimes, land. Many of the peasants inhabiting these highly controlled villages had been in hiding, deep in the jungle, for up to a year.
They left wearily, only after they no longer could withstand their fatigue
and hunger. In interviews with anthropologist Manz, they emphasized
"the devastation and demoralization of seeing their own fellow
villagers—relatives and former neighbors acting as willing or reluctant
army collaborators—destroying the crops that were to provide food for
those in hiding for the months ahead."[64] The program's effect, Figueroa
asserts, has been "nothing more than to stimulate the *campesina* population that fled to the mountains as a consequence of mass terror and
maintained ties with the guerrilla forces to abandon that attitude and
give itself up to military control. . . ."[65]

Reflecting on the social environment left in her country by the
state's decade of unbridled violence, one USAC student writes:
"Guatemala is a country that has grown up under dictatorial regimes . . .
for the majority this has turned into a culture (a culture of fear, culture

of terror) which gives birth to values, attitudes, and customs that
become manifest in conduct not always rational and very difficult to
understand."[66] Anthropologist Marcelo Suarez-Orozco, in his studies of
the effects of terror on sectors of the Central American populace, has discerned more clearly how this "culture of fear" plays out in its victims.
The anthropologist's interviews with young Guatemalans, Nicaraguans
and Salvadorans who escaped "the situation" in their countries for the
relative safety of the United States, reveal the terror instilled in the population by the horrifying incidents of the 1970's and 1980's. One subject
emphatically states: "'I was afraid even though there was nothing I was
guilty of; I was afraid. . . . They never came to our house, but I was still
afraid.'"[67] Another reveals "people were killed by both sides, the death
squads and the guerrillas. So one cannot be with one group or with the
other, the best thing is to be quiet and not be involved in anything."[68]
Suarez-Orozco identifies how such statements fit into a pattern of psychological responses to environments of extreme violence and insecurity.
"Terror works through an inner voice quoting the outer madness," he
writes. "The calculated unleashing of terror brings about shared denials
in a population. This is followed by the emergence of defensive rationalization about local events and, eventually, by the internalization of
terror."[69]   Importantly, the author notes that in this final, "internalization" stage, "terror returns in the form of a new consciousness of events
and images previously denied, forbidden and half-known," and that it
begins only once the immediate danger subsides, as when his subjects
fled "the situation."[70] Only through this final stage can terror's grip begin
to wane. One Argentine informant, referring to his country's "dirty
war," affirmed: "Argentina had suffered 'a wound and a wound only fes-
ters when left covered up.' A wound, he said, 'only heals properly if it
ventilates in the open, with plenty of light and fresh air to cure it.'"[71]

   With the subsidence of massive terror, perhaps Guatemala has
entered the final, healing, stage of Suarez-Orozco's paradigm. Given the
continued repression of the Guatemalan people by their government,
however, this notion is difficult to sustain. In the single year of 1991—
six years after the installation of a "democratic" state—"security forces"
murdered 575 people and forced the disappearance of 145 more.[72] In 1993
the use of threats and intimidation, so popular during the *luquista* peri-

od, returned as an important weapon of state terror: 359 occurred that year. These statistics suggest an ongoing reliance by Guatemala on low-intensity warfare tactics. Moreover, despite the efforts of groups such as GAM and CONAVIGUA, the absence of a "truth commission" thus far, such as those that investigated human rights violations in Argentina and El Salvador, has kept Guatemala's dark period of terror "covered up," with very little "light and fresh air to cure it." The eerie quietness of Guatemalans on the ghastly events of their country's recent past may signal that society, as of yet, has not psychologically begun to remove itself from danger; that, within Suarez-Orozco's model, they have persisted in the rationalization stage ("the best thing is to be quiet and not be involved in anything").

Dr. Sandra Bloom, an expert on the psychological impacts of war, asserts that just as

> trauma frequently becomes the organising principle in the psyche of the individual, so also in the psyche of a group or nation trauma can become a central organising principle.[73]

She describes the process of dissociation, in which individuals (or societies) undergoing severe psychological stress may detach themselves temporarily from the profound impacts of their experiences. In the short term this process permits an individual (or society) to continue functioning without becoming paralyzed by emotion. "This separation of mental contents," Bloom notes, though, "is unstable . . . the dissociated memories, thoughts, and effects press for reintegration into the main body of consciousness. This conflict manifests through the . . . compulsion to repeat trauma. . . ."[74]

Figueroa Ibarra has observed such dramatic impacts of terror on the everyday life of his country's people. He writes that "it is possible to think, even, that this has left a profound print on [the society's] idiosyncrasy, something which has not remained uncaptured by the sharpest speakers on the national conscience, like Otto René Castillo, when he explains the silence and melancholy of his co-patriots."[75] Within Guatemala, he has noted that the traumatizing effect of state terror

appears as a profound fear, which can include a falling into
paranoia, like a sensation of impotence, and weakness before
the powerful and terrible repressive machinery, a feeling of
conformity, so as not to try to change what it is already known
cannot be changed, passivity before inequality and oppression,
and finally an aversion to all political and social organizations
that deny or oppose the established system.[76]

Gabriel Aguilera Peralta also wrote of the psychological processing of
atrocities by Guatemalans. He states:

At the beginning of the chain of abductions and murders one
noted a stupor amongst the citizenry, which rapidly changed
into an intense fear for personal safety and an accustomation
to the daily bloody facts. As the wave advanced, not even the
most terrible deaths provoked a visible reaction outside of the
victim's family.[77]

The daily appearances of mutilated bodies, the massacres, disappearances, and constant threats occurring during Guatemala's darkest period,
then, naturally have had a profound impact on the society's capacity to
respond to abuses in the present.

A second legacy of state terrorism which inhibits Guatemalans from
decrying the injustices in their country involves the division of society
along a multitude of lines. The terrorist state grouped Guatemalan citizens into villains and patriots, civil patrollers and subversives, less than
human (indigenous) and human (*ladino*), Catholic and Protestant, formal
and informal, rural and urban, rich and poor, "criminal" and "just."
These divisions logically prevent Guatemalans from identifying with the
struggles of other "groups" and inhibit them from interpreting these
struggles as their own. Fernando López of the Guatemalan Archbishop's
Human Rights Office observes that society's most unified sector, the military, has manipulated social schisms in order to maintain its hegemony.
The vast poverty and illiteracy of the people, further, has facilitated this
manipulation.[78]

Ignacio Martín-Baró wrote of the fractures commonly seen within
societies plagued by strife:

war implies social polarization, the displacement of groups toward opposite extremes. . . . The already polarized nuclei seek and even demand that everyone define themselves in partisan terms. Thus, not making a commitment to certain groups is seen as a sign of commitment to certain other ones, and identifying with neither side entails the risk of being considered an enemy by both sides . . . common sense [becomes] replaced by partisan sense. . . .[79]

The repressive apparatus' exploitation of social tension in Guatemala can be seen readily today in the debate over human rights and the establishment of a "verification committee" to monitor abuses in Guatemala. Despite, or perhaps because of, local and international pressure for improved human rights reporting and education within Guatemala, ultra-conservative groups have tried to turn public opinion against the concept of rights. Recall the two letters in *Prensa Libre* that condemned street children and specifically decried their protection by human rights organizations. One letter writer did not beat a street child only because he "would have gone to jail for beating a street child," who would have been protected by agencies "and even by Human Rights."[80] The second quoted police officers: "'we can't do anything, if they complain, human rights send us to jail, they defend delinquents,'"and argued that everything in Guatemala is backwards, since criminals can hit and rob people under the protection of rights.[81] Many individuals condemn Casa Alianza and others for protecting the rights of street children. One private security guard, defending his mistreatment of a street child, complained that "these youths beat each other up to make other people look bad, and as they have people that defend them they do whatever they want."[82]

In the larger context of reactionary attacks on human rights, many rumors circulated after the recent child-snatching scare which blamed conservative propaganda for driving the people's paranoia. At the time of the frenzy, international rights groups were exerting great pressure for the establishment of a truth commission at the peace talks between rebels and the army. The army, one of the world's most murderous, naturally prefers no such commission, and thus may have tried to turn public opinion against foreigners and foreign intervention. Although unsubstantiated, these rumors of conservative interference might offer an explanation for the bombardment of stories about North American child-snatchers in the press at the time, which included such fear-inducing propaganda as diagrams of children's organs next to their reported values on the black market. During the height of the scare, *Prensa Libre* ran at least three to four articles daily on the topic.

A more recent example came in September 1996, with the scheduled execution of two Guatemalan inmates for the rape and murder of a four-year-old girl. Although all of the major newspapers, pushing deadlines, reported that the executions had occurred, a last minute appeal by international human rights bodies resulted in a stay for the purpose of reviewing certain questionable legal proceedings in the case. The leak of this news, several hours later, provoked an outcry among the populace, soon whipped into a frenzy by the media. Officials and private citizens, alike, angrily stated in the press and on television that international organizations had no right, and no business, subverting the national legal system.

A *Siglo Veintiuno* editorial illustrates this reaction. It first reports Chancellor Eduardo Stein's public condemnation of the Inter-American Court on Human Rights for its role in delaying the case, and then urges the government of Guatemala to "send a pointed message to the organization: We are not inclined to cede our sovereignty."[83] A column written by Estuardo Zapata for the same paper goes further. Preparing a letter to the slain four-year-old Marisol *on behalf of the people of Guatemala*, he vents: "Our system has fallen into international prostitution." He claims that Guatemalan justice is making fun of the girl and her family, as are the foreign "pro-human rights organizations." He asks Marisol, "why do the ex-aides of guerrillas now come forward with first communion faces defending your murderers and rapists?" Moreover, he writes, directly to those foreigners:

> *Go home* [without translation]. Leave by the same door you entered. We don't want you here. We did not ask you to come, nor have we welcomed you, *loosers*, who in your own countries are failures and now want to become here Robin Hoods and Mother Theresas.[84]

Nancy Scheper-Hughes describes a similar backlash against human rights in the shantytowns of Northeast Brazil. She writes that the work of rights groups there has been "readily subverted by the Right. Powerful conservative forces in Brazil translated 'human rights' into a profane discourse on special favors, dispensations, and privileges for criminals."[85] Moreover, she reveals how "under the political ideology of favors and privileges extended only to those who behave well, human rights cannot logically be extended to criminals and marginals, those who have broken, or simply live outside the law."[86] And thus, many inhabitants of the shantytowns that Scheper-Hughes studied conceived of human rights negatively, even when this conception proved "contrary to their own class and race interests."[87] The anthropologist recounts the dismay of one shantytown mother upon hearing that the president planned to enact prison reforms. This woman, it seemed, had forgotten "that her own sons had at various times suffered at the hands of police at the local jail and that the prison reform act was meant to protect *her* class, in particular."[88]

Scheper-Hughes ties this opposition to rights guarantees to growing fears of urban violence among shantytown residents. She asserts that the community expresses little "outrage" over police brutality and death squad activity in the shantytowns because its members acquiesce to "hegemonic discourse on criminality/deviance/marginality and on the 'appropriateness' of police and state violence. . . ."[89] Laura Gingold found similarities in the poor neighborhoods surrounding Buenos Aires. She notes that by the early 1980's, official police discourse, working through the media, had incorporated poor youths, particularly drug dependent, city-dwelling poor youths, into "the social construction of the criminal."[90] In order to distinguish themselves from this image of "the delinquent," Gingold asserts, those who occupy the same social space

interpret their own experience, establishing a rupture between an 'us,' normal, working, respectful of authority, and those 'outside.' . . . In these discourses they recreate the dichotomy 'us: normal,' and 'them: crooked.' . . . The right to kill delinquents was not questioned. Institutional violence directed at subjects behaving unconventionally was not questioned, it

was justified as a legitimate power of the police institution
that guaranteed security.[91]

Certainly, a parallel trend has emerged in Guatemala during the past
few years. Guatemalans, particularly those inhabiting poor neighborhoods on the city's fringe, have expressed deep concern and fear over
growing urban crime. A 1988 *Prensa Libre* editorial reflected on these sentiments:

> Social decomposition has acquired disturbing characteristics:
> daytime assaults and robberies. The kidnapping of young
> women has increased to an alarming degree. Honorable people
> cannot walk the streets safely; instead, they always walk in
> fear. Insecurity has become a permanent condition. Even the
> police dare not confront the criminals, unless they are in
> groups. Discouraged, honorable citizens ask themselves, when
> will this terrible state of affairs end? When will we have peace,
> work, liberty?[92]

Six years later a July 1994 letter to the editor of the same paper describes
the social climate in Guatemala City in similar terms:

> The simple fact that we find ourselves face to face with anoth-
> er neighbor, in some little-trafficked street raises uneasiness
> and puts both on guard, as the fear of being assaulted is mutu-
> al. And . . . on seeing a group approaching, neither the hour nor
> the street matter, especially if they dress in the style of the
> gangs that we see in the films they show us on TV. . . . But
> what sometimes passes over us is that each Guatemalan is pro-
> gressively infirm from this fear, with symptoms of a highly
> altered nervousness, that has made him untrusting and unso-
> ciable. . . . [93]

The outcome of such fear, especially in the context of Guatemala's ineffectual and irregular criminal justice system, resembles that in Northeast
Brazilian shantytowns. In a report on prevalent attitudes toward crime
in Guatemala, the former president of the judicial branch, Edmundo
Vasquez Martinez states "[people] have the impression that the tribunals
comprise an immense bureaucratic machinery in which they do not

want to become swallowed."[94] If we add to this the tendency of the police to act as "a repressive body in service of the government," the report suggests, the response to "social violence" is to "contain it by harsher means, greater police presence, and a decrease in procedural guarantees."[95]

Studies of punitiveness in the United States, although controversial in nature, also have linked decreasing concern with procedural rights to increasing fear of crime. Testing the validity of this assertion, Robert Langworthy and John Whitehead conducted a survey in 1986, the responses from which indicated "quite clearly that people who are fearful about the probability of their victimization tend to be more punitive."[96] More to the point, Ira Schwartz, *et al.*, studied attitudes toward juvenile justice in the United States expressed in a 1991 national telephone survey. Summarizing their findings, the authors reported:

> The data indicate as fear increases, support for due process tends to decrease. Also as fear increases, so does support for trying juveniles in adult courts and for incarcerating them in adult prisons. Simply put, fear of being victimized leads to punitive attitudes toward juveniles.[97]

In her studies, Scheper-Hughes found a heightened fear of victimization among the poor of Northeast Brazil, "a self-conscious sort of thinking with and through the body, a 'remembering' of the body and one's 'rights' in it and to it," which she links to the very real appearance of mutilated and dismembered bodies in the shantytowns.[98] Suarez-Orozco, similarly, discovered a very high level of fear expressed by the Central American youths in his study. Pictures of a young person standing beside an operating table, which generally elicit stories of accidents or medical school achievements in U.S. subjects, provoked haunting responses from Suarez-Orozco's group. Over 45 percent related the image to themes of torture and assassination, almost completely absent in other samples.[99]

Several subjects interviewed by Summerfield and Toser in their research on low-intensity conflict in Nicaragua also describe a *physical sadness* , "conveying how the horror generated by the war penetrated the

body as well as the mind." One woman stated that her "blood is frightened," and a man reported "episodes of intense anxiety, palpitations, and
a sensation that his body was suddenly much bigger."[100] Thus, the state's
brutal use of terror in the past appears to make its citizens overly preoc-
cupied with bodily harm and safety. Given this context, and the coincident possible links between fear of victimization and calls for stricter
punitive measures, the depiction by Guatemalan press and politicians of
street children as dangerous delinquents proves especially damaging for
the protection of these children's rights.

As mentioned, the Guatemalan military has exploited growing fear
of crime in the capital city, using it to consolidate its position in the
urban arena once again. Countless stories of assaults and burglaries by
local media sources inflame the insecurities sensed by the city's population after so many years of state-directed terror. Hoping to regain the
consensus lost during the last years of Cerezo's presidency, his successor,
Serrano Elías, created the heavy-handed *hunapú* security force to "pacify"
urban violence. The excesses of *hunapú* agents led to the force's disband-
ment the following year, but the state's intent to deal harshly with
offenders in order to fortify its popular support has remained. As noted,
government and police officials at this time blamed urban violence on
"gangs" of street children, thus conveniently vilifying the kids rather
than confronting the reality that social crime had increased in diverse
sectors as a result of deepening poverty.

In the near vacuum of state power stemming from Serrano's failed
attempt to assume dictatorial control in May 1993, and even after the
legitimate election of Alvaro Arzú Irigoyen as president in January 1996,
the calls for harsh treatment of juvenile delinquents resumed. The military, taking advantage of the environment of hostility and fear, has
begun patrolling the capital's poor, crime-ridden settlements. In July
1994, Defense Minister Mario René Enríquez announced a decision to
send members of Military Intelligence forces periodically into Mixco
"and other marginal areas of the capital to combat gangs and the constant robberies and delinquent acts they carry out. . . ."[101] According to
the Minister, he had received complaints from inhabitants of at least six
Mixco settlements urgently requesting the military's intervention to stop
increasing gang delinquency.[102]

At the same time, the very symbol of state terror, Efraín Ríos Montt, began exploiting the atmosphere of discontent to consolidate his own position in Guatemalan politics once more. On a platform which promised to control crime (as he did in the past) the ex-dictator and his party (the FRG), won the largest share of seats (35 percent) in the August 1994 congressional elections. Ríos Montt's colleagues subsequently voted him President of the Congress and he began campaigning for the Fall 1995 presidential elections. Recall that a renewed assassination spree on street children (four reported murdered within a month of the new congress' installation) coincided with the "law and order" dictator's return to power. His December 1994 statements to the press promising to execute all delinquents were most revealing, reminiscent of his "killing people legally" campaign.

The intervention of non-state actors

The environment of fear, condemnation, and growing misery in Guatemala overwhelmingly favors inaction and silence as appropriate responses to the injustices surrounding street children's lives. That anyone in Guatemala comes to the aid of street children in their daily struggles and in their moments of deepest danger speaks poignantly of humans' capacity to love and to care even in the most devastating circumstances. At times street children tell of the individuals who help and respect them. Perhaps they notice these people because they are so few in number. In this category they include street educators, the adults with which street children have the most non-exploitative contact. Claudia kept score; she knew that the hotel workers did not really help her, but that Bruce and *Seño* Eugenia, who visited her during some of her most troubling times on the street, did. A young boy that I met along Eighteenth Street one day also knew. In his world marked by betrayal and abandonment he trusted in one cafeteria owner, the one who saved leftovers for his dinner every night.

These children, despite their harsh and cruel realities, understand

and receive the care that others extend them. Recounting to the press that the Centro Capitol guards had attacked him, another street child made clear: somebody had helped him. "They pulled me along, kicking me," he said, "and one of the women that works in a restaurant shouted at them not to treat me that way. They told her not to butt in, it wasn't her business."[103] Someone tried to help Nahamán, too, even as he laid dying in the street, the scene of his vicious attack. Someone covered his body in white paper and flowers, preparing him for death—the only salvation still offered him.

Some people, even journalists, write of street children, but instead of condemning them, urge the support and solidarity of readers. José Eduardo Zarco, author of *Prensa Libre*'s "T-MAS" column and director of the paper, often addresses the issues surrounding street children's lives in Guatemala. He also provokes a response, at times, from private citizens. On 10 August 1994 the paper published the following letter written to Zarco:

> You know I work until very late and I have to cross the streets and avenues of this great city (if that's how you could describe it), and every night, somehow, I arrive saddened at my house, where my two children and wife await me. . . . When I mention this it is because I cannot get used to seeing each night the children in the streets looking for a curb, a little corner where they can pass the night and, as you mention, young girls prostituting themselves.

> One of these nights, between Seventh Avenue and Fifteenth Street, Zone 1, I found two of these children inside a cardboard box, trying to sleep and give each other warmth because it was already 12:15 in the morning. I stopped a moment and many things passed through my head . . . the first thing that I thought of was my two children who have a home, but these children only had old, used rags. I approached and took out my camera and took some photos, but the flash woke them . . . they sat up and stretched their small bodies in the intense cold of that hour. Their eyes were red . . . their words were . . . 'we have no clothes,' . . . 'we are hungry.' They were eight or nine years old.

I wanted in that moment to have something to eat to give them. I only had a few cents and I told them 'buy something,' can you believe, at that hour. . . . [104]

CHAPTER SEVEN

Restoring Humanity

We must discover through experience and not in books that in our society it is no use to throw in the towel, to give up.

Paulo Freire, "And the Street Educators," No. 1 of *UNICEF CEDC Methodological Series* (Bogota: UNICEF Regional Office, 1987), 32.

The most effective means of securing children's rights must not be legislation directed narrowly to this end but legislation that attacks the structural causes of poverty itself. Child labour legislation, for example, has never been effective in any country in the world without also being accompanied by welfare measures which remove the need to work.

Judith Ennew and Brian Milne, *The Next Generation* (London: Zed Books, 1989), 26.

I put my fingers into the wound of the people's hands and put my hand into their sides to confirm that, as a people, they were mortally wounded but still alive.

Ricardo Falla, *Massacres in the Jungle* (Boulder: Westview Press, 1994), 2.

There are no easy solutions to the widespread abuse of Guatemala's street children. Because street children encounter indifference and mistreatment on so many different levels, improving their relationships to the larger society will prove tremendously complex. The enormous social divisions and culture of terror that plague Guatemala following decades of civil strife and merciless state repression now inhibit many positive movements for change in the country. A dismantling of these barriers to social harmony and health will occur only over time, with a pacification of the government's social control tactics, the successful implementation of a peace plan, and the gradual erosion of ethnic tensions and inequalities. In the present, however, even as society struggles to recuperate from its horrifying past, policymakers and child advocates in Guatemala can begin employing a variety of short-term measures to curb the brutalization of street children, as well as longer-term plans to alleviate the destitution and despair which provoke their *callejización*— taking to the streets.

Improving conditions for children on the street

Violence and exploitation, addiction and trauma, limited advocacy and poor public image: these represent the chief problems that children encounter on the streets, as documented by the testimonies and numerous written sources cited in this work. Service providers, advocates, and government leaders must address each of these difficulties if children are to survive their immediate circumstances and eventually transition successfully off the street, into healthier and more stable living environments.

Violence and Exploitation: This text has demonstrated that a complicated set of societal forces has converged to make the repression of street children not only permissible but also, at times, seemingly desirable in Guatemala. Personal motivations for gain, further, have led to these children's exploitation in a multitude of forms. In the past decade, police and other security forces have represented the primary perpetrators of violence against street children, as well as some of the most common "child-users" (see chapter four). This fact reveals that the government, itself, has the capacity to diminish the present threats to children's safety on the streets. As the *employer* of national police and military personnel, the government has the authority, if not the responsibility, to impose immediate and appropriate sanctions (pay cuts, suspensions, termination, e.g.) on those officers engaging in illegal activity. Although some 400 officers lost their badges over corruption charges in the early 1990's—many others just as crooked remained.

After Casa Alianza began investigating cases of police brutality against street kids in 1990, after a few particularly brutal (although token) cases involving officers went to the courts, and after protests from the international community began mounting, a response was observed. "Private" individuals soon became the most reported attackers of street children rather than uniformed police. At the same time, these "new" perpetrators used the same tactics and language as police officers had, the atrocities against street kids continued clustered over time and space, and several of the same children remained targeted for attacks, all suggesting an on-going link with public security forces. Similar to when Lucas García used his infamous death squads to divert attention and blame from the government for human rights violations, more recent regimes seemingly have shifted focus away from police to private individuals in street children's cases.

That the government responded in any form to the investigations and protests from international groups, however, does offer hope. A response was observed; the government recognized the high stakes involved with attaching itself or its image to the brutalization of children. Continued and consistent pressure may provide the best-fitting key for unlocking the government's grip of terror over street kids, as a result. Human rights groups and foreign governments, particularly those like the United States' that wield much influence in Guatemala City, should play a central and vital role in communicating contempt for the continued abuse of street children and intolerance over the attempted covering up of responsibility in these crimes. Unfortunately, an examination of the United States-Guatemala relationship around human rights shows a history of ambiguity, at best, and not the certain terms demanded at present.

Washington's strong influence has marked modern relations with Guatemala since the 1950's. Immediately following the 1954 overthrow of Arbenz (designed and backed by the United States), U.S. advisers helped the repressive Carlos Castillo Armas regime to upgrade its intelligence capabilities and, thus, paved the way for decades of repression to follow. Amnesty International's Michael McClintock indicates that US Central Intelligence Agency (CIA) officers sorted through the previous progressive government's files and "determined how they could be put to use." One agency operative revealed:

> I returned to Guatemala for a one-month temporary assignment . . . as part of a team [to] assist the new government in sifting and evaluating the documents left behind when Arbenz and his friends abruptly went into the foreign embassies. The papers we found were an intelligence gold mine. . . .[1]

In 1960, President Miguel Ramón Ydígoras Fuentes allowed the United States to train its operatives for the Bay of Pigs invasion on Guatemalan soil. When some 3000 soldiers concerned for Guatemala's national sovereignty—although ironically led by U.S.-trained officers—revolted in the northeast Department of Zacapa, the same U.S. planes in Guatemala for the Bay of Pigs drills bombed the area and quelled the protest. The rebelling officers then fled to Honduras, where they formed Guatemala's first guerrilla movement, the MR-13.[2]

New armaments, funding and training from Washington continued to pour into the Guatemalan military sector during the mid-1960's. Between 1950 and 1978, Guatemala received $62 million in U.S. military assistance, more than twice that of any other Central American nation, and even more than Mexico.[3] The four schools that trained Latin American military personnel, moreover, emphasized "populace control" in the 1960's, 70's and 80's. A 1971 U.S. Senate investigation of human rights abuses in Brazil found that

> the United States provided training on 'counterguerrilla operations, defoliation, electronic intelligence, the use of informants, insurgency intelligence . . . interrogation of prisoners and suspects, handling mass rallies and meetings, intelligence photography, polygraphs, populace and resource controls,

psychological operations, raids and searches, riots, special warfare, surveillance, terror and undercover operations.'[4]

In Guatemala, the 2000 courses that the United States provided the
armed forces between 1950 and 1969, alone,[5] led to an increased shrewd-
ness on the part of the military. As noted, the army "invented" the practice of disappearance in the mid-1960's in order to repress popular resistance. The first known case occurred in March 1966, when twenty-eight
Communist Party members were abducted and never again seen.[6] Tens
of thousands of disappearances followed.

U.S. officials attempted for years to detract attention from the
almost continual escalation of abuses by Guatemalan authorities. Citing
Cuba's menacing presence in the region, foreign policymakers insisted on
maintaining a heavy flow of military assistance to Guatemala. At his
1973 confirmation hearing former U.S. Secretary of State Henry
Kissinger stated in clear terms the U.S. policy toward grave violators of
human rights, such as Guatemala's military dictators:

> In our bilateral dealings we will follow a pragmatic policy of
> degree. If the infringement on human rights is not so offensive
> that we cannot live with it, we will seek to work out what we
> can with the country involved in order to increase our influ-
> ence. If the infringement is so offensive that we cannot live
> with it, we will avoid dealing with the offending country.[7]

Even after the U.S. President Jimmy Carter's administration brought
human rights to the forefront of U.S. foreign policy, traces of this "prag-
matic" approach remained, for as political scientist Lars Schoultz noted:

> administration officials continued to argue that access to mili-
> tary bases and raw materials was an appropriate justification
> for military aid to repressive regimes elsewhere in the world,
> especially in the Middle East and East Asia. This suggests that
> the argument was not being permanently discarded from
> United States policy toward Latin America, but merely moth-
> balled, to be returned to active duty when a threat to the
> strategic posture of the United States develops in the
> hemisphere.[8]

The Reagan years (1981-89) quickly proved Schoultz right. Partly in response to the demoralizing events in Iran, and partly in response to the Sandinistas' victory in Nicaragua, U.S. President Ronald Reagan reinstated a strong, interventionist U.S. foreign policy.[9] He focused his aggression on Central America and re-fortified relations with right-wing factions there, alienated by the previous administration's strong position on human rights. Even after the five Central American presidents signed a peace accord in 1987 and urged the United States to temper its stance in the region, Reagan boldly persevered in his agenda. He deemed the Arias plan, as it was called, "fatally flawed" and renewed his requests for military aid to Nicaragua's contras "as the only way to bring about democracy." Moreover, Reagan proclaimed Ríos Montt "totally dedicated to democracy,"[10] and asserted that "complaints of human rights abuses by the Ríos Montt government were 'a bum rap,'" even as the dictator began his campaign of massacres in the highlands.[11]

The administration of U.S. President George Bush (1989-93) subsequently retreated from Reagan's hard-line policies, but the invasion of Panama under his presidency demonstrated Washington's continued manipulation of Central America to bolster U.S. interests. The U.S. Department of State, under President Bill Clinton's administration beginning in 1993, defined human rights and democracy-building as its "overarching foreign policy goals" in Guatemala.[12] The United States acted as a "friend" in the recent peace process, meeting with government and guerrilla leaders outside of sessions in order to spur progress. State Department officials also periodically report and, at least ostensibly, express concern over unresolved cases of human rights abuses. Yet, in March 1995 U.S. Congressman Robert Torricelli exposed the still sordid nature of CIA involvement in Guatemala with evidence linking a paid Guatemalan "asset" of that organization, Colonel Julio Alpirez, to the murder of U.S. citizen Michael Devine and the execution of Guatemalan rebel Efraín Bamaca, husband to U.S. attorney Jennifer Harbury.

Torricelli's revelations sparked public outcry and a hard look at the CIA' s use of foreign operatives. Guatemalan researcher and reporter Edgar Gutiérrez suggests, though, that the motivation or "logic" behind even this criticism of human rights violations lies much more in Washington's current interests than in concern over Guatemalan abuses.

He notes that with the "re-democratization" of Latin America and the end of the Cold War, Guatemala neither holds an important strategic interest nor poses a national security complication for the United States. Within this context the Torricelli scandal

> and all that fueled it help the plans for a re-engineering of (read: a limitation of power and funds for) the foreign intelligence apparatus of the United States, whose operations prove onerous for an economy in transition, such as that in the country. And of course, all that sounds like foreign savings elicits the sympathy of U.S. citizens.[13]

The contracting of "assets" like Alpirez, especially during periods when the United States formally had dissolved defense spending in Guatemala, illustrates well a key point in Tina Rosenberg's study on violence in Latin America. The military aid poured into Central America, the author notes, became little more than a laboratory experiment for the United States, one that still failed to test

> what stimuli can induce killers to abandon their killer instinct. Instead, it proved how little the killers must alter their behavior to continue to receive awards from the United States. The mouse, after all, also trains his scientist: when he rings the bell, the good doctor brings him cheese.[14]

Recent events promoting increased interdependence in the Americas, including the enactment of the North American Free Trade Agreement (NAFTA) and the Summit on the Americas, show a more promising opportunity for effective promotion of human rights in Guatemala. Although Guatemalan officials have demonstrated disregard and contempt for outside pressure in the past and even now condemn the State Department for pursuing human rights cases, they also express a keen interest in expanding economic ties in the hemisphere. Discontent within Guatemala's business community partially led to the ouster of Ríos Montt in 1983. Certainly with today's trends toward globalization its leaders will tolerate even less a government that hurts its international position. In fact, the business community played a formidable role in the 1993 rejection of Serrano's attempt to assume dictatorial powers. The United States and the international community, as a whole, should send clear signals, then, that new initiatives benefiting Guatemalan business will depend on the government's compliance with international human rights norms. Such steps will promote internal checks on abuses and circumvent the need for stronger sanctions in the future.

The human rights community must proceed with great caution, however, as illustrated by the recent incident involving a stay of execution for two men convicted of raping and murdering a four-year-old girl. In cases where strong public sentiment rides on a particular outcome, international groups may actually stir resentment for human rights issues if they so vociferously and forcefully adopt opposing or unsupported positions. The long-term goal of promoting respect for rights must remain in focus even when individual causes and momentary victories sway our vision.

More specific to street children's cases, international groups should shed light on the larger context in which the abuses occur. The police officers and "private individuals" who brutalize the children often do so in an effort to extract money or valuable objects from them. When children cannot or do not comply, the consequences range from increased harassment, to beatings, to torture. This police corruption involves more than just failed disciplinary action. Officers in Guatemala receive unreasonably low salaries which do not guarantee their survival. In 1994, a desk officer earned Q. 755 (roughly US$ 135) a month, little more than the minimum wage. Patrol officers earned Q. 850, but had to buy their own supplies. (Officers received eight bullets, an obsolete gun, and one uniform at the start of their service. The department deducted the costs of replacements, as well as insurance fees, from their salaries).[15] This abominable compensation, besides demonstrating disrespect for the life-threatening duties of a police officer, virtually ensured reliance on "outside" sources of income. Hence, in order to curb police corruption and exploitation of "easy" victims, such as street children, the government, in addition to taking those immediate and appropriate disciplinary measures suggested above, also would have to significantly increase police salaries.

Advocacy and image: Although several groups now work to inform Guatemala's children of their rights, very few offer them immediate assistance when they encounter abuse. Casa Alianza has acted almost exclusively in providing legal aid to street children. While in Guatemala I interviewed staff at various human rights and children's organizations, hoping to compare and contrast their handling of street children's cases. My fruitful meetings started and ended, however, with Casa Alianza. I went to the Archbishop's office, known for its investigation and reporting of human rights cases, but staff members informed me that street children, themselves, never have filed complaints directly with the office. Rather, the office gains information about their cases through Casa Alianza.[16] I then went to the Defender of the Rights of the Child, believing that that office surely would handle street children's complaints. Despite its recent inauguration of a special project to assist these kids, however, its staff members had little involvement with actual legal cases. As at the Archbishop's office, street children never reported their abuse directly to the Defender's office, only through Casa Alianza.[17]

Similarly, at UNICEF, staff devoted to helping "children in especially difficult circumstances" never extend legal assistance to them. Street children "have groups such as Casa Alianza aiding them legally," a staff member informed me.[18] At CEDIC, a group otherwise very involved with street children, Assistant Director Edgar Alay lamented his organization's inability to help children in this regard. CEDIC's involvement with street children began just a few years ago, he explained, and perhaps someday would expand to include human rights work (he didn't see how CEDIC could conscientiously avoid this responsibility). But for now, his group recommends children speak with ACA's legal aid office.[19] Thus, street children only have one organization to turn to when they encounter abuse, Casa Alianza.

Reactionary groups naturally have targeted ACA employees in their intimidation campaigns, then, and in their attempts to discredit the rights movement have branded the organization a shelter for thieves. If ten or twenty other agencies in Guatemala investigated street children's abuse, could these right-wing groups attempt to credibly claim that all were wrong in protecting children? If concerned policy analysts, like those at UNICEF and ChildHope, lauded the legal work of ACA rather than remaining (diplomatically) silent, could the government of Guatemala dismiss criticism of its repressive tactics as easily by paying only lip service to street children's needs? If street children had a dozen organizations they could turn to and trust in for legal help instead of just one, would they report more cases of abuse than they have in the past? Likewise, if a greater number of organizations prosecuted street children's cases, in addition to ACA, could law enforcement and court officials so easily retard or obstruct justice? In short, if more groups *actively* defended street children's rights, would their abusers act with the same impunity that they always have? In all likelihood, no.

Any plan to combat the horrifying mistreatment of street children, then, must expand legal assistance to those wishing to denounce. Street children must feel the protection of a community of organizations, rather than just one with which they may or may not feel comfortable and whose members have been as readily persecuted as they have in the past. In Brazil, many ngos have created "defense centers" responsible for tracking children's cases, protesting "institutional arbitrariness and violence," and monitoring the legality of procedures used in juvenile courts.[20] The countless ngo and church-based groups working with Guatemala's youth should make the same commitment to street children by establishing similar legal centers. The need for enhanced protection, after all, is painfully obvious.

UNICEF's Karl-Eric Knutsson sees the limited protection of and advocacy for street children, as well as the ease with which street children are abused and neglected, as rooted in their degraded public image. "They are treated with abuse," he asserts, "precisely because they are not properly valued."[21] A great many Guatemalans, clearly, do not value street children. Street children have no voice. Countless articles portraying their lives appear in Guatemalan newspapers and magazines yet journalists rarely speak with street children directly. At best, a reporter buys a meal for a child, then spends the remainder of the afternoon asking intrusive questions. Lawmakers draft new legislation and devise new programs intended to benefit street children, but they never consult with the children, themselves. Apparently, it has become more convenient for those in power and for those shaping public opinion to group all street children together, to classify them all little bandits or lost causes, than to attempt a more fundamental understanding of their lives. The individuality of street children and the values that each possesses remain unrecognized, as a result, and Guatemalans all too easily disregard the needs, goals, ambitions, and desires of these children. Although hauntingly present in the capital, street children have become less than real for Guatemalans. Knutsson concludes that "physical existence alone is not sufficient for something to be defined as 'real.' A quality of 'meaning' must be added. It does not take much reflection to realize that only what we actively assign purpose and meaning to has significant existence."[22]

The potentially powerful role that the media might play in communicating this "quality of meaning" to the presence of street children was recognized at UNICEF's 1993 conference on street and working children. Delegates there recommended that in countries where children continually suffer abuse on the streets, such as Guatemala, child advocates should form a "partnership" with the press for investigating and reporting this mistreatment.[23] In Guatemala, ngos, such as Casa Alianza or ChildHope, and rights groups, such as the Archbishop's office that have strong communications contacts, should sponsor regular conferences for local journalists. They might greatly improve the present tattered images of street children through discussing at such conferences the potential damage of past newspaper stories, even the well-intentioned ones, for street children. Advocates and journalists, together, should explore ways of improving their future portrayals of street children. In addition, the administrators of ngos frequently contacted for information on street children, such as Casa Alianza, should stress to their employees the importance of using positive language in their comments to the press. Many times reporters quote "advocates" merely reinforcing popular, negative stereotypes of street children.

Also in order to make street children more "real" for Guatemalans, greater contact must exist between the kids and the larger community. A Brazilian street child poignantly revealed the damaging "removal" process which occurs in his country. "We are the fruits of this very society," he said, but

> [e]veryone thinks that we are dangerous criminals and they

don't think that we need help. . . . Is it that society thinks that
we are different from the rest? Or do they think that we cannot be helped? . . . What else can people think if society pun-
ishes us, placing us behind a wall?[24]

In Guatemala, the same "walling off" of street children occurs. I discovered this directly the day that I visited TOM's observation center for
girls. Although I probably had passed by the center a dozen times before
the visit, I had never noticed the building and, of course, never suspected
that it housed a juvenile center; no sign identifies it as such. Further, the
day before the visit I had spoken to TOM Administrator Franklin
Azuldia, but still had to wait a half-hour before being admitted. Once
the center's director, Lesbia de García, tracked down Azuldia to confirm
his approval, she apologized for the delay and allowed me to enter. It
seems that outsiders (not TOM staff or family members of interned children) rarely visit the facilities. They must receive special permission to
do so. As we walked around the place, I mentioned my difficulty in finding it, in the absence of a sign out front. García replied that generally not
even the neighbors realize that the building houses a juvenile center—
until they notice the stream of police cars stopping there to "deposit"
new interns each day.[25]

   This "enclosed" atmosphere of juvenile facilities virtually exiles children within their own city, prohibiting contact between them and the
community that lies "outside" of the wall. While some community
members might voice resistance to more open detention centers,
UNICEF's Francisco Espert notes that sealing off interned children merely reinforces negative stereotypes.[26] In addition,

> the possibility of using the community's basic services such as
> health, education, recreation, and social participation becomes
> lost. While on the other hand, the sports installations and
> workshops of the institution, which operate at a level far
> below the actual capacity, fail to benefit community youths
> who, besides receiving training and recreation, would con-
> tribute, through direct contact, to the normal socialization
> process of the interned minors.[27]

Thus, an opening up of Guatemala's juvenile facilities would benefit the community, as well as street children, and would allow "outsiders" to identify more with them, to recognize their humanity.

A third method for improving the image of street children would return a voice, directly, to those who live or have lived on Guatemala's streets. The Defender of the Rights of the Child recently initiated a public awareness campaign to generate support for children's rights throughout the country. Staff members have developed posters and coloring books illustrating the different rights guaranteed under the UN Convention. CIPRODENI and Centro Ecuménico de Integración Pastoral (CEIPA) both broadcast weekly radio programs in order to promote children's rights in areas outside of the capital.[28] Similarly, UNICEF-Guatemala has begun airing a series of television and radio announcements aimed at increasing awareness of children's health and safety needs. The same medium should be used to spread concern for improving street children's treatment.

CEDIC has published a "comic" book series, "Un día en la vida de Juancho," narrating the daily trials of a teenage street boy. However, its circulation is limited and low rates of literacy in Guatemala make oral forms of communication more successful, in any case. Either quasi-state bodies, such as the Defender's Office, international agencies, such as UNICEF, or well-financed ngos, such as ChildHope, should organize and fund a public theater group for street children to express themselves, their concerns, and their difficulties. In addition to taping public broadcast spots, the group might use performance at local schools and church groups as a means of exposing street children's realities. In doing so, it would reveal the strengths and creativity of these children in responding to the harsh conditions they encounter at home, on the streets, and in institutions. It also would communicate the general *reluctance* to stealing and prostitution among street children and demonstrate their strong value systems. Diffusion of such messages, along with improved depictions in the press and greater interaction between interned children and the larger community, would make it increasingly difficult for Guatemalans to disregard the suffering of street children by stigmatizing them and labeling them "others." The recognition of street children and their basic needs, in turn, would generate, perhaps, greater outcry over their brutalization on the streets.

Addiction and trauma: Chapters four and six of this work reveal that a desire to improve the image and safety of the capital city (for both nationals and tourists) has led Guatemalan security forces in the past to "rid" the streets of homeless youth. Many police and private citizens become irate or disgusted when they see children inhaling glue or thinner. Others fear that kids become more violent while under the effects of these drugs. They respond, as a result by ignoring rather than helping street children, or worse, by scorning and terrorizing them. True, 96 percent of Guatemalan street children do admit regular drug use. Much more effective than pouring glue on their heads or forcing them to swallow bags of it, though, would be to break their drug use through clinical treatment. No concerned individual or agency presently may refer any addicted child to a public clinic for treatment, however, as none exists for this purpose.

Casa Alianza does run a private facility it calls a "detoxification" center, but the program provides nothing similar to a "medical detox." Children, almost all in their early teens or younger, stay at the center for up to six months, and in this sense the program resembles more a transitional or long-term "rehab" than a "detox." While an essential link in the chain of addiction services, such long-term treatment often proves a difficult, intimidating first step for anyone dependent on drugs or alcohol. A tired and sick child might willingly enter a true detox facility for five to seven days (now the standard length of stay), especially one that he/she knows will treat the physical and psychological symptoms of withdrawal. It takes a much greater leap of faith to enter a program designed to last several months, however, especially one removed from the child's normal and familiar environment. The location of ACA's center, in a rural community an hour's bus ride from the capital, although presenting clear therapeutic benefits poses at the same time, an additional psychological barrier for many "hard-core" street-oriented youth in need of its services.

Adolescents and children, moreover, like their adult counterparts, may need numerous interventions in order to make progress in recovery, due to the insidious nature of addiction. Service providers may need what often seems like unlimited patience in order to successfully break a child of the physical craving for and psychological obsession with a particular drug or drink. Street educators should continuously reach out to "active" youths, even those deemed "chronic relapsers." Programs should continue to accommodate them, but also should use the positive examples of kids who formerly lived on the street but who now have stabilized due to solid experience in recovery. Adolescents generally learn best and most willingly from their peers.

The government and/or private groups also might operate less restrictive juvenile centers and shelters, ones where children could enter even after using drugs or alcohol, provided they could follow basic safety rules and regulations. These centers might provide the first step to eventually getting them into treatment, while ensuring them of at least minimal food intake, health and hygiene services. Children might develop longer and more trusting relationships with staff in such "wet" (drug and alcohol permitting) facilities as well, since 54 percent of street youth surveyed by CEDIC stated they left programs because of the urge to use.

Hand in hand with drug treatment programs, the government should better regulate the sale of glue and other highly addictive substances now readily available on the streets. Pressure on the manufacturers of glue and solvents, like H.B. Fuller, to develop less toxic and addictive forms of their products also should remain strong. These two steps, taken together, might effectively begin to curb the now staggering growth of child addicts on the streets.

Beyond substance abuse issues, most street children suffer from the emotional impacts of deeply traumatic experiences, either in their homes, on the streets, or both. The inability to trust that underscores Ruth's testimony, the explosive anger and tendency toward violence brought out in Carolina's, the low self-esteem and sense of self-worth, and the difficulty in expressing one's needs, revealed through Elida's story, and the "black and white" thinking and resentment of authority shown in Claudia's, all have roots in traumas occurring during the young women's formative years. Incest, rape, beatings, abandonment, losses from death and alcohol, and neglect all link street children's stories. Their abuse most often repeats itself on the street, either at the hands of police, peers, or other private individuals engaged in exploitative practices.

Any effort to "re-integrate" street children into the community, and any initiative to improve the quality of their lives, must address these profound psychological scars. Group and individual therapy may provide effective treatment for stress-related symptoms, but only if on-going and offered in a safe environment, preferably once the child has removed him or herself from the abusive situation. For the lack of trust, anger, fear, and suppression of needs examined in therapy often prove essential for the survival of those children still exposed to violence, neglect, and exploitation. Psychiatric medications also may offer an effective component of treatment for some traumatized children, particularly those most affected by depression or anxiety.

Although potentially costly, and surely complex, mental health services for street children are essential and desperately needed. Government and private agencies, then, must begin to develop programs appropriate for the population. They might solicit the required financial and technical assistance for doing so from international funding sources and professional associations.

Slowing callejización

As observed throughout this text, children generally take to the street for two primary purposes, to escape volatile situations within their homes, or to improve the socioeconomic circumstances of their families. Alleviating the destitution and despair of children before they reach the streets requires long-term planning and commitment from Guatemala's leaders. Below I offer a few key components that such a movement might include.

Assisting "disintegrating" or single-parent households: Chapter five discussed in detail how the standard ideological model of childhood in Guatemala excludes all but a tiny fraction of the population, members of the upper class. This model, transplanted to Guatemala by elites with connections abroad, emulates the hardly representative Western two-parent structure in which the father single-handedly supports the family, the mother raises the children, and the children spend carefree days studying or playing. In Guatemala, particularly since the onset of the "debt crisis" and the subsequent implementation of structural adjustment policies, large numbers of families have strayed from this unrealistic model. Real wages decreased drastically for the poorest sectors of the population in the 1980's, and the average salary fell short of that required for even minimal subsistence. No longer can a single family member provide for household consumption needs, as in the idealized model, and additional members, usually the mother and older children, have begun to work as a result.

The inability of the male head-of-household to perform his socially defined role as breadwinner has increased emotional tensions within many poor families. While some households have endured these strained relations, precisely because of their members' mutual dependence, others have disintegrated. "Broken" homes resulting from these emotional and economic hardships suffer the further burden of social stigmatization in Guatemala, not only because they deviate from the idealized model of family life but also because they violate widely diffused and accepted religious norms. These norms hold marriage as sanctified and indissoluble and, thus, cover "dissolved" matrimonies, and the consensual unions which frequently stem from them, in a shroud of immorality. Chapter two of this book, along with CEDIC's 1993 survey and Ariza Castillo's study in the Dominican Republic, reveal that the majority of street children come from highly ostracized families—the ones which least conform to upper-class ideals and break most with revered religious norms.

The alienation of street children and their families, however, has accomplished nothing other than to provoke greater hostility and indifference from among the populace. Attaching stigmas to "broken" families has not decreased their presence, it only has allowed Guatemalans to avoid temporarily the blatant reality that social conditions in their country do not allow for conformity to an idealized family life. The sector of the population that *has* accepted this and has presented a clear alternative to the upper-class model, the Maya indigenous, also has responded with greater care to the needs of abandoned, neglected and orphaned children in its communities.

Grassroots movements, thus, must now begin to promote acceptance of and respect for the actual diversity of family life. They must begin to gradually nullify the current regime's emphasis on stigmatization. This will require a delicate break from concepts spread among the poor in the past that attribute responsibility for the tragedies of destitution, alcoholism and drug use, for example, to individual behavior. As illustrated, such notions dangerously obscure a deeper understanding of these social phenomena and distract attention from their structural causes. Leaders should begin to address more responsibly the issues of single parenthood, juvenile labor, and child neglect, for example. They must strive to break the social stigmas attached to these issues, for only in accepting their real presence and rejecting the conditions that foster them, will society adequately respond to families in need.

Although the Guatemalan Constitution and the U.N. Convention on the Rights of the Child require the government to intervene on behalf of struggling families, specifically those plagued by abuse, alcoholism and drug addiction, the state presently provides little support. The dire circumstances suffered by so many of Guatemala's street children in their homes reveal vividly the government's failure to respond to families in crisis. Ngos in Guatemala also often neglect involvement in "domestic affairs," even when families desperately and precisely need outside intervention in order to survive. In Graciela's case, and Claudia's, religious groups did step in to remove the children from their homes. Here, however, and in far too many other cases, removal from immediate danger posed as an end. Most programs do not reach out to counsel abusive or addicted family members. They institutionalize children, then do nothing to prepare the family for the child's successful reincorporation into the home. To foster a healthier and safer family environment for children, programs must provide more counseling for parents and stimulate mutual-support groups within communities. This, in turn, may prevent many children from abandoning their homes early, on their own.

Similarly, government and non-governmental organizations should assist single-parent households in order to relieve their growing burdens. As Ennew and Milne observed, government officials generally overlook the strengths of female-headed households, in particular, noting only what they lack, a father figure. If Guatemalan women received support instead of condemnation when trying to raise children on their own, some might avoid forming, out of economic necessity, the unstable second and third unions that so often lead to their and their children's abuse.

Greater support also would relieve a second burden for single mothers. UNICEF's study on poor women's coping strategies—*The Invisible Adjustment*—revealed that single mothers often must accept either part-time employment or low-paying jobs that they can perform in their homes (such as washing and ironing or piece-rate work) or they must leave their children improperly attended or alone while they work longer hours outside of the house. In order to avoid such scenarios, either ngos or public agencies should organize safe and reliable child care alternatives, such as day centers or cooperatives for working women, directly in the city's poorest neighborhoods. In addition, ngos should support new income-generating opportunities for single mothers, like crafts cooperatives or food production enterprises. This would raise not only the financial independence of women but also their self-esteem and would allow them more flexibility in their schedules to adequately care for their children.

Coordinating efforts for children in destitute communities: Despite the work of agencies such as CONANI and CIPRODENI, which provide oversight for agencies assisting children in Guatemala, a multitude of private and public organizations still operate in seemingly disparate fashion. Ngos, in particular, function according to their own agendas and sometimes fail to consider the true needs of the children they serve. Worse, many wish to prove to financial supporters that they are accomplishing development and thus compete rather than cooperate with one another, or opt for short-term projects offering highly visible gains rather than more time-consuming and complex ones that prove, in the long run, more beneficial to their constituents. While only a handful of ngos offer programs specifically for street children (ACA, CEDIC, Solo Para Mujeres, CEIPA, and ChildHope, less directly) a nearly endless number have mandates to assist "disadvantaged children" or specifically those from the city's poorest neighborhoods. Many others dedicate themselves to analyzing and assessing children's needs. Looking through the newspaper or telephone listings, or simply walking around the city, one notices dozens of organizations with names like Sociedad para el Desarrollo Integral de la Familia Guatemalteca (SODIFAG), Sociedad

Protectora del Niño, Casa del Niño, Hogar Mujercitas, El Camino (which provides sexual guidance to adolescents), Fundación Pediatra, PLANAN (*Niño* to *niño* program), La Novena, BIF, TOM, PAMI, and a plethora of church-based groups.

The actual work of these organizations remains less obvious than their highly visible logos, however. In their time of need a poor mother or father might not understand which of the groups to approach for assistance. They might be passed from one office to another, wasting their already limited time until finally giving up, unattended. Worse, if children seek assistance directly how will they know where to turn? To alleviate such confusion, public and private organizations, together, should develop a guide to their services and eligibility requirements. Ngos working in poor communities should then use the guide readily to advise residents on where to turn for help. In addition "youth promoters" from associations like CONANI, who personally visit families and children in the poorest settlements, as well as social workers striving to re-integrate children into their homes, should utilize and distribute copies of the guide to households.

Moreover, the directors of major child and youth-oriented groups should meet annually to discuss their work and plans for the upcoming year. CONANI, itself, has observed a need for greater "unification of criteria" and planning among these organizations.[29] Meeting annually would allow directors to re-assess the needs of Guatemala's youth, to evaluate how their work has met these needs, and to discern gaps that remain in their coverage. Responsibilities for addressing those gaps could be assigned at the conference in order to ensure on-going attention. Such a system would make public bodies and ngos more responsive to the true needs of Guatemala's youth, not just their own agendas.

Supporting self-help movements in poor settlements: A large percentage of Guatemala's street children lived in the squalor of the capital's poorest neighborhoods before fleeing their homes. They left behind the misery of underemployment and low family incomes that required them to work from an early age, the inadequate services that daily jeopardized their physical safety, and the overcrowded housing that provoked tensions, frustrations, and sometimes abuse within their families. As migrants flee the war-torn, economically marginalized countryside in growing numbers, officials in the city prepare little for their arrival. As discussed in this works's introductory chapter, the Guatemalan government has spent negligible amounts on urban housing and services during the past several decades. Worse, even when newcomers construct shelter and secure services on their own, government forces periodically evict them from their settlements, destroying their progress and annihilating their dreams.

The government obviously cannot or will not meet the growing demands of its urban population. New residents, on the other hand, eagerly and ably provide, through the sweat of their own labor, what the government does not. Many scholars note the successes of this "ground up" form of urban development, and in fact planners and policymakers in and outside of Latin America often romanticize "the informal." UNICEF's Juan Pablo Terra states, for example, that while "marginal neighborhoods are sometimes called tumors, giving the cancerous image of death . . . in reality they are the embryos that represent Latin America's future."[30]

Regardless of the language used to describe self-help strategies for development and survival, their flourishing relates, no doubt, to the harsh economic consequences of structural adjustment. Urban scholar Fernando Carrión writes of disturbing developments beginning in the 1980's:

> Urban policy is reduced to its non-existence: elimination of subsidies for services and infrastructure, with which the reproduction of the labor force falls increasingly on civil society rather than the State (strategies of extreme survival, stealing, prostitution) and the administration of the city disappears . . . the municipal government, that in principle ought to be in charge of the city's growth, has seen its tasks and possibilities becoming more limited, and because of this it has been losing legitimacy. . . .[31]

Planner Thomas Angotti concurs that

> Self-help is basically an acknowledgment that the State will

take little or no responsibility for the planning and development of poor neighborhoods. Self help actually describes the
way most metropolises in Latin America have been built—
spontaneously and without government assistance.[32]

The poorest quarters of cities like Guatemala do differ greatly from
those in the Western industrialized cities. A UNICEF report summarizes
that "[i]n relation to the deteriorated neighborhood, the spontaneous
neighborhood tends to suffer a greater lack of services but enjoys a possibility of progressive improvement, through the work of its very inhabitants. . . ."[33] Anthropologist Emilio Willems also notes this difference
and theorizes that:

> A slum dweller can never hope to own the building he lives in,
> but the squatter expects or hopes eventually to obtain legal
> title to the land on which his house is built. Shantytowns are
> forms of urban growth, slums are not.[34]

Threats of eviction or destruction will only slow the uncapitalized,
indigenous progress made by new settlers, since heightened uncertainty,
naturally, makes people more reluctant to invest in their properties.[35]
Thus, rather than so readily persecuting poor settlers and driving them
from their tracts of land, the government would more wisely encourage
their improvements to the abandoned and under-used properties that
scar the city. Without this form of growth—the one which currently
provides the only means of absorbing the steady flow of immigrants
from the countryside—Guatemala would become no more than a time
bomb waiting to explode under increasing pressures of overcrowding,
destitution and despair.

Offering this outlet and presenting at times hopeful possibilities for
development in the future, Guatemala's poor communities still provide
ripe conditions for immense suffering in the present. Infant mortality
and child malnutrition stem logically from the high unemployment, con-
taminated water supplies, and precarious physical conditions that mark
these settlements. Eliminating government coercion may provide a safe
context for the long-term development of poor communities, but they
also require immediate, more tangible support from both the govern-

ment and the non-governmental sector.

In their study of the urban environment's impact on Costa Rican children, Lungo and Pérez emphasize that in order to increase access to and awareness of services, support must occur directly in poor communities.[36] Some groups in Guatemala, such as CEIPA and CONANI, already have outreach programs in destitute sectors, and CEDIC made its start in Zone 12's *Guajitos* settlement. Large gaps in their coverage still exist though. New programs—especially those providing services for children—are desperately needed. They must complement, however, rather than disrupt or replace, the survival strategies of community members themselves.

What do you hope from the future?

Ruth

To graduate
look for a job,
support my son,
and have, buy a parcel,
a house for me
in order to have a place to live with my son
so that nobody says to me,
'Look, move out of there, because it's mine.'
Rather it's something that is going to be mine
and my son's.

Elida

If I set myself, like, to study,
to get ahead,
well, God willing,
to get a good job in order to give my son a better life.
Because . . . when I was pregnant, I suffered
because I didn't eat,

and that even affected the baby a lot,
in that an ulcer formed in him.
And then, I defended myself in washing and ironing
in houses.
And that was my work.
Well now, well
I would like . . . to be a bit more
in the sense of . . . knowing how to earn money.

Claudia

In November I graduate. . . .
I'm trying to see what . . .
what to do for tomorrow.
Let's say specialize in something in the morning
and . . . work at night.
And supposing, save
and set out to live with my daughter.

Let's say that
the baby's father was also in the street. . . .
They talked to him,
they found him a job,
and he's working, he's in the *Comunidad*.
And [with his earnings] each month they're going to buy him
something,
like a stove, things that he needs.
And if when I,
next year, begin to work,
I begin to save also,
you know, so that when the two of us leave
we can be together . . .
but leave, you know, ahead,
not with our hands empty.

Carolina

I want to move ahead. I want to graduate
in order to give the best to my son.
Because if I was in the street,
I don't want my son to experience
what I experienced.
Because life in the street is really sad,
it's really hard. . . .
And it's that I want to give more to my son. . . .
And now, yes, I am determined
to . . . to graduate,
to work,
give the best to my son. . . .
I am determined not to go back to the same. . . . .

Will we annihilate their hopes for the future with the same indifference and cruelty that destroyed their pasts?

Notes

CHAPTER ONE

[1] Tina Rosenberg, *Children of Cain* (New York: William Morrow, 1991), 12.

[2] Sara Terry, "Giovani's Story: The Life and Death of a Guatemalan Street Child," *The Boston Globe Magazine*. 2 May 1993, 45.

[3] Rosenberg, 35.

[4] CONANI, SEGEPLAN, UNICEF, *Nuestra Realidad*, (Guatemala: Dec 1992), 21.

[5] CONANI, 21, 32.

[6] See for example Maggie Black, *Street and Working Children* (Florence: UNICEF Child Development Centre, 1993), 15; Susanna Agnelli, *Street Children A Growing Urban Tragedy* (London: Weidenfeld and Nicolson, 1986), 33-5; and Diane Bendahmane, "The Quiet Revolution," 2-12 of *Grassroots Development*, vol. 18, no. 2 (1994), 5.

[7] According to Ana Raquel de Tobar, director of UNICEF-Guatemala's programs for Children in Especially Difficult Circumstances, a 1990-91 survey by the organization found 600 children living in Guatemala's streets. UNICEF *publishes* a figure of 1500 so as not to contradict other groups (Interview, June 1994). Higher estimates come from, among others, CEDIC, a local ngo servicing street children. (*See* "Factores que propician la callejización de la niñez guatemalteca." Guatemala: CEDIC, 1993).

[8] Deborah Levenson, "On Their Own, A Preliminary Study of Youth Gangs in Guatemala City," No. 4 in AVANCSO series *Cuadernos de Investigación* (Guatemala: Inforpress Centroamericana, 1988), 11.

[9] UNICEF, "First Project Report for the US Committee for UNICEF, Project for Street Children and Children at Risk," (Guatemala: UNICEF, Jan 1989), 2.

[10] Claudia Paz y Paz and Luis Ramirez García, *Derechos humanos: niños, niñas y adolescentes privados de libertad*, Unpublished report of the Instituto de Estudios Comparados en Ciencias Penales (Guatemala: Aug 1993), 86.

[11] CONANI, 6.

[12] AVANCSO, "Vonós a la capital," No. 7, *Cuadernos de Investigación*, (Guatemala: Inforpress Centroamericana, June 1991), 44.

[13] AVANCSO, 45-6.

[14] Carlos Figueroa Ibarra, "Violencia y Democracia en Centroamérica," in *Verdad y Vida* (Guatemala: ODHAG) April-July 1994, 11.

[15] AVANCSO, 30-1, 36.

[16] "Prisioneros de la calle," 7.

[17] CONANI, 6.

[18] UNICEF, *El niño en América Latina y el Caribe* (Santiago: UNICEF, 1979), 45.

[19] Emma Samayoa de Medina, "La problematica que presentan los menores que viven en las calles de la ciudad de Guatemala," thesis, School of Social Work, University of San Carlos (Guatemala: USAC, date unknown), 38; and Paz y Paz and Ramirez García, 6.

[20] Paz y Paz and Ramirez García, 6.

[21] CONANI, 7.

[22] Giangi Schibotto, *Niños trabajadores*, (Lima: IPEC, 1990), 338.

[23] Thomas Angotti, "The Latin American Metropolis and the Growth of Inequality," in *NACLA Report on the Americas*, Jan-Feb 1995, 16.

[24] Banco Centroamericano de Integración Económica, *Memoria Anual 1990-91*, 89-93, Inter-American Development Bank *Economic and Social Progress in Latin America,* 1996 Report, 359, and CONANI, 8.

[25] Juan Arancibia Córdova, "Consideraciones sobre el ajuste estructural en Centroamérica," *Revista Centoamericana de Economía*. Sept-Dec 1991, 19.

26 CONANI, 6-7.

27 Inforpress Centoramericana, *Guatemala 1986. El año de las promesas* (Guatemala: Inforpress Centroamericana, 1987), 33.

28 Arancibia, 28 and Paz y Paz and Ramirez García, 3.

29 Inforpress, 35.

30 Agnelli, 45.

31 Judith Ennew and Brian Milne, *The Next Generation* (London: Zed Books, 1989), 55.

32 Schibotto, 338.

33 Lourdes Benería, "The Mexican Debt Crisis: Restructuring the Economy and the Household," 83-104 of Benería and Feldman, *Unequal Burden* (Boulder: Westview Press, 1992), 96-7.

34 UNICEF, *The Invisible Adjustment. Poor Women and the Economic Crisis* (Santiago: UNICEF Regional Office, 1987), 59.

35 Mario Rolando Cabrera, "La pobreza y los niños," in *La República*, 12 Apr 1994.

36 Nancy Scheper-Hughes, *Death Without Weeping* (Berkeley: University of California Press, 1992), 219-33.

37 "Temor e indignación de padres de familia por robo de niños," *La República*, 23 Mar 1994, 4.

38 "Robo de niños cause violencia en Villa Nueva," *La República*, 5 Apr 1994.

39 Walter Lafeber, *Inevitable Revolutions* (New York: WW Norton, 1984), 125.

40 Ibid., 168.

41 Ibid., 168-9.

42 Frank Newman and David Weissbrodt, *International Human Rights* (Cincinnati: Anderson Publishing Company, 1991), 241.

43 Ibid.,153.

44 Ibid., 241.

45 Oficina de Derechos Humanos del Arzobispado de Guatemala (ODHA), *Informe Anual, 1993*, 271.

46 Lafeber, 257.

47 Figueroa Ibarra, 11.

48 Ricardo Falla, *Massacres in the Jungle* (Boulder: Westview Press, 1994), 2.

49 Figueroa Ibarra, 11.

50 "Guatemala ocupa primer lugar en violaciones de DH en 1993," *La República*, Guatemala. 6 July 1994.

51 Figueroa Ibarra, 11.

52 ODHA, "Fuerzas armadas: su rol dentro de la sociedad," *Verdad y Vida*, Guatemala. Apr/Jun 1994, 23.

53 Elizabeth Farnsworth, "Guatemala: Who Calls the Shots?" *Mother Jones*, Oct 1987, 22.

54 Inforpress, 13.

55 Figueroa Ibarra, 12.

56 Ibid., 12.

CHAPTER TWO

1 The children's names that appear in this paper are not actual, except where the child specifically authorized me to use his or her real name.

2 CEDIC, "Factores que propician la callejización de la niñez guatemalteca," (Guatemala: CEDIC, 1993), 24.

3 "Crece prostitución infantil en Guatemala," *Barricada*. 9 Mar 1994, 9.

4 CEDIC, 24.

5 Ibid., 24.

6 Interview with Marvin Castillo, 28 July 1994.

7 CEDIC, 8.

8 Interview with Edgar Alay, 11 Aug 1994.

9 CEDIC, 26.

10 Ibid., 30.

11 ChildHope, "Nuestros niños, nuestra esperanza," Bulletin, No. 9 and 10 (Guatemala: Jan 1994), 6

12 CEDIC, 30.

13 Ibid., 31-32.

14 Ibid., 35.

15 Paul McEnroe, "Latin America Glue Abuse Haunts HB Fuller," *StarTribune*, Minneapolis/St. Paul. 21 Apr 1996, A21.

16 Bonnie Hayskar, "Sticking with Addiction in Latin America," *Multinational Monitor*. Apr 1994, 26-9.

17 CEDIC, 33.

18 Ibid., 33.

19 Ibid., 33.

20 Rinaldo Sergio Vieira Arruda, *Pequenos Bandidos* (São Paulo: Global editora, 1983), 21.

21 Vieira Arruda, 23.

22 Giangi Schibotto, *Niños trabajadores* (Lima: IPEC, 1990), 173.

23 Vera da Silva and Helena W. Abramo, "Experiencia urbana, trabajo, e identidad. . . ," 197-214 of Vainstoc and Carrion, *La ciudad y los niños* (Quito: Ciudad, 1987), 202.

24 Carol S. North et al., "Violence in the Lives of Homeless Mothers in a Substance Abuse Treatment Program: A Descriptive Study," *Journal of Interpersonal Violence*. June 1996, 234-249.

25 Interview with Edgar Alay.

26 Ibid.

CHAPTER THREE

1 *Constitución política de la República de Guatemala*. 31 de mayo de 1985. "Version reformada," (Guatemala: Jimenez y Ayala editores, 1993). Articles 1 and 2, 1.

2 "Guatemala: English Translation of the 1985 Constitution by Peter Heller," in Blaustein et al., *Constitutions of the Countries of the World*, (Dobbs Ferry: Oceana Publications, 1986), 3.

3 *Constitución*, Articles 273-75, 70.

4 Ibid., Article 51, 10.

5 Ibid., Articles 54-56, 10-11.

6 Blaustein et al., 30.

7 "Convention on the Rights of the Child," in UNICEF, *The State of the World's Children 1991*. (Oxford: Oxford University Press, 1991), 77-96.

8 Claudia Paz y Paz and Luis Ramirez García, *Derechos humanos: niños, niñas, y adolescentes privados de libertad*, Unpublished report of the Instituto de Estudios Comparados en Ciencias Penales, (Guatemala: Aug 1993), 5-6, and UNESCO, Statistical Yearbook (London: UNESCO, 1993), Table 2-10.

9 Inter-American Development Bank, *Economic and Social Progress in Latin America, 1996 Report*, 50.

10 UNICEF, *The State of the World's Children 1992*, (Oxford: Oxford University Press, 1992), 7-8 and UNICEF "The Progress of Nations," (New York: UNICEF House, 1993), 29.

11 UNICEF, "The Progress. . . ," 9, 17, 23.

12 IADB, 339 and "Prisioneros de la calle," in *Siglo Veintiuno*, Guatemala. 9 Mar 1992, 5.

14 UNICEF, "The Progress. . . ," 10-11.

15 Deborah Levenson, "On Their Own," No. 4, AVANCSO series *Cuadernos de Investigación*

(Guatemala: Inforpress Centroamericana, 1988), 41-2.

[16] CONANI, UNICEF, SEGEPLAN, *Nuestra Realidad*, Guatemala. Dec 1992, 39.

[17] Emma Samayoa de Medina, "La problemática social que presentan los menores que viven en las calles de la ciudad de Guatemala." Thesis, School of Social Work, USAC, (Guatemala: date unknown), 48-9.

[18] Bonnie Hayskar, "Sticking with Addiction in Latin America," *Multinational Monitor*, Apr 1994, 26-9.

[19] Interview with Franklin Azuldia. 12 July 1994.

[20] Paz y Paz and Ramirez García, 83.

[21] Ibid., 11-12, and Mary Ana Beloff, "De los delitos y de la infancia" 104-113 in *Nueva Sociedad*, Jan-Feb 1994, 107.

[22] Beloff, 107.

[23] *Código de Menores*, Decreto 78-79 (Guatemala: Jimenez y Ayala editores, 1979), Articles 3 and 6, 5-6.

[24] Paz y Paz and Ramirez García, 15.

[25] Ibid., 2 and *Código*, Articles 42 and 49, 25-28.

[26] *Constitución*, 4.

[27] *Código*, Article 3, 5

[28] Paz y Paz and Ramirez García, 18-19. Here the authors reject the notion that the internment of juveniles does not represent punishment because it is, at minimum, a sanction, and the principle of legality extends to all sanctions.

[29] Ibid., 23.

[30] *Código*, Articles 35-6, 20-22.

[31] Paz y Paz and Ramirez García, 25.

[32] *Código*, 24.

[33] Paz y Paz and Ramirez García, 75, 82.

[34] Ibid., 39, 50, 58.

[35] Ibid., 59-62.

[36] Interview with Lesbia de García, director, Centro de Observación para Niñas, Zone 1, Guatemala. 13 July 1994.

[37] Carlos Rafael Soto, "El rostro de la vergüenza (II)," *El Gráfico*, Guatemala. 10 Mar 1993, 9.

[38] Paz y Paz and Ramirez García, 34.

[39] Casa Alianza, *Report to the UN Committee Against Torture on the Torture of Guatemalan Street Children 1990-1995*, Guatemala. Nov 1995, 54.

[40] Vieira Arruda, 72.

[41] Interview, 13 July 1994.

[42] Paz y Paz and Ramirez García, 105.

[43] Ibid., 106.

[44] Ibid., 86.

[45] "Alianza con los niños de la calle," 7-11 in *Noticias de Guatemala* (10 Jan 1992), 10.

[46] Paz y Paz and Ramirez García, 85.

[47] *Código*, Article 3, 5.

[48] Interview, 12 July 1994.

[49] Interview with Hector Dionicio, 11 July 1994.

[50] Procuraduría de los Derechos Humanos, "¿Qué es la defensoria de los derechos de la niñez?" Informative Bulletin (Guatemala: date unknown).

[51] Procurador de los Derechos Humanos, Press Release "Presentación del Anteproyecto del Código de la Niñez y Adolescencia," (Guatemala: date unknown), 1.

[52] Ibid., 2.

[53] Ibid., 3.

[54] Interview with Gloria de Castro, coordinator of the Pro-Convention Commission on

the Rights of the Child, Aug 1994.

[55] Ibid.; interview with Hector Dionicio, Sept 1996.

[56] Interview with Gloria de Castro.

[57] Lucy Barrios de Mendez, "Legislativo aprueba nuevo Código del niño, niña y adolescente," in *Siglo Veintiuno*, Guatemala. 12 Sept 1996, 14.

[58] Presidencia de la República de Guatemala, "Proyecto Escuela Juvenil de Formación Integral Niños de la Calle," Informative Brochure (Guatemala, date unknown).

[59] Interview with Franklin Azuldia.

[60] Ibid.

[61] Interview with Alba Pedrosa, director, "Proyecto: Apoyo a los Niños de la Calle," Aug 1994.

[62] Interview with Marvin Castillo, 28 July 1994.

[63] Maggie Black, *Street and Working Children* (Florence: UNICEF Child Development Centre, 1993), 38-9.

[64] Interview, Sept 1996.

CHAPTER FOUR

[1] Sarah Terry, "Giovani's Story," in *The Boston Globe Magazine*. 2 May 1993, 42-3. *Also* Children's Rights International, *Children Without Childhood*, 1990, 5.

[2] Ibid.

[3] Amnesty International, "Guatemala: Extrajudicial Executions and Human Rights Violations Against Street Children," *Special Report* (London: AI, July 1990), 4-7.

[4] "Alianza con los niños de la calle," *Noticias de Guatemala*, Jan 1992, 7.

[5] US Department of State, Country Reports on Human Rights Practices for 1990 (Washington: Feb 1991), 634.

[6] US Department of State, Country Reports on Human Rights Practices for 1991 (Washington: Feb 1992), 613.

[7] US Department of State, (1991), 617.

[8] US Department of State, Country Reports on Human Rights Practices for 1977 to 1985.

[9] "Alianza con. . .," 8.

[10] Ibid.

[11] US Department of State, Country Reports 1992 and 1993.

[12] "Prisioneros de la calle," 6.

[13] Ibid.

[14] Casa Alianza unpublished report, case number 43.

[15] "Niño de la calle denuncia en Honduras brutalidad de policías guatemaltecos," *Prensa Libre*, Guatemala: 29 Mar 1993.

[16] "Otro niño de la calle torturado por Policías Nacionales en Guatemala," in *Bulletin of the Centro de Informaciones Ecuménicas*, Mexico. No. 310, 26 July 1993.

[17] Guatemala Human Rights/USA, *Update*, 4 Apr 1994.

[18] Ibid.

[19] Ibid.

[20] "Intentan quemar vivo a niño de la calle," *Prensa Libre*, Guatemala: 11 Apr 1994.

[21] "Ofrecen recompensa de Q100 mil por denunciar o capturar a terroristas," *Prensa Libre* , 26 Sept 1994, 3.

[22] "Menor convaleciente en hospital relata promenores de la tragedia," *Prensa Libre,* 26 Sept 1994, 3.

[23] ODHAG, 17.

[24] Ibid.

[25] Ibid., 11.

26 Ibid., 15.

27 Ibid., 20.

28 "Alianza . . . ," 9.

29 Ibid., 9.

30 Ibid., 9.

31 Carlos Rafael Soto, "El rostro de la vergüenza (II)" in *El Gráfico*, Guatemala. 18 Mar 1993, 9.

32 "Las niñas de la calle: una historia de dolor . . ." in *Siglo Veintiuno*, Guatemala. 24 July 1993, 4-5.

33 Amnesty International, 1990, 2.

34 "Niños de la calle, entre maltratos y mendicidad," in *El Nuevo Diario*, 8 Mar 1993, 10.

35 "Prisioneros . . . ," 7

36 Laura Gingold, "Feos, sucios y malos," in *Nueva Sociedad*, Jan-Feb 1992, 104-6.

37 Gingold, 114.

38 "Policías privados propinan golpiza a niño de la calle," in *Siglo Veintiuno*, Guatemala. 10 Dec 1993.

39 Susanna Agnelli. *Street Children: A Growing Urban Tragedy* (London: Weidenfeld and Nicolson, 1986), 63.

40 "Harris: amenazan de muerte a defensores de niños de la calle," *Prensa Libre*, Guatemala. 20 Mar 1993, 24.

41 "Violence Against the Children of the Poor," International Child Resource Institute Bulletin, Berkeley. Spring 1994.

42 "Director de PN reconoce existencia de corrupción en esa institución," *Prensa Libre*, Guatemala. 12 Sept 1994.

43 Amnesty International, 1990, 23.

44 "Prisioneros de la calle," 7.

45 Comments made in an informal telephone interview, Sept 1994.

46 International Child Resource Institute Bulletin, Spring 1994.

CHAPTER FIVE

1 Asunción Lavrin, "Mexico," Hawes and Himer, eds., *Children in Historical and Comparative Perspective* (New York: Greenwood Press, 1991), 424.

2 Guillermo Páez Morales, "Children in Colombia," No. 2 of UNICEF CEDC *Outreach Series* (Bogotá: UNICEF Regional Office, 1992), 154.

3 Paéz Morales, 11.

4 Elizabeth Anne Kuznesof, "Brazil," Hawes and Himer, eds., *Children in Historical and Comparative Perspective* (New York: Greenwood Press, 1991), 164.

5 Páez Morales, 141.

6 Páez Morales, 14.

7 Susan De Vos, *Household Composition in Latin America* (New York: Plenum Press, 1995).

8 Ignacio Martín-Baró, "Religion as an Instrument of Psychological Warfare," Tod Sloan, translator, in Aron and Corne, eds., *Writings for a Liberation Psychology* (Cambridge: Harvard University Press, 1994), 136-8.

9 Martín-Baró, 140-41.

10 Ibid., 146.

11 Deborah Levenson, "On Their Own," No. 4 of AVANCSO series *Cuadernos de investigación* (Guatemala: Inforpress Centroamericana, 1988), 48.

12 Martín-Baró, 142.

13 Phillip Berryman, "The Coming of Age of Evangelical Protestantism," in *NACLA Report on the Americas*, May-June 1994, 7.

[14] Berryman, 7.

[15] Celia Muñoz and Ximena Pachón, *La niñez en el Siglo XX* (Bogotá: Planeta, 1991), 172.

[16] Nancy Scheper-Hughes, *Death Without Weeping* (Berkeley: University of California Press, 1992), 357.

[17] "Familia, vida, y solidaridad," letter from the Latin American Bishops Conference, Santo Domingo, 18 June 1994, as reprinted in *Renacer Católico* (Parish newsletter, Sanarate, El Progreso, Guatemala, July/Aug 1994), 3.

[18] "Familia . . . ," 4.

[19] "Carta a las familias de Su Santidad Juan Pablo II," 2 Feb 1994, as reprinted in *Panorama Centroamericano* (Guatemala: Jul-Aug 1994), 102.

[20] "Carta . . . ," 105.

[21] Claudia Paz y Paz and Luis Ramirez García, *Derechos humanos: niños, niñas y adolescentes privados de libertad*, Unpublished report of the Instituto de Estudios Comparados en Ciencias Penales (Guatemala: Aug 1993), 4.

[22] "Carta . . . ," 128.

[23] Emilio Willems, *Latin American Culture, An Anthropological Synthesis* (New York: Harper and Row, 1975), 52.

[24] Judith Ennew and Brian Milne, *The Next Generation* (London: Zed Books, 1989), 49.

[25] Levenson, 20.

[26] Instituto Interamericano del Niño, *La conducta anti-social del menor en América* (Montevideo: IIN, 1964), 5.

[27] Maggie Black, *Street and Working Children* (Florence: UNICEF Child Development Centre, 1993), 38.

[28] Comision Económica para América Latina y el Caribe (CEPAL), "Situación y perspectivas de la familia en América Latina y el Caribe," 8 June 1993, as reprinted in *Panorama Centroamericano* (Guatemala: July/Aug 1994), 34-5.

[29] CEPAL, 40-5.

[30] Giangi Schibotto, *Niños trabajadores* (Lima: IPEC, 1990), 51.

[31] Laura Gingold, "Feos, sucios y malos," in *Nueva Sociedad*, Jan-Feb 1992, 113.

[32] Marina Ariza Castillo, "Familias y pobreza, menores deambulantes en República Dominicana," in *Nueva Sociedad*, Jan-Feb 1994, 90-5.

[33] Paulo Freire, "And the Street Educators," No. 1 in UNICEF series *Care Alternatives for Street Children* (Bogotá: UNICEF, 1987), 19.

[34] Mary Ana Beloff, "De los delitos y de la infancia," *Nueva Sociedad*, Jan-Feb 1994, 104-5.

[35] Schibotto, 113.

[36] Ibid., 128.

[37] Rinaldo Sergio Vieira Arruda, *Pequenos Bandidos* (São Paulo: Global editora, 1983), 165.

[38] CONANI, UNICEF, SEGEPLAN, *Nuestra Realidad* (Guatemala: December 1992), 6.

[39] "Más de un millón de niños trabajan," *La República*, Guatemala, 16 Aug 1993.

[40] Rolando Castillo, "Casa Hogar una esperanza para niños de la calle," in *La República*, 9 Jan 1994, 10.

[41] "La sociedad los crea y los rechaza," in *Siglo Veintiuno*, 24 July 1993.

[42] Vieira, 63.

[43] Schibotto, 179.

[44] Ibid., 67.

[45] Vieira, 162.

[46] Carlos Alberto Luppi, *Malditos Frutos do Nosso Ventre* (São Paulo: Icone, 1987), 164-5.

[47] Vieira, 161.

[48] Rigoberta Menchú, *I . . . Rigoberta Menchú*, Elisabeth Burgos-Debray, ed., (London: Verso, 1984), 14-15.

[49] Ibid., 8-11.

[50] T. Berry Brazelton, "Implications of Infant Development Among the Mayan Indians of

Mexico," Leiderman et al., eds., *Culture and Infancy, Variations in the Human Experience* (New York: Academic Press, 1977), 155, 179.

[51] "¿Qué piensan los niños latinoamericanos sobre la familia?" (Bolivia: Defensa de los niños internacional, Nov 1993), 66.

[52] Menchú, 13, 9.

[53] Ibid., 7.

[54] Ibid., 11.

[55] Ibid., 10-11.

[56] Brazelton, 154.

[57] Menchú, 15.

[58] Ibid., 17.

[59] Interview with CEIPA street educator Carlos Mansón, 6 Aug 1994.

[60] Ricardo Falla, *Massacres in the Jungle* (Boulder: Westview Press, 1994), 98-100.

[61] Ibid., 101.

[62] Interview, Carlos Mansón.

CHAPTER SIX

[1] Jonathan Kozol, *Rachel and Her Children* (New York: Fawcett Columbine, 1988), 129-39.

[2] Ibid., 129-31.

[3] "La sociedad los crea y los rechaza," in *Siglo Veintiuno*, 24 July 1993, 6.

[4] Nancy Scheper-Hughes and Daniel Hoffman, "Kids Out of Place," in *NACLA Report on the Americas*, May/June 1994, 17.

[5] Jonathan Kozol, *Amazing Grace* (New York: Harper Perennial, 1995), 38-39.

[6] Ibid., 41.

[7] Vera da Silva Telles and Helena W. Abramo, "Experiencia Urbana, trabajo e identidad . . ." Ana Vainstoc and Diego Carrion, *La ciudad y los niños* (Quito: Ciudad, 1987), 200.

[8] da Silva and Abramo, 207.

[9] Scheper-Hughes, 239.

[10] Laura Gingold, "Feos, sucios y malos," *Nueva Sociedad*, Jan-Feb 1992, 115.

[11] Gingold, 114-15.

[12] Richard Sennett, *The Uses of Disorder* (New York: Alfred A Knopf, 1970)

[13] Sennett, 18-20, 32.

[14] Ibid., 45.

[15] "A platéia não se comove," *Istoé*, 4 Aug 1993, 56-7.

[16] "A platéia. . . " 56-7.

[17] Scheper-Hughes, 240.

[18] Sarah Terry, "Giovani's Story: The Life and Death of a Guatemalan Street Child," *The Boston Globe Magazine*. 2 May 1993, 45.

[19] Carlos Nobre, "Rio exterminou 6.033 menores em dez anos," *Jornal Do Brasil*, 28 Apr 1996, 29.

[20] "La sociedad los crea y los rechaza," in *Siglo Veintiuno*, 24 July 1993, 6.

[21] "Niños de la calle, delincuentes impunes," letter to the editor in *Prensa Libre*, 23 May 1994.

[22] Letter to the editor in *Prensa Libre*, 11 Apr 1994.

[23] Interview with Marvin Castillo, 28 July 1994.

[24] "Crece prostitución infantil en Guatemala," in *Barricada*, 8 Mar 1994, 9.

[25] "50 percent de los menores contraen enfermedades venérias," *La Hora*, 9 Mar 1993, 7.

[26] Manolo García, "Pequeñas esclavas nocturnas," *Prensa Libre Revista Domingo*, 17 July 1994, 8-9.

[27] Bonnie Hayskar, 26-9.

[28] Ibid., 26-9.

[29] Paul Jeffrey, "Glue Maker's Image Won't Stick," *Multinational Monitor*, Dec 1995.

[30] Diana B. Henriques, "Black Mark for a 'Good Citizen,'" *The New York Times*. 26 Nov 1995, section 3, 11.

[31] Paul McEnroe, "Latin America Glue Abuse Haunts H.B. Fuller," *StarTribune*, Minneapolis/St. Paul. 21 Apr 1996, A21.

[32] "Fuller's Glue," editorial in *StarTribune*, Minneapolis/St. Paul. 3 May 1996.

[33] Alfred Kaltschmitt, "Pegamento con aceite de mostaza (II parte)," *La República*, 10 Aug 1993.

[34] Alonzo Salazar, "Young Assassins of the Drug Trade," *NACLA Report on the Americas*, May-June 1994, 27.

[35] Salazar, 28.

[36] "Prisioneros de la calle," *Siglo Veintiuno*, 9 Mar 1992, 7

[37] "La sociedad los crea y los rechaza," 7.

[38] Carlos Figueroa-Ibarra, *El Recurso del Miedo* (San José: EDUCA, 1991), 15-16.

[39] Figueroa-Ibarra, 131.

[40] Ibid., 16, 135-9.

[41] Ibid., 138-9.

[42] Ibid., 39.

[43] Ibid., 135.

[44] Ibid., 38-9.

[45] Ibid., 40.

[46] Ibid., 40.

[47] Ibid., 42.

[48] Ibid., 16.

[49] Michael McClintock, *The American Connection, Volume Two: State Terror and Popular Resistance in Guatemala* (London: Zed Books, 1985), 180.

[50] Figueroa-Ibarra, 26.

[51] Ibid., 27.

[52] Ibid., 29-32.

[53] Ricardo Falla, *Massacres in the Jungle* (Boulder: Westview Press, 1994), 38.

[54] Figueroa-Ibarra, 143.

[55] McClintock, 230.

[56] Ibid., 230.

[57] Figueroa-Ibarra, 160; McClintok, 234.

[58] Figueroa-Ibarra, 245.

[59] Falla, 8, 38.

[60] Manuel Uribe and Andrés Segovia, *Terrorismo de Estado en América Latina* (Quito: Ediciones Rosa Vivar, date unknown), 178.

[61] Falla, 186.

[62] Ibid., 186.

[63] Beatriz Manz, "Exodus, Resistance, and Readjustments in the Aftermath of Massacres," Epilogue of Falla, *Massacres in the Jungle*, 197-202.

[64] Manz, 198.

[65] Figueroa-Ibarra, 286.

[66] Vilma Aurora López Cantoral, "Los menores de edad 'de y en la calle' en la Ciudad de Guatemala y la atención institucional," Thesis, School of Social Work, USAC, Guatemala, 1989, 42.

[67] Marcelo Suarez-Orozco, "Speaking of the Unspeakable, Towards a Psychosocial Understanding of Responses to Terror," *Ethos* 18 (3) 1990, 366.

[68] Suarez-Orozco, 364.

[69] Ibid., 366.

70 Ibid., 366.
71 Ibid., 370.
72 Oficina de Derechos Humanos del Arzobispado de Guatemala, *Informe Anual* (Guatemala: 1993), 314.
73 As quoted in Ian Lee Doucet, "Psychoanalysis, Child Abuse and War," *Medicine and War*, Vol. 8 (1992), 286.
74 As quoted in Doucet, 286.
75 Figueroa-Ibarra, 11.
76 Ibid., 36.
77 Gabriel Aguilera Peralta, *El Proceso de Terror en Guatemala* (Guatemala: CIDAL, 1971), 23.
78 Inteview with Fernando López, 26 July 1994.
79 Ignacio Martín-Baró, "War and Mental Health," chap. 6 of Aron and Corne, eds., *Writings for a Liberation Psychology* (Cambridge: Harvard University Press, 1994), 112-14.
80 Letter to the editor in *Prensa Libre*, 23 May 1994.
81 Letter to the editor in *Prensa Libre*, 11 Apr 1994.
82 "Policías privados propinan golpiza a niño de la calle," *Siglo Veintiuno*, 18 Dec 1993.
83 "¿Dos sistemas de tribunales?" editorial in *Siglo Veintiuno*, 12 Sept 1996.
84 Estuardo Zapata, "Marisol, violada y asesinada (otra vez)," *Siglo Veintiuno*, 12 Sept 1996.
85 Scheper-Hughes, 227.
86 Ibid., 228.
87 Ibid., 225.
88 Ibid, 227.
89 Ibid, 225.
90 Gingold, 106.
91 Ibid., 114-115.
92 Deborah Levenson, "On Their Own," No. 4 of AVANCSO series *Cuadernos de Investigación* (Guatemala: Inforpress Centroamericana, 1988), 2.
93 "La ciudad del miedo" in *Prensa Libre*, 7 July 1994.
94 "El fantasma de la violencia," *Crónica*, 2 June 1989, 11.
95 Ibid., 11-13.
96 Robert Langworthy and John T. Whitehead, "Liberalism and Fear as Explanations of Punitiveness," *Criminology* v. 24, no. 3 (1986), 583.
97 Ira Schwartz, Sheyang Guo and John Johnson Kerbs, "Public Attitudes toward Juvenile Crime and Juvenile Justice: Implications for Public Policy," in *Hamline Journal of Public Policy and Law*, vol. 13, no. 2, (1992), 251.
98 Scheper-Hughes, 232.
99 Suarez-Orozco, 372.
100 Derek Summerfield and Leslie Toser, "'Low-Intensity' War and Mental Trauma in Nicaragua: A Study in a Rural Community," *Medicine and War*, Vol. 7 (1991), 89-90.
101 Elder Interiano, "Inteligencia militar combatirá a pandilleros" in *La República*, 6 July 1994, 2.
102 Interiano, 2.
103 "Policías privados propinan golpiza a niño de la calle," in *Siglo Veintiuno*, 18 Dec 1993.
104 Ervin San Juan Yat, "Los niños del olvido," letter to the editor in *Prensa Libre*, 10 Aug 1994.

CHAPTER SEVEN

1 Michael McClintock, *The American Connection, Volume Two: State Terror and Popular Resistance in Guatemala* (London: Zed Books, 1985), 33.
2 Ibid., 49-50.

[3] Lars Schoultz, *Human Rights and United States Policy toward Latin America* (Princeton: Princeton University Press, 1981), 215.

[4] Ibid., 232.

[5] Caesar Sereseres, *Military Development and the United States Military Assistance Program for Latin America: The Case of Guatemala, 1961-69* (Dissertation, University of California, Riverside, 1971), 200.

[6] McClintock, 79-80.

[7] Schoultz, 110.

[8] Ibid., 249.

[9] Robert A. Pastor, *Whirlpool* (Princeton: Princeton University Press, 1992), 65.

[10] Ibid., 76.

[11] America's Watch, "With Friends Like These . . . ," excerpted in Bonnie Szumski, ed., *Latin America and U.S. Foreign Policy* (St. Paul: Greenhaven Press, 1988), 62.

[12] United States Department of State, "U.S. Policy Toward Guatemala," Nov 1994.

[13] Edgar Gutiérrez, "Los aparatos de inteligencia en la transición guatemalteca," *Verdad y Vida,* July-Sept 1995, 9.

[14] Tina Rosenberg, *Children of Cain* (New York: William Morrow, 1991), 270.

[15] Interview with Peg Willingham, Guatemala Desk Officer, U.S. Department of State, 30 Jan 1995.

[16] Interview with Fernando López, ODHAG, 26 July 1994.

[17] Interview with Gloria de Castro, Alba Pedrosa, Aug 1994.

[18] Interview with Ana Raquel de Tobar, June 1994.

[19] Interview with Edgar Alay, Aug 1994.

[20] Irene Rizzini et al., "Brazil: A New Conception of Childhood," in Szanton-Blanc et al., *Urban Children in Distress*, 92.

[21] Karl-Eric Knutsson, "Preface" in Cristina Szanton-Blanc et al., *Urban Children in Distress* (Switzerland: Gordon and Breach, 1994), xvi.

[22] Knutsson, xvi.

[23] Maggie Black, *Street and Working Children* (Florence: UNICEF Child Development Centre, 1993), 49.

[24] From Carlos Alberto Luppi, *Malditos Frutos do Nosso Ventre* (São Paulo: Icone editora, 1987), 43.

[25] Interview with Lesbia de García, 13 July 1994.

[26] Francisco Espert, "Apertura y humanización institucional," No. 7 of UNICEF, CEDC *Methodological Series* (Bogotá: UNICEF, 1987), 41.

[27] Espert, 41.

[28] CIPRODENI, "Una mano con la niñez," *Informational Bullentin* (Guatemala: Sept-Oct 1992), 10 and interview with Carlos Mansón, CEIPA, Aug 1994.

[29] CONANI, SEGEPLAN, UNICEF, *Nuestra Realidad* (Guatemala: Dec 1992), 37.

[30] UNICEF, *El niño en América Latina y el Caribe* (Santiago: UNICEF, 1979), 8.

[31] Fernando Carrión, *Investigación urbana en el area andina* (Quito: Ciudad,1988), 42.

[32] Thomas Angotti, "The Latin American Metropolis and the Growth of Inequality," in *NACLA Report on the Americas*, Jan-Feb 1995, 18.

[33] UNICEF, *El niño . . .* , 45.

[34] Emilio Willems, *Latin American Culture: An Anthropological Synthesis* (New York: Harper and Row, 1975), 261.

[35] Willems, 271.

[36] Mario Lungo and Marian Pérez, "Pensamos en una ciudad que contribuya a restituir a los niños pobres el derecho a la recreación," in Vainstoc and Carrion, eds., *La ciudad y los niños* (Quito: Ciudad, 1987), 144.

Bibliograhy

"50% de los menores contraen enfermedades venérias," in *La Hora*, Guatemala. 9 Mar 1993.

"A platéia não se comove," in *Istoé*. São Paulo: 4 Aug 1993, 56-7.

Agnelli, Susanna. *Street Children. A Growing Urban Tragedy.* London: Weidenfeld and Nicolson, 1986.

Aguilera Peralta, Gabriel. *El Proceso del Terror en Guatemala.* Guatemala: CIDAL, 1971.

"Alianza con los niños de la calle," in *Noticias de Guatemala.* 10 Jan 1992, 7-11.

Amnesty International. "Guatemala: Extrajudicial Executions and Human Rights Violations Against Street Children." London: Amnesty International Secretariat, July 1990.

Angotti, Thomas. "The Latin American Metropolis and the Growth of Inequality," in *NACLA Report on the Americas.* Jan-Feb 1995, 13-18.

Arancibia Córdova, Juan. "Consideraciones sobre el ajuste estructural en Centroamérica," in *Revista Centroamericana de economía.* Sep-Dec 1991, 16-29.

Ariza Castillo, Marina. "Familias y Pobreza," in *Nueva Sociedad.* Jan-Feb 1994, 90-103.

Asociación Casa Alianza. *Report to the UN Committee Against Torture on the Torture of Guatemalan Street Children, 1990-1995.* Guatemala: Nov 1995.

Asociación Casa Alianza. Unpublished Report of Case Files. Guatemala: July 1994.

AVANCSO. "Vonós a la capital." No. 7 of AVANCSO series *Cuadernos de investigación.* Guatemala: Inforpress Centroamericana, June 1991.

Banco Centroamericano de Integración Económica. *Memoria Anual 1990-91.*

Barrios de Mendez, Lucy. "Legislativo aprueba nuevo Código del niño, niña, y adolescente," in *Siglo Veintiuno,* Guatemala. 12 Sept 1996.

Beloff, Mary Ana. "De los delitos y de la infancia," in *Nueva Sociedad.* Jan-Feb 1994, 104-113.

Bendahmane, Diane. "The Quiet Revolution," of *Grassroots Development*. Vol. 18, no. 2 (1994), 2-12.

Benería, Lourdes. "The Mexican Debt Crisis: Restructuring the Economy and the Household," in Benería and Feldman, eds., *Unequal Burden.* Boulder: Westview Press, 1992.

Berryman, Phillip. "The Coming of Age of Evangelical Protestantism," in *NACLA Report on the Americas.* May-Jun 1994, 6-10.

Black, Maggie. *Street and Working Children.* Florence: UNICEF Child Development Centre, 1993.

Brazelton, T. Berry. "Implications of Infant Development Among the Mayan Indians of Mexico," in Leiderman et al., eds., *Culture and Infancy in the Human Experience.* New York: Academic Press, 1977.

Cabrera, Mario Rolando. "La pobreza y los niños," in *La República*, Guatemala. 12 April 1994.

Carrión, Fernando. *Investigación urbana en el area andina.* Quito: Ciudad, 1988.

"Carta a las familias de Su Santidad Juan Pablo II," reprinted in *Panorama Centroamericana.* Guatemala: Jul-Aug 1994.

Castillo, Rolando. "Casa Hogar una esperanza para niños de la calle," in *La República*, Guatemala. 9 Jan 1994.

CEDIC. "Factores que propician la callejización de la niñez guatemalteca." Guatemala: CEDIC, 1993.

_____. "Un día en la vida de Juancho." Guatemala: CEDIC, 1993. Centro de Informaciones Ecuménicas. "Otro niño de la calle torturado por Policías Nacionales en Guatemala," in *Bulletin*, no. 310. Mexico: 26 July 1993.

ChildHope. "Nuestros niños, nuestra esperanza," nos. 9 and 10. Guatemala: Jan 1994.

Children's Rights International. *Children Without Childhood*. Special Report, CRI, 1990.

CIPRODENI. "La sociedad guatemalteca debe poner un 'hasta aquí' a la desaparición de niños," in *La República*, Guatemala. 12 April 1994.

_____. "Una mano con la niñez." *Bulletin*, Guatemala. Sept-Oct 1992.

Código de Menores. Guatemala: Jimenez y Ayala editores, 1979.

Comision Económica para América Latina y El Caribe. "Situacion y perspectivas de la familia en América Latina y el Caribe," reprinted in *Panorama Centroamericana*. Guatemala: July-Aug 1994.

CONANI, SEGEPLAN, UNICEF. *Nuestra Realidad*. Guatemala: Dec 1992.

Constitución Política de la República de Guatemala, Versión Reformada. Guatemala: Jimenez y Ayala editores, 1993.

"Convention on the Rights of the Child," in UNICEF, *The State of the World's Children*. Oxford: Oxford University Press, 1991.

"Crece prostitución infantil en Guatemala," in *Barricada*. 9 March 1994.

da Silva Telles, Vera and Helena W. Abramo. "Experiencia urbana, trabajo e identidad . . .," in Vainstoc and Carrion, eds., *La ciudad y los niños*. Quito: Ciudad, 1987, 197-214.

Defensa de los Niños Internacional. "¿Qué piensan los niños latinoamericanos sobre la familia?" Bolivia: Nov 1993.

"Destacan explotación de niños trabajadores," in *Prensa Libre*, Guatemala. 3 May 1993.

De Vos, Susan. *Household Composition in Latin America*. New York: Plenum Press, 195.

"Director de la PN reconoce existencia de corrupción en esa institución," in *Prensa Libre*, Guatemala. 12 Sept 1994.

"¿Dos sistemas de tribunales?" editorial in *Siglo Veintiuno*, Guatemala. 12 Sept 1996.

Doucet, Ian Lee. "Psychoanalysis, Child Abuse and War," in *Medicine and War*. Vol. 8 (1992), 282-293.

"El fantasma de la violencia," in *Crónica*. 12 June 1989, 11-16.

"El problema de los niños de la calle," in *El Gráfico*, Guatemala. 23 Mar 1993.

"El vía crucis de los niños lustradores," in *Prensa Libre*, Guatemala. 2 Oct 1993.

Ennew, Judith and Milne, Brian. *The Next Generation*. London: Zed Books, 1989.

Espert, Francisco. "Apertura y humanización institucional," no. 7 of UNICEF CEDC *Methodological Series*. Bogotá: UNICEF, 1989.

Espinola, Basílica, et al. *In the Streets, Working Children in Asunción*. Bogotá: UNICEF, 1987.

Falla, Ricardo. *Massacres in the Jungle*. Boulder: Westview Press, 1994.

"Familia, vida, y solidaridad, " letter from the Latin American Bishops Conference, Santo Domingo, 16 June 1994. Reprinted in *Renacer Católico*. Sanarate, El Progreso, Guatemala: July-Aug 1994.

Farnsworth, Elizabeth. "Guatemala: Who Calls the Shots?" in *Mother Jones*. Oct 1987, 16, 22, 57.

Figueroa-Ibarra, Carlos. *El Recurso del Miedo*. San José: EDUCA, 1991.

_____. "Violencia y democracia en Centroamérica," in *Verdad y Vida*. Guatemala: Apr-July 1994, 9-13.

Freire, Paulo. "And the Street Educators." No. 1 of UNICEF CEDC *Methodological Series*. Bogotá: UNICEF, 1987.

"Fuller's Glue," editorial. *StarTribune*, Minneapolis/St. Paul. 3 May 1996.

"García Laguardia demanda efectiva protección para los niños de la calle," in *La República*, Guatemala. 12 Apr 1994.

García, Manolo. "Pequeñas esclavas nocturnas," in *Prensa Libre Revista Domingo*, Guatemala. 17 July 1994, 8-9.

Gingold, Laura. "Feos, sucios y malos," in *Nueva Sociedad*. Venezuela: Jan-Feb 1992, 104-119.

Guatemala Human Rights Commission/USA. *Update*, Washington. 4 Apr 1994.

"Guatemala ocupa primer lugar en violaciones de DH en 1993," in *La República*, Guatemala. 6 July 1994.

Gutiérrez, Edgar. "Los aparatos de inteligencia en la transición guatemalteca," in *Verdad y Vida,* Guatemala. July-Sept 1995, 9-12.

"Harris: amenazan de muerte a defensores de niños de la calle," in *Prensa Libre*, Guatemala. 20 Mar 1993.

Hayskar, Bonnie. "Sticking with Addiction in Latin America," in *Multinational Monitor*. Apr 1994, 26-9.

Heller, Peter B. "Guatemala: English Translation of the 1985 Constitution," in Blaustein and Flanz, eds., *Constitutions of the Countries of the World*. Dobbs Ferry: Oceana Publications, Sept 1986.

Henriques, Diana B. "Black Mark for a 'Good Citizen,'" in *The New York Times*. Section 3, 26 Nov 1995.

Inforpress Centroamericano. *Guatemala 1986. El año de las promesas*. Guatemala: Inforpress Centroamericano, 1987.

Instituto Austriaco Guatemalteco. Seminario: Los niños de la calle una realidad alarmante. Guatemala: IAG, 1992.

Instituto Interamericano del Niño. *La conducta antisocial del menor en América*. Montevideo: IIN, 1964.

"Intentan quemar vivo a niño de la calle," in *Prensa Libre*, Guatemala. 11 April 1994.

Inter-American Development Bank. *Economic and Social Progress in Latin America. 1996 Report*.

Interiano, Elder. "Inteligencia militar combatirá a pandilleros," in *La República*, Guatemala. 6 July 1994.

International Child Resource Institute. "Violence Against the Children of the Poor" in *Bulletin*, Berkeley. Spring 1994.

Jeffrey, Paul. "Glue Maker's Image Won't Stick," in *Multinational Monitor*. Dec 1995.

Kaltschmitt, Alfred. "Pegamento con aceite de mostaza (II Parte)," in *La República*, Guatemala. 10 April 1993.

Kozol, Jonathan. *Amazing Grace*. New York: Harper Perennial, 1995.

_____. *Rachel and Her Children*. New York: Fawcett Columbine, 1988.

Kuznesoff, Elizabeth Anne. "Brazil," in Hawes and Himer, eds., *Children in Historical and Comparative Perspective*. New York: Greenwood Press, 1991.

"La ciudad del miedo," letter to the editor in *Prensa Libre*, Guatemala. 7 July 1994.

"La niñez clama por atención," in *La República*, Guatemala. 4 Aug 1993.

"La sociedad los crea y los rechaza," in *Siglo Veintiuno*, Guatemala. 24 July 1993.

Lafeber, Walter. *Inevitable Revolutions*. New York: WW Norton and Co., 1984.

Langsworthy, Robert and John T. Whitehead . "Liberalism and Fear as Explanations of Punitiveness," in *Criminology*. Vol. 24, no. 3 (1986), 575-91.

"Las niñas de la calle: una historia de dolor . . ." in *Siglo Veintiuno*. 24 July 1993, 4-5.

Lavrin, Asunción. "Mexico," in Hawes and Himer, eds., *Children in Historical and*

Comparative Perspective. New York: Greenwood Press, 1991, 421-45.

Levenson, Deborah. "On Their Own. A Preliminary Study of Youth Gangs in Guatemala City." No. 4 of AVANCSO series *Cuadernos de investigación.* Guatemala: Inforpress Centroamericana, Sept 1988.

López Cantoral, Vilma. *Los menores de edad "de y en la calle" en la ciudad de Guatemala y la atención institucional.* Thesis. Guatemala: School of Social Work, University of San Carlos, 1989.

"Los niños de la calle necesitan una oportunidad para reincorporarse," in *Siglo Veintiuno.* Guatemala: 24 July 1993.

"Los niños, nuestras eternas cicatrices," in *Siglo Veintiuno,* Guatemala. 30 May 1994.

"Los niños olvidados," in *El Gráfico,* Guatemala. 3 Oct 1993.

Lungo, Mario and Pérez, Marian. "Pensamos en una ciudad que contribuya a restituir a los niños pobres el derecho de la recreación," in Vainstoc and Carrion eds., *La ciudad y los niños.* Quito: Ciudad, 1987.

Luppi, Carlos Alberto. *Malditos Frutos do Nosso Ventre.* São Paulo: Icone, 1987.

Manz, Beatriz. "Exodus, Resistance, and Readjustments in the Aftermath of Massacres," epilogue in Ricardo Falla, *Massacres in the Jungle.* Boulder: Westview Press, 1994.

Marroquin, Gonazalo. "Que vivan los niños," in *La República,* Guatemala. 1 Oct 1993.

Martín-Baró, Ignacio. *Writings for a Liberation Psychology,* Adrianne Aron and Shawn Corne, eds. Cambridge: Harvard University Press, 1994.

"Más de un millón de niños trabajan," in *La República,* Guatemala. 16 Apr 1993.

McClintock, Michael. *The American Connection, Volume Two: State Terror and Popular Resistance in Guatemala.* London: Zed Books, 1985.

McEnroe, Paul. "Latin America Glue Abuse Haunts H.B. Fuller," in *StarTribune,* Minneapolis/St. Paul. 21 Apr 1996.

Menchú, Rigoberta. *I . . . Rigoberta Menchú.* Elizabeth Burgos-Debray, ed. London: Verso, 1984.

"Menor convaleciente en hospital relata promenores de la tragedia," in *Prensa Libre,* Guatemala. 26 Sept 1994.

"Morte consumada," in *Istoé,* São Paulo. 4 Aug 1993, 63.

Muñoz, Celia and Pachón, Ximena. *La niñez en el siglo XX.* Bogotá: Planeta, 1991.

Newman, Frank and Weissbrodt, David. *International Human Rights.* Cincinnati: Anderson Publishing Co., 1991.

"Niño de la calle agredido por policías particulares," in *La Hora,* Guatemala. 17 Dec 1993.

"Niño de la calle denuncia en Honduras brutalidad de policías guatemaltecos," in *Prensa Libre,* Guatemala. 29 Mar 1993.

"Niños de la calle, delincuentes impunes." Letter to the editor in *Prensa Libre,* Guatemala. 23 May 1994.

"Niños de la calle, entre maltratos y mendicidad," in *El Nuevo Diario.* 8 March 1993.

Nobre, Carlos. "Rio exterminou 6.033 menores em dez anos," in *Jornal Do Brasil.* 28 Apr 1996.

North, Carol S., et al. "Violence in the Lives of Homeless Mothers in a Substance Abuse Treatment Program," in *Journal of Interpersonal Violence.* June 1996.

Oficina de Derechos Humanos del Arzobispado de Guatemala. "Fuerzas armadas: su rol dentro de la sociedad," in *Verdad y Vida,* Guatemala. Apr-July 1994, 22-3.

_____. *Informe anual.* Guatemala: ODHAG, 1993.

"Ofrecen recompensa de Q. 100 mil por denunciar o captar a terroristas," in *Prensa Libre,* Guatemala. 26 Sept 1994.

Páez Morales, Guillermo. "Children in Colombia." No. 2 of UNICEF CEDC *Outreach Series*. Bogotá: UNICEF, 1987.

Palomba, Federico. "Tendencias evolutivas en la protección de los menores." Unpublished paper, date unknown.

Pastor, Robert A. *Whirlpool*. Princeton: Princeton University Press, 1992.

Patton, Michael Q. *Qualitative Evaluation and Research Methods*, second edition. California: Sage Publications, 1990.

Paz y Paz, Claudia and Luis Ramirez García. *Derechos humanos: niños, niñas y adoles centes privados de libertad*. Unpublished report of the Instituto de Estudios Comparados en Ciencias Penales. Guatemala: August 1993.

"Policías privados propinan golpiza a niño de la calle," in *Siglo Veintiuno*, Guatemala. 10 Dec 1993.

Presidencia de la República de Guatemala. "Proyecto Escuela Juvenil de formación integral niños de la calle." Informative brochure. Guatemala: date unknown.

"Prisioneros de la calle." Special report in *Siglo Veintiuno*, Guatemala. 9 March 1992.

Procuradaría de Derechos Humanos. "¿Qué es la Defensoria de los Derechos de la Niñez?" Informative brochure. Guatemala: date unknown.

Procurador de Derechos Humanos. "Presentación de anteproyecto del Código de la Niñez y Adolescencia." Press release. Guatemala: date unknown.

"Robo de niños causa violencia en Villa Nueva," in *La República*, Guatemala. 5 Apr 1994.

Rosenberg, Tina. *Children of Cain*. New York: William Morrow and Co., 1991.

Salazar, Alonzo. "Young Assassins of the Drug Trade," in *NACLA Report on the Americas*. May-June 1994, 24-28.

Samayoa de Medina, Emma. *La problemática social que presentan los menores que viven en las calles de la ciudad de Guatemala*. Thesis. Guatemala: School of Social Work, University of San Carlos, date unknown.

San Juan Yat, Ervin. "Los niños del olvido," letter to the editor in *Prensa Libre*, Guatemala. 10 Aug 1994.

Scheper-Hughes, Nancy. *Death Without Weeping*. Berkeley: University of California Press, 1992.

_____ and Daniel Hoffman. "Kids Out of Place," in *NACLA Report on the Americas*. May-Jun 1994, 16-23.

Schibotto, Giangi. *Niños trabajadores*. Lima: IPEC, 1990.

Schoultz, Lars. *Human Rights and United States Policy Toward Latin America*. Princeton: Princeton University Press, 1981.

Schwartz, Ira, Sheyang Guo and John Johnson Kerbs. "Public Attitudes toward Juvenile Crime and Juvenile Justice: Implications for Public Policy," in *Hamline Journal of Public Policy and Law*. Vol. 13, no. 2 (1992), 241-61.

Sennett, Richard. *The Uses of Disorder*. New York: Alfred A. Knopf, 1970.

Sereseres, Caesar. *Military Development and the United States Military Assistance Program for Latin America: The Case of Guatemala, 1961-69*. Dissertation, University of California, Riverside, 1971.

Soto, Carlos Rafael. "El rostro de la vergünza (II)," in *El Gráfico*, Guatemala. 10 Mar 1993, 9.

Spradley, James P. *The Ethnographic Interview*. New York: Holt, Rinehart and Winston, 1979.

Stanley, Barbara and Joan E. Sieber, eds. *Social Research on Children and Adolescents*. California: Sage Publications, 1992.

Suarez-Orozco, Marcelo. "Speaking the Unspeakable, Towards a Psychosocial Understanding of Responses to Terror," in *Ethos*. Vol. 18, no. 3 (1990), 353-83.

Summerfield, Derek and Leslie Toser. "'Low Intensity' War and Mental Trauma in Nicaragua," in *Medicine and War*. Vol. 7 (1991), 84-99.

Szanton-Blanc, Cristina, et al. *Urban Children in Distress*. Switzerland: Gordon and Breach, 1994.

Szumiski, Bonnie, ed. *Latin America and U.S. Foreign Policy*. St. Paul: Greenhaven Press, 1988.

Tedlock, Dennis. *Breath on the Mirror*. San Francisco: Harper Collins, 1993.

"Temor e indignación de padres de familia por robo de niños," in *La República*, Guatemala. 23 Mar 1994, 4.

Terry, Sara. "Giovani's Story: The Life and Death of a Guatemalan Street Child," in *The Boston Globe Magazine*. 2 May 1993, 14-17 and 37-49.

"Torturados por la sociedad," in *Siglo Veintiuno*, Guatemala. 24 July 1993.

UNESCO. *Statistical Yearbook 1993*. London: UNESCO, 1993.

UNICEF. *El niño en América Latina y el Caribe*. Santiago: UNICEF, 1979.

_____. "First Progress Report for US Committee for UNICEF, Project for Street Children and Children at Risk in Low Income Areas." Guatemala: Jan 1989.

_____. *The Invisible Adjustment*. Santiago: UNICEF, 1987.

_____. *The Progress of Nations*. New York: UNICEF House, 1993.

_____. *The State of the World's Children*. Oxford: Oxford University Press, 1992.

United States Department of State. Country Reports on Human Rights Practices. Washington: U.S. State Department, 1977-85, 1990-93.

_____. "U.S. Policy Toward Guatemala." Statement, Nov 1994.

Uribe, Manuel and Segovia Andrés. *Terrorismo de Estado en América Latina*. Quito: Ediciones "Rosa Vivar," date unkown.

"Víctimas de fuerzas de seguridad," in *El Gráfico*, Guatemala. 23 Mar 1994.

Vieira Arruda, Rinaldo. *Pequenos Bandidos*. São Paulo: Global editora, 1983.

Willems, Emilio. *Latin American Culture: An Anthropological Synthesis*. New York: Harper and Row, 1975.

Zapata, Estuardo. "Marisol, violada y asesinada (otra vez)," in *Siglo Veintiuno*, Guatemala. 12 Sept 1996.

Index